2018

Block Scheduling and Its Impact on the School Library Media Center

Block Scheduling and Its Impact on the School Library Media Center

MARIE KEEN SHAW

Greenwood Professional Guides in School Librarianship
Harriet Selverstone, Series Adviser

GREENWOOD PRESS
Westport, Connecticut • London

Library of Congress Cataloging-in-Publication Data

Shaw, Marie Keen.
　　Block scheduling and its impact on the school library media center
　/ Marie Keen Shaw.
　　　　p.　cm. — (Greenwood professional guides in school
　librarianship, ISSN 1074–150X)
　　　Includes bibliographical references and index.
　　　ISBN 0–313–30494–7 (alk. paper)
　　　1. School libraries—United States.　2. Instructional materials
　centers—United States.　3. Block scheduling (Education)—United
　States.　I. Title.　II. Series.
　Z675.S3S538　1999
　027.8′0973—dc21　　　　　　98–22900

British Library Cataloguing in Publication Data is available.

Library of Congress Catalog Card Number: 98–22900
ISBN: 0–313–30494–7
ISSN: 1074–150X

First published in 1999

Greenwood Press, 88 Post Road West, Westport, CT 06881
An imprint of Greenwood Publishing Group, Inc.

Printed in the United States of America

The paper used in this book complies with the
Permanent Paper Standard issued by the National
Information Standards Organization (Z39.48–1984).

P

In order to keep this title in print and available to the academic community, this edition
was produced using digital reprint technology in a relatively short print run. This would
not have been attainable using traditional methods. Although the cover has been changed
from its original appearance, the text remains the same and all materials and methods
used still conform to the highest book-making standards.

Contents

Acknowledgments

This book is dedicated to my husband, A. J., who sustained and encouraged me, and to my sons, Joe and Ken, who were confident in my ability and shared the family computer during this project. I thank my parents, sisters, and brothers who are enthusiastic about my success.

I also acknowledge the many friends and colleagues who readily shared with me their best thoughts for block scheduling and lesson design, in particular Alice Pembrook, Edythe Rose, Michael Landow, and other staff at East Lyme High School in East Lyme, Connecticut. I am appreciative of the school library media specialists who contributed to this book, especially Karen Libby, Patricia Gautier, and Linda Brake, who related their own experiences in the case studies in Chapter 12.

In reseaching material for this book I made contact, through a listserv, with many interesting and dedicated library media specialists who work in block-scheduled schools. Twelve agreed to help me in data collection for the book by contributing their ideas and opinions to a series of surveys I submitted to them over the course of a year. These practitioners are excited about block scheduling and the impact it has on their students and program, and they offer wonderful advice as well as their statistics. The participants are:

Elisa Baker
Ursuline High School
Santa Rosa, CA 95403

Connie Baldwin
Scotland High School
Laurenburg, NC 28352

Sonya Boyd
Shaw High School
Columbus, GA 31909

Linda Brake
Evergreen High School
Vancouver, WA 98684

Terri Brunner
Centralia High School
Centralia, MO 65240

Patricia Gautier
Edward Little High School
Auburn, ME 04210

Karen Libby
Kingswood Regional High School
Wolfeboro, NH 03894

Susan Meyer
Vines High School
Plano, TX 75075

Jayne Moore
Division of Instruction and Staff
    Development
Maryland State Department of
    Education
Baltimore, MD 21201

Sandra Parks
Harrisonburg High School
Harrisonburg, VA 22801

Carol Petrie
West Brunswick High School
Shallotte, NC 28479

Eileen Sexton
Duncanville Ninth Grade School
Dallas, TX 75249

Introduction

As we come to the close of this century, high school graduates are entering a world that expects them to think creatively, be able to extract information from many sources, be technology literate, and apply their knowledge and skills in either college or the workplace. The traditional classroom environment where the teacher lectures and the students are passive learners no longer prepares students adequately for their future.

The majority of high school communities are in the process of examining their mission and are concluding that they must restructure to educate children appropriately. Curriculum is being modified or broadly rewritten. Block scheduling, which provides fewer classes per day or semester but longer, sustained learning time, is being adopted by schools in record numbers. Along with block scheduling is often the philosophical change of teaching through information and materials, or resource-based learning. Students study a wide variety of resources, write, discuss, formulate ideas, create projects, and demonstrate their knowledge and skills with the active guidance and support of their teachers. The longer time for concentrating on a topic or subject in the block is conducive to cooperative learning and delivering instruction to multiple learning styles of students.

The school media specialist is at the center of change with block scheduling. Students and teachers rely on the resources of the library media center to support their teaching and learning. An existing, viable program in a traditional schedule will only become more essential to its users. Decisions have to be made as to how best the library media program can support the instructional and curricular changes that are made when teachers put lecture in a secondary position to active resource-based learning.

This book is directed to secondary school library media specialists who are undertaking the transition to block scheduling. They must have all the elements in place for a successful program that will contribute to student learning in this new environment. Although the book is written primarily for the high school level, middle and elementary school library media specialists will find suggestions and ideas that could prove helpful to them with only slight modification. Across the country K–12 educators are examining how they deliver instruction and often conclude that they must restructure the traditional school day in order to meet the goals they have for students. This book examines the essential components of the library media program in a block-scheduled school and provides useful handouts, lesson plans, and the experiences of four practitioners through their case studies.

When I began researching and writing this book, I had less than two years of experience as a library media specialist in a block-scheduled high school. I sought out the wisdom of many colleagues via the school library media specialists listserv. From a large group of respondents to my initial overtures, I selected twelve practitioners who were either working in a block-scheduled high school or were on the planning teams to move their school to the block system. Over fifteen months, these contributors affirmed for me the ideas and thoughts I had, and they gave me valuable insights, which I share in this book.

This book is organized as follows: Chapter One discusses the need for high school communities to examine how well they are doing and the need for most schools to restructure in order to meet their mission and goals for students in the twenty-first century. It provides an overview of block scheduling along with the types of schedules that are being used. Chapter Two addresses the need for library media specialists to be on the planning committee or team for block scheduling. From this vantage point, they can be knowledgeable about the new directions the school is taking and plan for the policies, resources, and staff the library media program will need to meet these goals. The methods and materials teachers use to instruct will radically change; Chapter Three examines how the library media specialist can support the faculty. In addition, the roles of the library media specialist—information specialist, instructional consultant, and teacher—are applied to a block-scheduled high school.

Professional development specific to and useful for library media specialists is brought to our attention in Chapter Four. What do we need, and how do we find it when we are often the only professional in our department? What will support staff need to learn to be supportive in the block? Chapter Five focuses on expected curricular changes as teachers design lessons to be much more dependent on student discovery and activities. How can we keep up with the plethora of new activities and provide the best materials when radical changes are occurring simultaneously across all the curricula in the school?

Chapters Six and Eleven were written to help library media specialists get through the day-to-day issues that the block schedule will bring. Chapter Six addresses staffing, collection development, and budgetary concerns. Chapter Eleven discusses the need for teacher and student flexibility in the library media center during a 90-minute block and how that affects the schedule, the issues of study hall if the school retains them, what happens when a substitute brings a class to the library media center, and how library media specialists can aid both teachers and students with performance assessment.

Resource sharing and networking are critical in a block-scheduled school, as Chapter Seven points out. Chapters Eight, Nine, and Ten describe the tremendous need for and dependency on technology to deliver the best information. An overview of technology planning and what it can do for a block-scheduled school is found in Chapter Eight, while Chapter Nine discusses the importance of the Internet and multimedia technology to students, who are required to gather information from global sources and construct well-designed presentations to demonstrate their knowledge and abilities. Chapter Ten stretches us to look at distance-learning possibilities in schools, which may have gained substantial instructional time by changing to block scheduling but have not made a parallel increase in staffing for enriching the curriculum or to provide additional courses.

Case studies of four practicing library media specialists from around the country who are working in block-scheduled schools are contained in Chapter Twelve. The contributors are candid about the benefits and the drawbacks of block scheduling on the library media program and staff, and much can be garnered from their experiences. The book concludes with Chapter Thirteen, which contains five lesson plans, four of them interdisciplinary between the library media program and an academic area. These plans were selected because each lesson could not offer students its excellent learning opportunities without the sustained time the block provides. An introductory lesson to the library media center for incoming ninth-grade students is provided. It is successful because the 90-minute period allows students to become engaged in the resources and activities.

Block Scheduling and Its Impact on the School Library Media Center

Restructuring and the Block Schedule: An Overview

"How do you use your library in the block?" a library media specialist recently asked the subscribers of a listserv. There were numerous and varied responses to this question. One surefire answer was that the library media program will change. What that change will be can be anticipated and directed by library media specialists with appropriate planning.

The decision to restructure the high school environment can be viewed as an opportunity for library media specialists to examine instruction, services, and facilities and capitalize on them to make them even better. As the high school undergoes innovation, media specialists may be able to seize the moment to make needed modifications.

In order for high school staff to accomplish meaningful change that will result in improved learning for students, many factors have to be in place. One strategist for successful change states, "Staff members who can attend simultaneously to multiple aspects of school redesign—curriculum, pedagogy, assessment, and school culture—are more likely to see the kinds of results for which they hope" (Wasley, Hampel, and Clark 1997, p. 694). If the library media specialist has this broad perspective and maintains high goals for student learning, professional development, resource-based learning, instruction, curriculum, technology, management, networking, and collection development, he or she will be a leader in the successful implementation of school restructuring that the block schedule supports.

RESTRUCTURING—TO WHAT END?

It would be unusual for a high school today not to be considering whether there is a need to restructure. We are bombarded in both the popular and professional literature with stories of how disengaged teenagers are from school and their learning. Our own day-to-day experience confirms that students approach their learning differently than students did ten or twenty years ago. Teachers have to work much harder to create a positive learning environment that provides differentiated and appropriate instruction and where the student can confidently and comfortably test new knowledge and try ideas. Restructuring "involves fundamental alterations in the relationships" among teachers, students, parents, administrators, and communities (Hargreaves 1998, p. 4).

We are challenged to examine the benefits and the process of restructuring a traditional factory-model high school. The school day is not unlike an assembly line, which allocates little pieces of learning again and again and again. Among the many obstacles, there are four challenges schools face today: growth, diversity, inclusion, and social dislocations:

First is the mismatch between growth and resources. Classrooms, schools, and sometimes districts are too large. They have grown beyond human scale for effective teaching, learning, and the management of these activities. Second is the phenomenal expansion of ethnic, linguistic, and cultural diversity in the classroom and the school. Third is the expectation of full inclusiveness. We have come to believe that all children can learn and should stay in school to do so. Fourth is the set of social changes or dislocations that have occurred over the past three decades: single-parent families, latchkey children, poverty and poor health, drugs, gangs, and violence. (Donahoe 1993, p. 301)

This author contends that school improvement can be accomplished when there is a formal arrangement that provides *time* in the school day for teachers and students to create an interactive culture and supporting infrastructure to improve student learning.

A MOVEMENT WHOSE TIME HAS COME

School restructuring should be an ongoing, evolutionary process. In fact, any organization—educational, business, or governmental in nature—must periodically and systematically examine whether it is accomplishing its mission. Is there something that should be done, some change made, so that the clients or end users will derive the best product by associating themselves with this institution or organization? Gordon Cawelti (1995) states that

the centerpiece of high school restructuring focuses on establishing clear standards and performance assessments for an integrated curriculum appropriate to the students' futures. Supportive factors that contribute to this system change should include more flexible schedules, extensive technology, and expanded use of community resources. (p. 7)

He sees block scheduling as a critical organizational element to successful restructuring. Schools that provide longer periods of time have the flexibility needed to offer varied instructional and learning activities (1995, p. 11).

Just a few years ago a block-scheduled high school was rare. In 1993–94, only an estimated 15 percent of high schools were following some type of block schedule. The majority of these schools were located in the West and South, and the purpose for adopting the block was to resolve an existing problem, such as lowering the student dropout rate. In 1995–96 when my own school, East Lyme High School, restructured and adopted the block, we were one of two high schools in Connecticut to do so. Within two years 50 percent of the nation's high schools were using a form of block scheduling (Eineder and Bishop 1997, p. 50).

THE ECONOMY

The 1980s influenced educational reform for the 1990s with economic reform and revitalization as the political arena around the world rapidly changed from a defensive posture to one of joining economic forces with traditional foes for mutual gain and benefit. Business assessed its traditional practices, including services and the readiness of its workforce. Manufacturing was replaced by the commodities of communication and technology services on a global level.

PREPARING STUDENTS FOR WORK

The demand continued for skilled, versatile workers with advanced training. Many employees who were victims of downsizing had to retrain. These potential new students did not fit the two- or four-year college schedule, and a different track had to be developed. Technical colleges developed weekend courses that attracted students making a career change (Mabry 1988, p. 3). Colleges found that they had to rethink their traditional schedule of courses and adapt to the needs of a new category of older student.

As employers identified critical business, communication, information, and technology skills necessary for employees, the pressure mounted on secondary schools to graduate students who would have the knowledge and skills to be competent employees. With a significantly reduced armed forces and a shrinking need for blue-collar labor, nonskilled graduates could not be guaranteed employment. Business, state legislatures, and higher education scrutinized high schools in the 1980s and brainstormed ways to keep students in school and improve the quality of their education.

THE COPERNICAN PLAN

In 1989 the Copernican Plan was developed by Joseph Carroll who advocated for change in the American high school. Just as Copernicus's ideas changed the perception of our solar system, this plan proposed the restructuring of all the major systems of the high school, including the schedule. Students would concentrate on one or two subjects at a time in a "macroclass." Integral to the Copernican schedule is a seminar program in which students discuss complex global issues (Carroll 1989, p. 16). Now, almost ten years after its first implementation, schools around the country continue to find that students' needs are best met with long blocks of time for academic and elective studies. Integral to the Copernican Plan is the replacement of the traditional Carnegie unit credits with stated course objectives or student outcomes. Students move closer toward graduation as they achieve these standards and objectives (Gee 1997, p. 794).

THE PROBLEM OF TIME

"There is never enough time" is a lament heard again and again by teachers and students. Restructuring the school day will not solve all the issues associated with this problem, but it will provide more control over the schedule. Gary D. Watts and Shari Castle suggest strategies for dealing with the dilemma of time in Table 1.1.

"BLOCK"—WHAT DOES IT MEAN?

The word *block* is a relatively new educational term, one that many veteran teachers did not have in their professional vocabulary when they undertook teaching. Nevertheless, educators have been using the word *block* for over five years, defining it as a segment of time for instruction that is usually twice as long in length as the traditional period. Combined with the word *schedule*, we immediately think of a restructured high school day that offers students approximately 90 minutes of uninterrupted time devoted to one course or curriculum area. A block-scheduled high school is more than just a change in the arrangement of the day or the manner in which students are moved throughout the building. It is a conscious effort by the administration, the teachers, and the community to create positive change in the curriculum students learn, the instructional methodology teachers practice, and the school climate of the building. Much has been written about how a school can successfully implement a block schedule (Schoenstein 1995, pp. 15–19). The most important factor for a high school undertaking block scheduling is not to lose sight that the block schedule is only a *vehicle* to accomplish change. After the adoption of block scheduling, periodical monitoring must oc-

Table 1.1
Strategies for Creating Time in the School Day

Strategy	Resolution
Freed-up or release time	This strategy is used for a temporary assignment and can involve teachers' "covering" for each other, or the employment of a substitute teacher.
Restructured or rescheduled time	This is the permanent and formal alteration of the time frame of the traditional calendar, school day, or teaching schedule (block schedule).
Common time	Planned, designated specific time periods for team, department, or interdisciplinary planning.
Better-used time	This strategy encourages staff to examine if they now receive the maximum potential from allocated time. For example, faculty meetings can be better utilized for professional development.
Purchased time	This requires funds for hiring additional teachers to reduce class size or to extend planning periods.

Source: Adapted from Gary D. Watts and Shari Castle, "The Time Dilemma in School Restructuring," *Phi Delta Kappan* (December 1993): pp. 307–8.

cur to determine if the school has reached the intended goals that were sought with restructuring.

BLOCK SCHEDULING FORMATS

Moving large groups of people from one place to another without chaos requires a schedule, be it in a sports complex, an airport, or a high school. We in education all know that the schedule of the building is a very controlling device; it rules where teachers and students are at any given time. For all students to learn a wide variety of subjects each day, a schedule must be adhered to.

There are several different formats of block scheduling that are being used across the country. What is common to each is that the instructional period has been extended to a longer amount of time, usually ninety minutes. Students and teachers do not meet for every class each day; instead, the daily focus is on a limited number of courses. The two most popular formats are the alternate-day schedule and the 4 × 4 semester plan. Other forms of block scheduling are the combination schedule, modified block schedule, trimester plan, and reconfiguring the year. Districts should research the pros and cons of each type of plan. For example, a school that decides that offering English and math to all students for the entire year is important should seriously consider the alternate-day schedule. If creating the environment for students and teachers whereby they only have to concentrate on half the courses at any given time is strategic, then the 4 × 4 schedule or trimester schedule should be looked at. Many schools will opt for a modified version of the block that best suits their students' needs.

Common Block Schedules

Alternating-Day Schedule. Also referred to as the A/B plan, this format carries the curriculum through the entire school year, with half the classes being offered on day 1 and the other half of the courses offered on a day 2. It retains the 180-day calendar as a continuous session and divides the day into four main blocks of instruction, each 80–90 minutes long.

4 × 4 Schedule. Also referred to as the accelerated schedule, students enroll in four courses that meet for 90 minutes each day for half the year. It reorganizes the 180-day school calendar into two terms with 90 days per term. Teachers usually teach three courses per semester. Year-long courses are completed in one semester. Students enroll in four new courses in the second semester.

Combination Schedule. This schedule divides most of the day into three or four large blocks of instructional time, with some traditional 45-minute periods remaining. Like the 4 × 4, courses within long blocks meet for a semester, and the courses remaining in the traditional 45-minute periods are carried through the entire year.

Modified Block Schedule. This block schedule accommodates everyone. During one week, a school using this format may have two or three full block days with the remaining time spent in a traditional day of seven or eight periods. Some schools rotate the order of classes. This modified schedule is sometimes used by schools to test their readiness for block scheduling. Other users have determined a value to retain some attributes of a traditonal schedule.

Trimester Plan. Students take two or three core courses every 60 days to earn six to nine credits or courses per year.

Reconfiguring the Year. Some districts reconfigure the 180-day school year into a combination of long terms and short terms to provide time for remediation, enrichment, or intense study. This plan is also called the 75-75-30 plan, whereby there are two 75-day terms (fall and winter) and a 30-day spring term. The 75-day term could have three 112-minute block classes, one 48-minute period, 24 minutes for lunch, and 12 minutes total to change classes, for a total of 420 minutes. The 30-day term provides for the study of one or two subjects through one 224-minute block, 24 minutes for lunch, and one 112-minute block. (Rettig and Canady 1996, p. 14; *Basics of Block Scheduling* 1997, p. 5)

WHY ARE HIGH SCHOOLS CHANGING TO THE BLOCK?

The Copernican Plan, perhaps too radical for most public high schools at its onset, initiated an earnest dialogue in the 1990s among educators about the structure of the high school day. They asked if under the traditional schedule teachers could meet the educational needs of 120 to 180 students in short periods of daily contact time. Is the hectic pace overwhelming to both students and teachers? What can be accomplished in such a short amount of time? Some would argue that schools have done a pretty good job under the traditional schedule, and in some districts they will continue to do so. On closer examination, however, the traditional schedule often fails a large number of students. As the 1994 report of the National Education Commission pointed out, "Schools will have a design flaw as long as their origination is based on the assumption that all students can learn on the same schedule."

There is a wealth of research about block scheduling and why high schools should consider restructuring the day. The reasons fall into two categories. The first is to try to create a solution to existing problems or seek improvements in areas that impede student performance or teacher instruction. The second category is not as straightforward, but it has to do with tweaking a system that isn't broken. The old adage, "If it isn't broke, don't fix it," does not encourage educational renewal or growth. Individual school districts may find that they are examining block scheduling not to solve a problem but to raise the standards of the learning environment from very good to excellent.

How Block Scheduling Can Improve the Environment

- It eliminates fragmented instruction.
- It increases overall available instruction time by reducing the number of class beginnings and endings.
- Tardiness and attendance are often improved.
- Some schools report a reduction in suspension and dropout rates.
- Student attention spans are maintained better.
- Teachers can manage instructional time more effectively. Block scheduling encourages team teaching and interdisciplinary courses.
- Teachers and students can engage in a number of different activities and instructional approaches within an extended instructional period.
- Students have more time and opportunity for active participation.
- Teachers and students can focus their attention on fewer subjects because teachers have fewer preparations and students have fewer homework assignments to juggle each evening.
- Teachers work with a smaller number of students each day or each term so they can better attend to individual instructional and developmental needs.

- Many schools report better academic achievement.
- There are more opportunities for students to complete teacher-supervised group activities and projects in class.
- There is time for extended activities that can give students school-to-career experiences.
- Students can enroll in a greater number and variety of courses. Some formats of the block offer more opportunities for acceleration.

BLOCK SCHEDULING AND THE LIBRARY MEDIA PROGRAM

This book focuses on how the library media facilities and resources are directly affected by block scheduling. The restructuring that occurs with block scheduling is often a positive renewal of curriculum and instruction; teachers differentiate their instructional methodology (how they teach) as well as the content of the curriculum (what they teach). Much of what students formerly learned through teacher lecture is now learned through resource-based activities. Time is now available in class for inquiry and discovery to teach and learn. The research skills of students are challenged as they use a wide variety of information resources to uncover content material, compare and contrast opinions, and draw their own conclusions based on the information they obtain.

Library media centers are the technology and information centers of the school. They link students to the information within the confines of the building and resources that can be thousands of miles away. Block scheduling can serve as a renewal for all teachers, as is often heard in a school that is making a change that "all teachers feel like first year teachers." There is a tremendous need to support the faculty in their experimentation with new instructional techniques and their design of many more student-centered learning activities. The math teachers who now want their students to research the history of calculus, gather data from a variety of sources to create graphs, or write a biographical paper on women mathematicians will seek resources that the typical school library never had to acquire to any extent. Now there are whole classes of mathematics students in great need of support in their studies. The challenge for the library media specialist is to prepare for the unknown assignments and the intense focus that will come to the program once block scheduling is implemented.

BIBLIOGRAPHY

Print Sources

The Basics of Block Scheduling. Professional Issues in Public Education. Hartford, CT: Connecticut Education Association, Summer 1997.

Canady, Robert Lynn, and Michael D. Rettig. Block Scheduling: A Catalyst for Change in High Schools. Princeton, NJ: Eye on Education, 1995.

Carroll, Joseph M. *The Copernican Plan: Restructuring the American High School.* Andover, MA: Regional Laboratory for Educational Improvement of the Northeast and Islands, 1989.

Cawelti, Gordon. "High School Restructuring: What Are the Critical Elements?" *NASSP Bulletin* 79, 569 (March 1995): pp. 1–15.

Donahoe, Tom. "Finding the Way: Structure, Time, and Culture in School Improvement." *Phi Delta Kappan* (December 1993): pp. 298–305.

Eineder, Dale V., and Harold L. Bishop. "Block Scheduling the High School: The Effects on Achievement, Behavior, and Student-Teacher Relationships." *NASSP Bulletin* (May 1997): pp. 45–54.

Gee, William D. "The Copernican Plan and Year-Round Education." *Phi Delta Kappan* 78, 10 (June 1997): pp. 793–796.

Hargreaves, Andy. "Renewal in the Age of Paradox." *Educational Leadership* 52, 7. Online. Internet. January 1, 1998. *http://www.ascd.org/pubs/el/hargreav.html*

Irmsher, Karen. "Block Scheduling." *ERIC Digest*, no. 104 (March 1996).

Mabry, Theo, N. "Alternative Scheduling." *ERIC Digest* (April 1988). (ED296766.)

National Education Commission on Time and Learning. *Prisoners of Time: Research. What We Need to Know.* Report of the National Education Commission on Time and Learning. Washington, DC: U.S. Government Printing Office, September 1994. (ED378685.)

Rettig, Michael D., and Robert Canady. "All Around the Block: The Benefits and Challenges of a Non-Traditional School Schedule." *The School Administrator* (September 1996).

Schoenstein, Roger. "Making Block Scheduling Work." *Education Digest* 60, 6 (February 1995): pp. 15–19.

Wasley, Patricia, Robert Hampel, and Richard Clark. "The Puzzle of Whole-School Change." *Phi Delta Kappan* (May 1997): pp. 690–697.

Watts, Gary D., and Shari Castle. "The Time Dilemma in School Restructuring." *Phi Delta Kappan* (December 1993): pp. 306–310.

Internet Sites

ASCD (Association for Supervision and Curriculum Development): Research database. *http://www.ascd.org/issue/research.html*

Center for Applied Research and Educational Improvement (CAREI), University of Minnesota: Block scheduling. *http://carei.coled.umn.edu/BSMAIN.HTM*

INSTRUCT (Implementing the NCTM School Teaching Recommendations Using Collaborative Telecommunications): Block schedule information. *http://instruct.cms.uncwil.edu/block.html*

NEA (National Education Association): Search feature of current topics. *http://www.nea.org/* (Select Block Scheduling and submit to the Search Database.)

University of Virginia—Block Scheduling Research. *http://curry.edschool.virginia.edu/~dhv3v/block/research/*

Wasson High School—block scheduling. *http://www.classroom.net/classweb/WASSON/myhome.html*

Planning for the Block

2

Each high school will have its own approach to planning for block scheduling, and there are many resources available to draw on. All the research suggests that planning cannot be overlooked. Equally important is the leadership role of the administration to meet the needs of many diverse groups—teachers, students, the board of education, parents, and the community—as they go through the process of understanding, accepting, and supporting the need for restructuring. "Changing a school's organizational schedule to a block requires extensive education of all community players including the school board, which generally must approve the move; parents, who went to school under the 50-minute traditional schedule and have to be convinced of the block's benefits; teachers, who must teach in different ways; and students, who must adjust to longer class periods and new ways of learning" (Phillips 1997, p. 4).

As administrations vary, so do the management styles of school districts. The average tenure of an urban school superintendent is two and one-half years (Renchler 1992). Board of education members may serve terms of two to four years, and their views often reflect the political climate of the time. It can be difficult to find sustained, long-term management policies in many school districts. The process of restructuring can take many years, and thus there is a need for a formalized acceptance of the long-range goals and objectives that will be sustained with new personnel.

Canady and Rettig (1995) suggest that alternative schedules can vastly improve the quality of the time students spend in school. When the schedule is properly designed for a high school, it can:

- Result in more effective use of time, space, and resources (human as well as material).

- Improve the instructional climate.
- Help solve problems related to the delivery of instruction.
- Assist in establishing desired programs and instructional practices.

THE FUTURE

With a complex world awaiting them, children today must have superb preparation. Problem solving is multifaceted and information is constantly changing. In 1954 information doubled every twenty years. Today it doubles every thirty to thirty-six months, and by the year 2000, information will double every twelve to eighteen months (Breivik 1998). The traditional approach to problem solving, whereby one consults an "expert"— be it the content in a book or the opinion of a knowledgeable person—is not an assured or correct process today. Global information is prolific, immediate, ever changing, and accessible from a wide variety of sources that can conflict or support an idea or opinion. Schools must be responsive in training students to be divergent thinkers, ready to face a workplace that demands creativity, teamwork, and continuous learning and growth of its employees. No longer does the culmination of a course of study certify a person to be an expert in a specialized field forever. One has to be able to use information and resources to reshape one's expertise and knowledge on a multitude of topics.

Schools adopt block scheduling for a variety of unique and individual reasons that reflect the needs of their learning communities, but all agree that it better prepares young people for the world of work. As of September 1997 forty state departments of education reported that some schools within their jurisdiction were trying a form of block scheduling (Phillips 1997, p. 1). The time the block provides gives students the opportunity to problem-solve together and research information that supports their theories and ideas.

As we prepare students for the world of work, we must be active contributors to creating an educational structure that provides the opportunities they need to be multiskilled and flexible. Major transitions are prevalent in the business community and higher education. Whether we agree or disagree that change is necessary, we live in a time when people have multiple careers, temporary consultants are commonplace, and management is rewarded for innovation and change.

GUIDELINES FOR IMPLEMENTING BLOCK SCHEDULING

Donald Hackmann (1995) sets out ten guidelines to follow for implementing block scheduling:

1. *Employ a systems thinking approach.* Don't implement a block schedule because it's the latest trend, but because it empowers teachers to rethink and restructure their system.

2. *Secure the support of your superiors beyond the faculty's jurisdiction.*

3. *Understand the change process.* Allow teachers sufficient time to assess how they feel about the new paradigm and to prepare for it. It is also important to make the change when the momentum peaks.

4. *Involve all the stakeholders.* Ensure that all interested parties are involved; explain the rationale for any change to the school board, central office administrators, teachers, parents, and students; and actively support teachers as they struggle with the demands of changing instructional methods.

5. *Consult sources outside the school.*

6. *Brainstorm creative alternatives.* Pay attention to why the block schedule will remedy problems of the traditional schedule.

7. *Examine the budgetary implications.*

8. *Plan faculty inservices.*

9. *Include an evaluation component.*

10. *Celebrate your successes.*

It is important for library media specialists to know the direction of restructuring in the district and to work with the administration for positive change. The administration needs the support of the instructional leaders of the school. They will be part of the planning process, implement the programs, and serve as evaluators who monitor the progress and the impact that block scheduling has on the school community.

Appropriate planning for the implementation of block scheduling is vital. Students and faculty should be able to state the important objectives for changing the schedule. If the proposed new schedule is not too complex and radically different from the past (such as moving from an eight-period day to an alternating A/B schedule), it may be of value to try out the proposed schedule for a week or two before a final acceptance (Wasley 1997, p. 49).

At East Lyme High School, the planning time frame for active research and investigation was relatively short. I was a member of the initial team chosen by the principal to clarify goals and objectives for restructuring our school and then to investigate the means to accomplish these ideals. The process we used was to attend a national conference, research existing alternative schedules, visit schools that had already implemented block scheduling, bring in experts for staff development, report to the faculty regularly, and finally make a formal recommendation to the faculty. Of the nineteen anticipated outcomes we had for restructuring at East Lyme High School, seven affected the library media program:

1. More time for cooperative group projects and individualized instruction

2. Opportunities to integrate subject matter

3. A calmer atmosphere for students and teachers

4. More continuity of lessons, projects, labs, group discussions, and activities

5. More choice for students
6. Increased communication among teachers
7. Increased personal responsibility for all students. (Mistretta and Polansky 1997, p. 26)

THE SCHOOL MEDIA SPECIALIST PLANS FOR THE BLOCK

Library media specialists play an essential role in the transition to block scheduling and later in sustaining and supporting the renewed interest in instruction and learning. They are concerned about how block scheduling will affect the library media program. As teachers move away from the traditional lecture approach to resource-based learning, the library media center and its educational support and services will be in great demand. Most library media centers are already overburdened, lacking enough staff and materials. What will the impact be with block scheduling?

Research, adequate funding, staffing, and communication are key to a successful transition. The library media specialist is called on to assure faculty and administration that the library media center will be able to support resource-based learning. If this cannot be accomplished under the existing configuration, there have to be specific recommendations for improvement so that the library media program can grow to meet the demands that come with implementation of the block. If block scheduling is viewed as an opportunity to assess the program and its component parts, the library media specialist can both gain positive feedback about the strengths of the existing program and develop an action plan that will make the library media center ready to embrace the challenges of the block.

ASSESSING THE EXISTING PROGRAM

During the block-scheduling planning, the library media specialist should articulate the strengths and weaknesses of the current program. Adapting block scheduling can be an opportunity to redirect services and renew the goals and objectives of the library media program. An analysis or evaluation of the current program should be done on a periodic basis, but often there is not enough time to step back and do this. The process of school reform can provide just the opportunity for this exercise. Following are questions that could be asked so that contingencies can be planned for.

Questions to Ask When Planning for the Block

1. What is the daily usage of the library media center? How many classes typically visit each day? How many classes typically visit each period?
2. How many students use the library media center during their study hall each day? Each period? What percentage of the student body is this?

3. Know your customers! What departments use the library media center more frequently? From the previous year's schedule book, note how many classes in each department visited the library media center over a year. Can you detect a trend as to *when* certain departments typically use the library media center? (See Figure 2.2.)

4. What departments are your most frequent customers? Using the information you've gathered, list the departments by the percentage of use (e.g., "English Department: 35 percent of the total class usage").

5. Which classes or departments require most time for direct instruction? Looking again at class usage, do a rough calculation of the percentage of classes that required direct instruction from the library media specialist. How many were independent in their research, and how many visited to select materials only? From these numbers, roughly calculate the percentage of your time that you spend as a teacher of media, technology, and information services as opposed to a director or manager of the library media center.

6. Create a spreadsheet of the circulation statistics versus student population over the past five years. Is there statistical evidence that without block scheduling the circulation is in a growth period? If so, what is the reason? An increased student population or changes in the manner in which the library media program is being used for curriculum support? Try to analyze why the program is developing in a certain direction.

7. What kind of materials circulate the most? If you cannot quantify them with data, take a walk through the stacks, and jot down the books that you know are most heavily used.

8. How do students use periodicals and newspapers: primarily for pleasure reading or as research materials? Do you subscribe to digitized formats and use technology to support periodical use now? Do you have sufficient numbers of titles for the use they are given? If not, what do you need more of?

9. How often do you use interlibrary loan materials from other libraries, and what kind of materials do students borrow? Is the process cost-effective in terms of staff and resources? Does the library media center have the right technology in place to support interlibrary loan?

10. How does each library media staff member use his or her day? What functions does each person accomplish? What functions tend not to be done very well? Are these problems because there is a lack of time, insufficient staff, poor work habits, insufficient training, or something else?

11. What is the ratio of computers to students in the library media center? In the school? Are you near the goal that your district or school technology plan strives to meet? If not, how far off are you? Are there funding plans in place in order to meet the goal?

The information collected during this assessment will give you valuable insight as to how you and your staff deliver services and instruction. It will also be helpful to have quantifiable data when working on or with the planning team for block scheduling. If the library media center is to support block scheduling successfully, adequate resources must be allocated that will allow an already busy and effective program do even more.

Just as classroom teachers worry about their ability to teach in a longer period of time, library media specialists too have anxious moments about the impact the block will have on their ability to support the learning of all students. This reality check of the data will give library media specialists information to advocate for the support and changes they will need in order to make the adaptations the faculty and students will demand with resource-based learning.

PLANNING TEAMS

In order for block scheduling to be successful, there must be careful thought and planning involved before the transition. Without proper planning, a high school is almost certain to meet disaster. The staff of Reed-Custer High School in Illinois spent five years investigating block scheduling. Their process of investigation and reflection reached these conclusions:

- The key to success would not be adopting a block schedule but rather *adapting* one to fit the school's particular needs.
- Block scheduling in one form or another addresses many of the most pressing problems facing students, teachers, and administrators today.
- When block scheduling fails, it is often for four reasons:
    —Schools jump into it too hastily.
    —Administrators impose it from the top, unsympathetic to the teachers', students', or community's feelings.
    —Teachers aren't given training in instructional strategies for the new delivery system.
    —It is implemented without sufficient examination of other school policies (Freeman and Scheidecker 1996, pp. 60–61).

If the school has a school improvement team (SIT), that team will most likely be the body that investigates block scheduling. SITs usually are composed of representatives from the faculty, students, administration, and parent communities. The SIT may form subcommittees to help it determine whether block scheduling is appropriate, but the final recommendation rests with this body, which will bring it to the superintendent and board of education for final approval.

A task of the planning team is to investigate the potential problems that a block schedule could have on the school and to make recommendations designed to remedy these anticipated concerns. The planning team may look at the impact on scheduling of classes, lunch period, study halls, professional development for staff, and library media center, to name a few.

Because the library media center has the potential to continue as it is or to become the center of learning activities with block scheduling, it is essential for the library media specialist to be a member of the planning team in order to share verifiable data about the use of the facility and its materials. The library media specialist must also make projections for the financial support that will be needed to transform the library media center into a support facility. Teachers and administration alike need to be assured that the library media specialist has the knowledge and skills to support resource-based learning and serve as a consultant for differentiated instruction. By being a member of the planning team, the library media specialist will affirm his or her role and be able to bring those very legitimate concerns to the forefront of the planning stage, rather than reacting to problems once block scheduling is in place and resources may have been directed to other parts of the building. The time and effort given to being a member of the planning team will pay back enormous dividends to the library media program.

The library media specialist should be a member of the planning committee so that he or she is aware of the outcomes sought by changing to a block schedule. Are resource-based learning and differentiated instruction goals of the committee? Collaborative planning for new curriculum and instruction can take place. Anticipate that departments that may not be traditional users will now look to the library media center for resources. What is feasible to achieve with existing resources of materials, staff, technology, and budget? Are there immediate modifications that have to be made for block scheduling outcomes to be realized, and is there a priority order?

When asked if they were participants on a special committee to investigate block scheduling, my survey respondents overwhelmingly said they were. The one person who said she was not said that she should have because block scheduling has an impact on students and the library media program, and she could have served as a research librarian for the committee to find information and people who had experience with block scheduling.

The survey respondents were very positive about their influence and contributions when they served on planning committees of their schools, whether at the building level or district level. Curriculum and instruction will undoubtedly change with the block schedule, and the school media specialist can support these changes by providing ideas and materials. Teachers in block-scheduled schools need to change their teaching styles from lecture to differentiated instruction, and this often means more frequent short-term library assignments. One respondent said, "The library media specialist should be a member in their instructional-consultant role. I found a lot of fear from teachers as they were uncomfortable using 90 minutes for resource/activity based learning." She went on to say that library media specialists can provide leadership when they show teachers how to integrate information problem solving into the curriculum. Another reason for library media specialists to be on the planning team is to learn what staff development teachers will need to make the transition to block scheduling. Media specialists can support teachers by sharing their knowledge of resource-based learning and teaching or arranging for outside speakers who can demonstrate multiple instructional strategies to teachers.

Library media specialists who visit schools that are block scheduled gain new ideas and insights and can bring back a sense of the enthusiasm that abounds in blocked schools. A library media specialist in Florida, whose school moved to block scheduling in August 1994, expresses her thoughts about the lack of media specialists who represented schools as visitors to observe block scheduling. Among the large number of teachers who came, there were only two library media specialists.

This lack of attention bothered me because having experienced the change, I knew what a major role the media center would play for any school contemplating making a similar change. I felt that the importance of the media center or library was being overlooked. (Galt 1996, p. 13)

I concur. East Lyme High School welcomed visitors biweekly during our second year of block scheduling. Each visiting group wanted to talk to me about the impact block scheduling had on the library media center, but it was a rare occasion that the visitor was a library media specialist. This lack of visibility bothered me, for I knew that when I had visited several block high schools as a planning team member, I realized that the library media program would have to change, but that it would change for the better. The visits also gave me the information I needed to articulate to my administration that staffing, technology, and budget would have to be increased significantly if we were to be able to fulfill our new mission as an instructional center for resource-based learning.

THE BASICS OF BLOCK SCHEDULING

The Connecticut Education Association (CEA) has published a pamphlet, *The Basics of Block Scheduling*, which outlines the process for planning and implementing a change to block scheduling. It gives these recommendations from five high schools in Connecticut that have recently adopted block scheduling:

- Form a block scheduling study committee that includes administrators, teachers, parents, students, a board of education member, and a representative of the teachers' association.
- Develop a consensus about what purpose block scheduling is intended to serve.
- Do research on block scheduling.

- Reexamine the outcomes established for block scheduling.
- Describe in detail what the schedule looks like in concrete terms and what people will be doing within the schedule.
- Develop the schedule.
- Determine what will be needed to prepare for and implement the change.
- Set a time line for implementing the schedule changes.
- Discuss and decide how you will evaluate whether the changed schedule is helping to bring the outcomes you desire.
- Make a plan for orientating teachers, students, and parents to the proposed change.
- Frequently assess the progress to identify concerns of the stakeholders, and address those concerns quickly and on a personal basis.

When the library media specialist is a member of the planning team, realistic expectations may be made for resource-based learning. The specialist has an opportunity to be an instructional leader in the school in a positive, proactive manner. He or she can facilitate the changes needed for the position to one of teacher, information specialist, and instructional consultant (*Information Power* 1988).

Just as there are subcommittees of the planning team that investigate curriculum issues, such as global language and mathematics instruction, there should be a special subcommittee that examines the library media program. The tasks of this subcommittee could include the following:

- Assess existing library data that quantify circulation, student use, class use, and other meaningful reports that provide information on the use of the library media program.
- Perform a time-on-task analysis that indicates how staff spend their day on services for patrons and other responsibilities.
- Analyze the budget.
    —Are the existing funds adequate for the services provided in a non-blocked environment?
    —If your state has guidelines for library media program spending or technology spending, is the high school within these guidelines?
    —Contact high schools in your region, especially any that are block scheduled, and compare your budget to theirs. Where do you exceed their spending? Where do you fall short?
- Examine the ratio, use, and expected increase of technology and online services.
- Look at potential partnerships with the community, including the public and academic libraries, for resource sharing.
- Determine how the library media center is being used now. Is it a vibrant learning center, or is it primarily a location for study hall students? How will the changes of the block affect current use patterns?

Obvious comparisons can be made in order to make the case for increased staff or funding. For example, you can look at circulation of materials as just one snapshot of how resources will have to be reallocated. On average, circulation of materials for blocked high schools increases 25 percent. Not only does this have an implication for budget to acquire more books and multimedia, but it also has a subtle, yet realistic impact on staffing, as the following analysis demonstrates:

Average time to select a book now: 3 minutes

Average time to check out a book: 30 seconds

Average time to shelve a book: 2 minutes

Average time to create and distribute an overdue notice: 3 minutes

If it currently takes the staff 8½ minutes to complete a circulation item from selection to shelving and if circulation increases by 25 percent, it is a quick calculation to make the point that more staff time will be spent on this behind-the-scenes activity. What else will the staff be expected to do to support resource-based learning? What demands will be made on instructional support of the library media specialist, the need for students to have an information specialist, and the role the school media specialist has as a consultant to the teachers? These are the kinds of discussions the library media subcommittee should have in order to prepare for the changes block scheduling will bring.

ONGOING ASSESSMENT OF THE BLOCK

During the first year of block scheduling, all departments must continually assess the benefits and problems associated with block scheduling. As a whole community of learners, there should also be a building-level committee that monitors the effect the block is having on the school in its entirety.

A special committee to monitor the implementation of block scheduling was established at East Lyme High School. During the first year, it met monthly, and each meeting resulted in some modifications or recommendations that, when implemented, corrected a concern or staved off a potential problem. Teachers and students served on the committee, and all staff knew that they could join it at any time.

In addition, it is important for the library media specialist to make special contact with the faculty to give them an opportunity to express how the library media program is responding to their new instructional and curriculum needs. I had been asked to conduct professional development for area media specialists a year into block scheduling, and I used that opportunity not only to gain insight to share, but to take a reading on how

Figure 2.1
Assessing Our Program for Block Scheduling

On the October 25th Professional Development day, I will be a co-presenter to area school media specialists on the topic of how block scheduling affects the role and resources of a high school library media program. As we are still new to the block, I would greatly appreciate your comments and suggestions. Not only will your comments help me prepare my remarks, but they will also give me valuable feedback as to how well we are doing to meet your needs. Thank you for taking your time to help me!

Name_____ Department_____

1. Have you changed your student expectations because of the block, and if so, do you require different kinds of research experiences from the Library Media Center?
_____
_____

2. Has the block allowed you to bring your classes (or send groups of students) to the Library more often?
_____

3. Can you comment on the materials and resources of the Library with regard to adequacy, depth, appropriateness to your curriculum changes, etc.
_____
_____
_____

4. What additional resources should be acquired to keep current with your curriculum or instructional needs?
_____
_____

5. Is interlibrary loan (borrowing books from other libraries) important for you and your students? What are the successes (or problems) that you or your students encounter?
_____
_____

6. Are there success stories I can share, such as certain research projects you feel worked well because of the support given by the Library Media staff and/or materials?
_____
_____

7. Please offer suggestions as to how the Library Media program can help you.
_____
_____

Figure 2.2
Class Visits to the Library Media Center, by Department

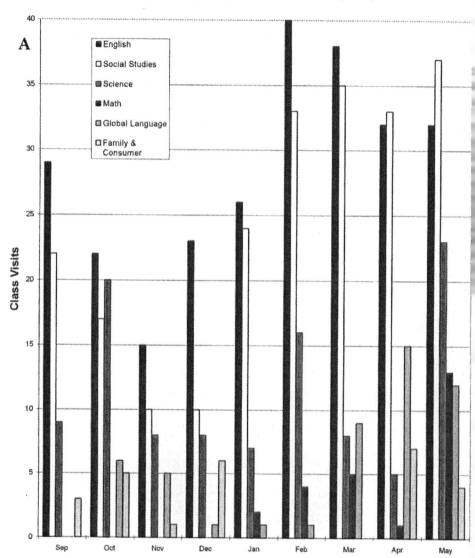

Figure 2.2 Continued

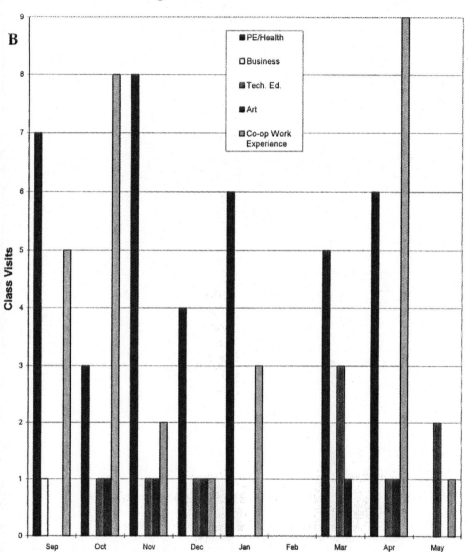

Source: School library media center scheduling book.
Note: Graph A: scale is 0–40. Graph B: scale is 0–9.

we were doing for our own community of learners. Figure 2.1 contains the survey each teacher received. The response rate was very high, and the input invaluable. This communication device served as a quick assessment to ask the staff how we were doing.

Two excellent ideas from Centralia Regional High School in Centralia, Missouri, helped their faculty adjust to block scheduling and assess its impact. The library media specialist kept an information bank of ideas, programs, handouts, and so forth, and all teachers were asked to contribute to it as well as take materials from it. The bank served an important function of readily giving access to all teachers of successful lessons or techniques, particularly in a large high school that is departmentalized.

Centralia Regional High School also established a regular sharing time for all teachers. On the fourth Wednesday in the fall of the first year of block scheduling, there was a 25-minute time set aside after school in the library media center. All teachers were encouraged to attend and share ideas on what did and did not work with their specific block schedule efforts (Brunner 1997).

These kinds of efforts pay back tremendous dividends. Every teacher, no matter how experienced, is a new teacher when block scheduling begins.

Figure 2.2 shows the number of classes in each department that used the Frances Hart Ewers Library Media Center in 1996–97. The charts were distributed to the curriculum instructional leaders and administration for future planning purposes. The goal was to distribute the number of assignments by each department more evenly throughout the school year. The Frances Hart Ewers Library is the library media center at East Lyme High School, East Lyme, Connecticut, where I work.

BIBLIOGRAPHY

Print Sources

Baker, Robert C. "Block Scheduling: Impact on Library Media Programs." *Florida Media Quarterly* 21, 2 (1996): p. 10.

The Basics of Block Scheduling. Professional Issues in Public Education. Hartford, CT: Connecticut Education Association, Summer 1997.

Breivik, Patricia Senn. "Information Overload." Burlington, VT: University of Vermont. Online. January 1, 1998. Internet. *http://www.uvm.edu/~jrc/workshop/overload.htmlrl*

Brunner, Terri. *Block Schedule Information.* Centralia, MO: Centralia High School, 1997 (handout).

Canady, Robert Lynn, and Michael D. Rettig. "The Power of Innovative Scheduling." *Educational Leadership* 53, 3 (November 1995): pp. 4–10.

Freeman, William, and David Scheidecker. "Planning for Block Scheduling." *Clearing House* (November 1, 1996): pp. 60–61.

Galt, Joan. "Block Scheduling: Comments from Inside the Media Center." *Florida Media Quarterly* 21, 2 (1996): pp. 12–13.

Hackmann, Donald. "Ten Guidelines for Implementing Block Scheduling." *Educational Leadership* 53, 3 (November 1995): pp. 24–27.

Information Power: Guidelines for School Library Media Programs. Chicago: American Association of School Librarians and Association for Educational Communications and Technology, 1988.

Mistretta, Gerald, and Harvey Polansky. "Prisoners of Time: Implementing a Block Schedule in the High School." *NASSP Bulletin* 81, 593 (December 1997): pp. 23–31.

Phillips, Ione D. "On the Block." *Techniques* (September 1997): pp. 1–6.

Renchler, Ron. "Urban Superintendent Turnover: The Need for Stability." *Urban Superintendents' Sounding Board* 1, 1 (Winter 1992). (ERIC ED346546.)

Scroggins, Gary V., and P. J. Karr-Kidwell. *Implementation of Block Scheduling in a Four-Year High School: A Literary Review and a Handbook for Administrators, Teachers, and Parents*. Ohio. 1995. (ERIC ED387879.)

Wasley, Patricia A. "Alternative Schedules: What, How, and to What End?" *NASSP Bulletin* 81, 588 (April 1997): pp. 44–50.

Internet, Listserv, and Newsgroup Sites

Arizona Educational Media Association (AEMA-L). *listserv@asuvm.inre.asu.edu*

BLOCKLIST. *listserv@tc.umn.edu*

Illinois School Library Media Association Discussion List (ISLMANET-L). *listserv@postoffice.cso.uiuc.edu*

k12 Library Newsgroup. *k12.library* (name of newsgroup)

Kentucky Library Media Specialists Discussion List (KYLMS). *listserv@lsv.ukv.edu*

LM_NET. *listserv@listserv.syr.edu*

Media Forum Discussion List (MEDIA-L). *listserv@listserv.aol.com*

Peter Milbury's School Librarian Web Pages. *http://www.cusd.chico.k12.ca.us/~pmilbury/lib.html*

The Library Media Specialist and Instructional Change

3

This chapter discusses the roles of the library media specialist as instructional consultant and teacher in a block-scheduled high school where traditional teaching changes. Library media specialists are instructional consultants when they plan with teachers. Classroom goals should always be the focus of the library media specialist's teaching and library media services (Dalbotten and Wallin 1990).

Many schools decide to move to a block schedule for the purpose of improved student learning and acquisition of lifelong skills. The traditional method of instruction, lecture, is not resource oriented nor does it encourage students to produce evidence of their knowledge and skills. Authentic methods of instruction are those that "require students to produce (not just reproduce) knowledge relevant to their lives through disciplined inquiry, and to achieve in ways that are of value to themselves and to society." When a teacher uses authentic methods of instruction, the "classroom is a more challenging and collaborative environment for students to learn how to use knowledge and not merely to possess it" (Duis 1995, pp. 136–138).

INSTRUCTIONAL CONSULTANT ROLE OF THE LIBRARY MEDIA SPECIALIST

In 1995–96 there were slightly over 50,000 library media specialists serving 45 million students in the United States, with a ratio of approximately 1:882 for all levels of public schools. Some states, such as Kansas, had a much lower ratio of 1:476. California had an extraordinarily high and unacceptable ratio of 1:6,179 due to the devastating impact over the past twenty years of Proposition 13 and the Class Size Reduction Act of 1996

(Gorman 1995, p. 27; Goldberg 1997, p. 14). The ratio has an enormous impact on the library media specialist's effectiveness in meeting the responsibilities of all the roles.

In a block-scheduled high school, where the demand for library media services skyrockets, the numbers are underrepresented because of the intense need that teachers and students have for the library media specialist to assist them in resource-based learning. One library media specialist in a school of 800 students in a traditional high school does not have the same demand placed on him or her as the library media specialist with the same number of students in a block-scheduled high school.

A 1994 report on the impact of the library media program and student academic achievement noted that students who achieved higher scores on standardized tests also attended schools where the library media specialist had an instructional role (Lance 1994, p. 4). The report, however, does not specify which aspects of the role are the most relevant to achievement. The following list defines the responsibilities set out by the National Reading Research Center for the library media specialist as instructional consultant:

- Participates in designing literacy curriculum and instructional strategies
- Ensures that information skills are integrated into the content areas
- Participates in selecting topics for unit experiences (thematic units, inquiry units, literature units, content area units, etc.)
- Participates in developing unit plans
- Participates in gathering books and other resources for units
- Participates in carrying out unit plans
- Participates in assessing unit experiences (DeGroff 1996, pp. 5–6)

Based on my own experience, I would wager that the first two responsibilities—participating in curriculum development that integrates the state and national standards on literacy—have the most impact on student achievement. Further, the ability to read, view, and listen to complex information, to research, and to use information to make decisions are skills that are highly desired of students. In our instructional consultant role, we can ensure that students become knowledgeable and practice these skills across the curriculum. Just one example of how these skills can be promoted is to have a school requirement in every course of a technology objective and a research-writing objective. These two guidelines will provide numerous opportunities for collaborative planning with teachers.

Most library media specialists demonstrate their leadership as instructional consultants when they provide professional development to the staff. Ever-emerging new and complex technologies require that teachers be continually offered opportunities to learn their educational uses (Pickard 1994,

p. 28). I have found that with block scheduling, teachers are very interested in designing thoughtful, creative, and meaningful activities that use all the resources of the library media program, especially the technology. When the library staff establishes credibility with teachers to help them with technology, the teachers will share with their students their confidence in us as technology leaders and resource teachers.

INSTRUCTIONAL LEADER AND ASSESSMENT

The appropriate role the library media specialist has in the assessment of student work is a tricky question. Can we fully participate and be leaders in instructional design if we do not grade students' work (Pickard 1994, p. 28)? I contend that we can. In the block schedule, there is literally no time for the library media specialist to take on grading students' projects, even though we would like to see to completion the activity that we helped plan. The end product is often the most rewarding part of the experience, and it is frustrating not to "read the end of the chapter" with the students as they demonstrate what they have learned. Many times the assessment is performance based—a skit, an oral report, or a debate. It is unreasonable to expect the library media specialist to participate routinely in these classroom assessments or to evaluate long written projects. I believe we are in a similar position as others in the building who are also responsible for curriculum yet do not grade individual work. Administrators do not assess all students' progress, nor do curriculum instructional leaders or department heads. Yet they often are the people making broad curricular and instructional decisions. I believe that as library media specialists, we have to accept that we can occasionally formally assess the final project. We do, however, constantly assess all students informally for their information literacy skills. Daniel Barron (1991) suggests that the instructional consultant role of the library media specialist more accurately can be described as an "instructional partner" with teachers and administrators. We must initiate and rely on our dialogue with teachers, who best know their students, about the success or failure of the activity that required resource-based learning.

A library media specialist may easily have three or four classes each block using the library media center, and it is an enormous task to plan with teachers and prepare materials and technology for them. To assess individual students' work would be impossible and unnecessary. Carol Simpson (1996) put the issue in this way:

School librarians expand their areas of influence to include the classroom when they collaborate with classroom teachers to meet the information needs of students. Suggesting resources, locating and acquiring needed materials, recommending strategies, facilitating use of technologies, and instructing students and teachers in optimal information-seeking methods replace the traditional librarian tasks. Librarians assist teachers and students to search out their information needs, critically evaluate the materials they locate, and use technological means to synthesize their findings into new knowledge. Librarians must become more proficient in the use of the new technologies to promote them and instruct students and teachers in their use. As students become more self-directed learners, the librarian acts as a resource person in the students' quest for supporting information and the development of appropriate presentation strategies. Consulting duties added to an already burgeoning schedule gives the librarian more than enough work to fill the day.

Assurance

The library media specialist will play an important role in the transition to block scheduling. Teachers will relax and be much more accepting of the changes if they have the support of the library media program as they examine and redesign their instructional methods.

The library media specialist, as an instructional consultant, can assure teachers that block scheduling provides them opportunity to develop their ideas and that they should not discard the excellent instructional activities they have already amassed. Resource-based learning and block scheduling will allow them to take their best efforts and modify them to accommodate teaching in a sustained period of time. As you flip from being an instructional consultant to an information specialist, you will be essential in ensuring that the restructuring of the high school occurs for the benefit of all.

LIBRARY MEDIA SPECIALIST AS TEACHER

We are the teachers of information literacy, and we have some or all the responsibility for teaching technology and computer skills. In the restructured high school that incorporates resource-based learning into the curriculum, the *process* can be as important as the *content*. With the block schedule and with the recent infusion of technology, our role as teacher expands tremendously.

According to the National Reading Research Center (DeGroff 1996, pp. 5–6), the library media specialist as teacher has these responsibilities:

- Teaches children how to select and locate books, resources, and information
- Teaches colleagues how to select and locate books, resources, and information
- Teaches parents and adults how to select and locate books, resources, and information
- Promotes and supports life-long reading and learning
- Promotes and supports critical thinking and reading

- Teaches appreciation for freedom of information
- Teaches understanding of and respect for copyright and privacy
- Teaches parents and others techniques for reading to children

Missing on this list, and on the list for instructional consultant, is the ever-growing responsibility not only to plan for technology but to instruct students and teachers in its use.

Robert Baker (1996), a library media specialist in a block-scheduled high school, wrote this about the impact that block scheduling has on information skills instruction:

An advantage of block scheduling is that it provides time for creative teaching opportunities for information skills. . . . After we introduce a concept or skill, we can provide immediate hands-on applications for maximum learning and reinforcement.
Media production and communication skills have also become more important. . . . Teachers and students were most concerned with ideas or techniques for communicating their ideas and information to the class. We prepared samples to show students the possibilities of each type of presentation method. . . . [T]he media specialist instructs each group in the techniques for using the equipment or program. (p. 10)

The extended time that the block affords has made a very positive impact on how I can teach information skills. In the traditional schedule, by the time the teacher took care of attendance, homework, and other transitions, announced the assignment in the classroom, and moved the class across the school into the library media center, I was fortunate *if* there was twenty minutes available to instruct students in appropriate information skills. I recall saying again and again, "Tomorrow we will pick up where we left off, and you will be able to use the materials we just saw." Of course, the next day when the class arrived, I was fortunate if the students remembered the colors of the books they saw, let alone what their value was to their research and how to use them. With the block schedule, there is immediate reinforcement of my instruction because there is time to use the materials or technology in depth to reinforce their purpose and utility for the project at hand. There is also time for me to assess students informally in all stages of their research and technology use to determine if they are finding appropriate information and to discuss with them how they intend to use it.

The Frances Hart Ewers Library Media Center was always a busy place before block scheduling. When we made the transition, it became even more essential to students and teachers. Now, however, the kinds of activities that take place are focused on instruction, learning, and critical thinking skills. I believe that we are on our way to an effective integration of information literacy where the skills are directly related to the content-area curriculum and to classroom assignments and the skills themselves are tied together in a logical and systematic information process model (Eisenberg and Johnson 1996).

An important personal benefit for me was to participate in the numerous professional development workshops our school scheduled for our transition to block scheduling; like the faculty, I learned many new instructional techniques. I am also much more aware of asking myself the questions, "What do I want students to accomplish?" and "How and what are the best ways to do so?" Relating library and technology instruction to the classroom focus is essential; that is, information skills should not be taught in isolation without a curricular context. The following summary of the research process promotes the library media specialist as teacher (Farmer 1995, pp. 11–13):

- *Take time to think.* Critical thinking is much more important than a push-button printout. Thinking should be documented. Compose search strategies on paper.
- *Take time to talk about information.* Students need to discuss their progress and problems. These quick assessments reinforce the idea that information worth getting is worth thinking about.
- *Process over product.* Library media specialists help students determine the best resources for a given topic.
- *Determine if the resource is useful.* Evaluate the resource with the student for many attributes, such as index, subheadings, and table of contents.
- *Take a critical look at the specific content of a source.* Assess the resource for point of view, perspective, author's background, fact or opinion, and depth of information.

Information literacy will be required of students in whatever school-to-career transition they make. We as teachers can introduce and reinforce information literacy and technology in the block schedule better than before because we have the sustained time to be thorough and flexible and to help students make logical sequences and connections to the information process.

CHANGES IN CLASSROOM INSTRUCTION

A concern for teachers who work in high schools that are preparing to adopt block scheduling is whether they will be able to change their instructional methodology to accommodate the increased amount of time in a block. One of the major disadvantages of a block schedule is the initial resistance to change and the requirement that teachers change their teaching strategies (Irmsher 1996).

Block scheduling promotes teachers to take on the role of a facilitator or consultant who *directs* the learning of their students. This is not unlike an orchestral conductor who has numerous subsets of musical activity occurring at once. The conductor facilitates the orchestra to meet the objective of a unified performance of a work. In a block-scheduled school, the teacher now has uninterrupted time to facilitate the learning in a differentiated classroom.

Lecture

Lecture, once a revered pedagogy, is now often criticized as an ineffective way for students to learn. Teachers should not discard lecture, but, as Lisa Birk (1997, p. 58) suggests, they should examine ways to make lecture valid. Fifty years ago lecture meant that the teacher orates and the student writes. In recent times teachers have relied too often on one-way communication, primarily, I believe, because as the content expanded in the curriculum and the classroom model did not change, teachers felt enormous pressure to cover everything in the same time constraints of the industrial model classroom. Birk recommends that teachers use an "interactive" lecture: the teacher still does most of the talking, but now engages students with questioning and storytelling. An interactive lecture might last the whole period or just 10 minutes, depending on the teacher's purpose and the students' needs.

Not all lectures are unproductive, of course, and, in fact, for some learning styles, the lecture is an excellent form of teacher instruction. Yet the more interactive the lecture is, with the teacher using probing questions and encouraging students to react verbally to information, the more appropriate is its use. Teachers and administrators must distinguish between traditional lecture and interactive lecture. The library media specialist can support teachers with interactive lecture by supplying up-to-date or anecdotal material to teachers. One way I do this is to offer teachers the service of having the table of contents of new magazines photocopied and placed in their mailboxes. This gives busy teachers who may normally not find the time to come to the library media center the opportunity to scan the titles of new articles in their field of study. Often teachers take the ideas they glean from the current literature and use it in their interactive lectures.

Instructional Strategies

In many studies, and certainly in schools that are block scheduled, teachers have a lot to say about how the extended time has given them the incentive to change or modify their instructional strategies. The impact of block scheduling on teaching and learning is still unclear because it is so new, but teachers and administrators report that it has given them an opportunity for change and innovation (Fritz 1997).

A survey conducted in California encouraged teachers to comment on the block and its effect on their teaching strategies. Teachers said the block gave them time to engage students in activities that helped make the subject come alive and the freedom to diversify their methods of instruction. Moreover, there was less stress overall for the teachers because of the reduced number of student contacts each day. In addition, teachers find that block scheduling allows them to conduct small-group activities so that content can be delivered differently than in the traditional classroom (Staunton 1997, pp. 77, 82–83). All of these comments can carry over to the library media center. The high number of activities correlates to the increased demand for library and technology services and materials. Teachers who wish to try new ways of instruction often will incorporate technology and need the support from the computer teachers or library media staff.

There are many suggestions for instructional strategies for teachers. Library media specialists should be aware of these strategies and try practicing them. Consider the following two sets of strategies.

STIR Method

Karen Flowe (in Phillips 1997, p. 2) recommends three to five different activities in a 90-minute block:

- *Stimulation:* 10 to 20 minutes on stimulating curiosity
- *Involvement:* 50 to 60 minutes on activities
- *Response:* 10 to 20 minutes on a concluding activity to reinforce the day's learning

Most of the activities students are engaged in in the library media center fit in the band of involvement in this model.

Instructional Strategies for Block Scheduling

Hackmann and Schmitt (1997, p. 4) offer these strategies:

1. Continuously engage students in active learning: think-pair-share, learning journals, guided notes, active questioning.
2. Include group activities to encourage student participation: cooperative learning, writing groups, case studies, role playing, simulations.
3. Incorporate activities addressing the multiple intelligences.
4. Use creative thinking activities.
5. Move outside the classroom.
6. Employ authentic forms of assessment.
7. Integrate and reinforce basic skills throughout the curriculum.
8. Incorporate technology.
9. Share resources and ideas with colleagues.
10. Plan ahead for support activities.

Although nowhere in this list does it say, "Take students to the library media center," I strongly believe library media specialists can support items 2 through 10 in all three roles. We should extend ourselves to those opportunities to help teachers with their planning and instruction. It does not always have to be in an interdisciplinary, team teaching situation. We can influence solid classroom instruction through planning, sharing ideas, and providing the appropriate materials and supporting environment.

Interdisciplinary Teaching

The library media specialist promotes interdisciplinary teaching between the discipline of information and technology and curricular areas. We also can be a catalyst for integration among all other departments. Resource-based teaching goes beyond having the library media specialist retrieve materials requested by teachers and students and the teaching of library skills in isolation. It requires the full integration of library research, reference, and technology skills into the curriculum (Ray 1994, p. 20).

The structure of the high school has traditionally kept departments separate, and in large high schools there are teachers who never interact with each other because it has not been "logical" for their departments to work together. But the world of work does not neatly departmentalize, and employers today expect their workers to solve a problem or think of an issue from a variety of points of view or options. Many schools that restructure have a goal of interdisciplinary teaching and curriculum integration, but they are not prepared to dissolve departments or other internal structures. The library media specialist has the advantage of a working relationship with all the teachers in the building, and thus knows individuals' teaching styles and the expectations they have of their students. A department head knows the teachers very well in the department, but often does not have the experience of working with people in other disciplines, and thus does not have the knowledge of who can work well together. Being a matchmaker often takes only a conversation to lead teachers toward each other. I encourage library media specialists to promote and facilitate integrated activities through any discipline. The block schedule affords the sustained time whereby teachers can share activities or even units. Teachers can request that classes be held at the same block or to double-block with a teacher in another subject area and share the same students, such as an American studies class that would be held for 180 minutes and team-taught by English and social studies teachers.

Here are some guidelines for promoting interdisciplinary teaching:

• Develop a file of the assignment sheets teachers distribute to their students for library projects.

- Organize this file in an accessible way for you—by subject, perhaps, or by grade level if your school has teams.
- Examine trends or patterns in teacher expectations. Look for logical partnerships for interdisciplinary teaching. For example, is there an American literature English teacher who in the past required historical background to understand a novel better?
- Purchase new materials that are colorful and attractive. Promote new online technologies (or even old ones). Give teachers examples of how students could benefit from using a library media center resource that would give them insight into a topic from various points of view.
- Offer professional development activities after school. Make them fun! One favorite was a series of Internet workshops that built up to the teachers' being able to plan a lesson using the Internet as the primary resource.

Make teachers comfortable and help them become knowledgeable about the resources so that they have confidence in assigning tasks to their students who will use the same resources. At the workshops, purposefully have teachers from different disciplines share a computer or work toward a common goal. They will catch on that they are experimenting and modeling exactly what they expect their students to do: work in groups toward common goals.

BIBLIOGRAPHY

Print Sources

Baker, Robert C. "Block Scheduling: Impact on Library Media Programs." *Florida Media Quarterly* 21, 2 (Special Issue Series) (1996): p. 10.

Barron, Daniel. "The School Library Media Specialist as Instructional Consultant." *School Library Media Activities Monthly* 8, 4 (1991): pp. 48–50. (ERIC EJ436265.)

Birk, Lisa. "What's So Bad About the Lecture?" *Education Digest* 62, 9 (May 1997): pp. 58–61.

Bryant, Robert Harold. "A Comparative Study of Teaching Strategies Used in Block and Traditionally Scheduled High Schools in the State of Wyoming." Doctoral dissertation, University of Wyoming, 1995. (Dissertation Abstracts AAG9630597.)

Craver, Kathleen W. *School Library Media Centers in the 21st Century.* Westport, CT: Greenwood Press, 1994.

Dalbotten, Mary, and Joan Wallin. *Classroom Instructional Design: Tools for Teacher/Media Specialist Interaction.* St. Paul, MN: Minnesota State Department of Education, 1990. (ERIC ED337128.)

DeGroff, Linda. *Getting to Know the School Library Media Specialist.* (Microform.) Washington, DC: U.S. Department of Education, Office of Educational Research and Improvement, Spring 1996. (ERIC ED396253.)

Duis, Mac. "Making Time for Authentic Teaching and Learning: Gateways to Experience." *Kappa Delta Pi Record* 30, 3 (Spring 1995): pp. 136–138. (ERIC ED390806.)

Eisenberg, Michael, and Doug Johnson. "Computer Skills for Information Problem-Solving: Learning and Teaching Technology in Context." *ERIC Digest* (March 1996): pp. 1–6. (ED392463). *http://www.ed.gov/databases/ERIC_Digests/ed392463.htmlrl*

Farmer, Lesley. "Information Literacy: More than Pushbutton Printouts." *The Book Report* 14, 3 (November/December 1995): pp. 11–13.

Fritz, Donald L. *Teaching in Ninety Minutes: Conversations with Teachers Using Block Scheduling.* Doctoral dissertation, University of Nebraska, 1997. (Dissertation Abstracts AAG9730270.)

From Library Skills to Information Literacy: A Handbook for the 21st Century/California Media and Library Educators. Castle Rock, CO: Hi Willow Research and Publishing, 1994.

Gardner, Howard. "Reflections on Multiple Intelligences: Myths and Messages." *Phi Delta Kappan* 77, 3 (November 1995): pp. 200–203.

Goldberg, Beverly. "Advocacy Pays Off for L.A. School Libraries." *American Libraries* 28, 11 (December 1997): pp. 14–17.

Gorman, Michael. "The Domino Effect, or Why Literacy Depends on All Libraries: California Universities Have Been Hit Hard by Cuts in School and Public Library Funding." *School Library Journal* 41, 4 (April 1995): pp. 27–30.

Hackmann, Donald G., and Donna M. Schmitt. "Strategies for Teaching in a Block-of-Time Schedule." *NASSP Bulletin* 81, 588 (April 1997): pp. 1–9.

Information Power: Guidelines for School Library Media Programs. Chicago: American Library Association, 1988.

Irmsher, Karen. "Block Scheduling in High Schools." *OSSC Bulletin* 39, 6 (July 1996): pp. 1–69. (ERIC ED399673.)

Lance, Keith Curry. "The Impact of School Library Media Centers on Academic Achievement." *ERIC Digest* (May 1994): pp. 1–7. (ED372759.) *http://www.ed.gov/databases/ERIC_Digests/ed372759.htmlrl*

Marshak, David. *Action Research on Block Scheduling.* Larchmont, NY: Eye on Education, 1997.

Phillips, Ione D. "On the Block." *Techniques* (September 1997): pp. 1–6. Online. EBSCO MasElite.

Pickard, Patricia. "The Instructional Consultant Role of the Library Media Specialist: A Progress Report." *School Library Media Activities Monthly* 10, 5 (January 1994): pp. 27–29.

Ray, Judith Thomas. "Resource-Based Teaching: Media Specialists and Teachers as Partners in Curriculum Development and the Teaching of Library and Information Skills." *Reference Librarian* 44 (1994): pp. 19–27.

Simpson, Carol. "The School Librarian's Role in the Electronic Age." *ERIC Digest* (November 1996). (ERIC ED402928.)

Staunton, Jim. "A Study of Teacher Beliefs on the Efficacy of Block Scheduling." *NASSP Bulletin* 81, 593 (December 1997): pp. 73–80.

Staunton, Jim, and Teresa Adams. "What Do Teachers in California Have to Say About Block Scheduling?" *NASSP Bulletin* 81, 593 (December 1997): pp. 81–84.

Internet Sites

Hints and Tips for 90 Minute Block Classes. *http//ftp.classroom.com/Classroom-Connect/ Wasson.Block/Hints.and.Tips.txtrl*

A Learner Centered Approach to School Restructuring: The Role of the School Library Media Specialist. Draft position paper approved by AASL. *http:// www.cyfc.umn.edu/Other/libmedia.html*

Role of School Libraries in Information Literacy and Essential Learnings, Washington Library Media Association. *http://www.wlma.org/literacy/roleesl.htm*

Wasson Block Text Files. *http://www.classroom.net/classweb/WASSON/textfiles.html* or *http://www.classroom.net/classweb/WASSON/myhome.html*

Professional Development
for the Block

4

> If visions of reform hold any prospect of influencing American
> schools, new learning will need to occur at multiple levels. Policy
> makers will have to learn, as well as children; teachers, as well as par-
> ents. Administrators, curriculum developers, school board members—
> everyone will have to learn. Basic assumptions and orientations will
> need to be reconsidered and rebuilt. (Wilson et al. 1996, p. 469)

Volumes have been written about the need for teachers to be trained in
multiple intelligences, assessment, differentiated instruction, class management, learning styles, curriculum writing, and development—to name
just a few—in order to be successful teachers in the block. Is it important
for library media specialists to avail themselves of the same professional
development that fellow classroom teachers are participating in?

Yes! Yes! Yes! As the classroom teachers are spreading their wings and
discovering new ways to instruct, we as instructional leaders in our buildings must fully understand how these new methodologies will change the
way that teachers and students expect to be supported by the library media program. In our role as information and technology consultants, we
must be aware of the varied and new directions that teachers are taking.
We should avail ourselves of a wide variety of professional development
opportunities, even if they do not seem to be directly related to library media. For example, when I questioned why attending a workshop on assessment would be important to me, I learned that assessment is no longer
just giving grades; it is a process of thinking in a rubric that continually
monitors the progress of a student. Can we use rubrics in the library media center? Of course we can, and they are a very useful means for library

media specialists to determine the level of information skills a student has mastered. Not only have I learned a very practical and useful way of assessing student achievement in my own program, but I am "talking the talk and walking the walk" with my fellow faculty. I am a resource to them as they devise new assessment techniques with new activities for meeting curriculum goals and objectives.

CHARACTERISTICS OF EFFECTIVE PROFESSIONAL DEVELOPMENT

If you are a member of your school or district planning committee for professional development, you can have great influence on the types of activities and learning you and your teachers will experience. Abdal-Haqq (1996, pp. 1–2) views effective professional development in this way:

- Is ongoing.
- Includes training, practice, and feedback; opportunities for individual reflection and group inquiry into practice; and coaching and other follow-up procedures.
- Is school based and embedded in teacher work.
- Is collaborative, providing opportunties for teachers to interact with peers.
- Focuses on student learning, which should in part guide assessment of its effectiveness.
- Encourages and supports school-based and teacher initiatives.
- Is rooted in the knowledge base for teaching.
- Incorporates constructive approaches to teaching and learning and recognizes teachers as professionals and adult learners.
- Provides adequate time and follow-up support.
- Is accessible and inclusive.

A planning committee has the responsibility to interview the presenter and evaluate the potential of each workshop prior to its delivery to ensure it meets these criteria. If it is going to fall short, it will not be successful, and could even do permanent damage because teachers will resent having spent their very valuable time ineffectively. Nevertheless, teachers must have a wide variety of professional development for block scheduling. "A change to block scheduling causes teachers to re-examine curriculum and redefine priorities," and consequently, "teachers must (and most do) make changes in their teaching when schools implement block scheduling. Nearly three-fourths of teachers in a block schedule, over time and with appropriate staff development and support, lecture less and engage students in more active learning" (Rettig and Canady 1997, pp. 33–34).

THE LIBRARY MEDIA SPECIALIST

Where does one go to find professional development specifically for library media specialists? In her article Joan Galt states, "There was no one to help me adjust to the change. I needed to try to define how to prepare myself and the media center for block scheduling" (Galt 1996, p. 12). Interestingly, as important an impact that block scheduling has on the library media program, there is very little written to help in the transition phase and later with the implementation of the block. Yet the library program is vital to students, who will now be required to participate actively in their learning. In my extensive research for this book, I found few articles specific to block scheduling and the high school library media program.

Professional development is a key component for the success of block scheduling. Administrators know that they have to support all the departments, but foreign language and math get the most focus. They ask, How will students be able to sustain their global language or mathematics skills over months of inactivity with the 4 × 4 schedule? How will students achieve on AP tests or SATs under block scheduling? In order to work out these important issues, teachers are encouraged to visit other blocked schools and participate in professional development workshops held to address these kinds of questions and plan new instructional strategies.

Where departments have several members, there are strength and support for collaboration and the sharing of ideas. The high school media specialist, however, often is the lone professional in his or her department and does not have the benefit of working through the issues that are raised with block scheduling with a group of other library media specialists. Visits to block schools are helpful, but it has been my experience that the library media specialist is a member of the "away team" only infrequently. Is that because the existing job is so intense that he or she cannot afford the time to leave the library media center for a day? How often do we say to our colleagues, "I really wanted to attend that conference, but I can't take the day off"? As much as I hear myself in this statement, I encourage library media specialists to view visits to other schools as essential.

Collaboration

Just as we network for resource sharing, we must network for our own professional development with block scheduling. Look to your neighbors. Are there other high schools within a comfortable travel distance that you can visit to observe their use of the block schedule? Call on your peers in the profession. Do not feel that you are intruding on this person's time and space. Forward important questions before your visit so your host can be prepared to give you the information you seek. I found that some of the more successful visits occur when the visitor just sits back and evaluates the activity; I find invaluable the feedback from the observer. Regional educational service centers can be asked to organize professional development for the high school media specialists it serves. When a critical mass is reached for an audience, you will be more successful at attracting a quality speaker.

State professional organizations for school media specialists should be encouraged to put block scheduling on any upcoming conference agenda for attracting guest speakers for workshops or having a keynote speaker for the event. Many of the issues that surround the change that block scheduling brings are also of interest to middle and elementary school media specialists.

Block scheduling affects many areas, particularly management of the library, collection development, and information skills instruction (Baker 1996, p. 10). Technology advances are always very useful professional development topics, but in making the transition to block scheduling management, collection development and information skills are essential to the success of the library media program in the new environment. Don't overlook contacting your state department of education consultant for school media services. This person is current with the new ways of delivering exemplary school media programs. Your consultant can share ideas and experiences and lead you to other practitioners whom they know are successful with the block.

Do go to conferences. The 1996 Association for Supervision and Curriculum Development (ASCD) national conference had many speakers on the topic of block scheduling, including Michael Rettig, Assistant Professor of Education, James Madison University, and Robert Canady, Professor of Educational Leadership, University of Virginia. Although their keynote speech focused on their recent research, concepts were reinforced for resource-based learning, supportive services that are needed, differentiated instruction, and other attributes that affect the library media program. There is no substitute for human contact and conversation. Supplemental to it, however, are a wide variety of excellent electronic resources the library media specialist can use.

Listservs

There are ways to network with those in the profession without leaving your school. Listservs, which are akin to electronic bulletin boards, have been very helpful to me in meeting library media specialists who have much to say about block scheduling. By posting questions or comments on the listservs, I have found many colleagues all over the United States and abroad who are wrestling with some of the same issues I am. In fact, some data for this book come from library media specialists I "met" through listserv contact. Some listservs offer a digest feature that condenses individual messages on a topic into one large e-mail, very helpful for a busy person. These digests are often archived and can be obtained later.

Here are a few comments about listservs if you are not already a user:

1. Any message you post on the listserv can be read by any member of the listserv. Some new members are not clear on this concept and post information that is not useful to a wide audience. You can respond to an individual by copying the sender's address into a unique e-mail message.

2. There are many ways to learn about listservs. I periodically scan a web site called *tile.net/lists*, which coordinates thousands of listservs and newsgroups. It is easily accessible, and one can locate a listserv by title, subject, or alphabetical listing. All the information you need to join is provided, along with the number of current members, the country it emanates from, where the site is hosted (often a university), how to join, and the administrative and computer contact. This site has available all the listservs associated with the school library media profession.

3. The number of members will directly affect the amount of e-mail you receive. For example, a listserv that has over 7,000 members will generate approximately seventy-five letters per day. Be sure that your e-mail server has the capacity to receive these letters and that you have the time to download them at least every other day to keep up with the mail. You can always leave the listserv or suspend the mail.

Two listservs that are very helpful to library media specialists who are working through the issues of block scheduling are LM_NET and BLOCK-LIST. LM_NET was established several years ago by Peter Milbury at Syracuse University. Almost 8,000 library media specialists are active members of LM_NET. Although it is not dedicated to block scheduling, it is a useful forum for exchanging comments and asking questions. I received many responses and ideas for block scheduling from the members of LM_NET.

BLOCKLIST is dedicated to the issues of block scheduling in all disciplines. I have monitored it for over a year, and found that there are occasional comments concerning library media centers. Other issues discussed are the various types of schedules, student achievement, and standardized testing. This listserv is administered through the University of Minnesota and is interesting to follow because there are often strong opinions stated among the members about the merits of block scheduling.

When looking at *tile.net/lists* one will find numerous listservs that focus on high school educational issues, and these may also be useful to gain information about block scheduling.

To join a listserv, access *http://www.tile.net/lists* to search the many listservs available. Send an e-mail message to the listserv address as indicated. For example, to join LM_NET, send an e-mail message to *listserv@listserv.syr.edu*.

In the message of the e-mail, type the command *sub LM_NET your name.* Within 24 hours you should receive a message from LM_NET (or the listserv you are joining) asking you to confirm your desire to join. Typically all you have to do is click Reply, and type OK in the message line. This has to be done within 48 hours. If not, the listserv administrator will not add you to the membership.

You are now a member of the listserv and will begin to receive the postings. If at any time you want to suspend your membership, simply follow the directions given to SET NOMAIL. When you are ready to restore membership, send a SET MAIL message to the listserv administrator.

Table 4.1 notes recommended listservs.

Other Internet Resources

A few of the best web sites about block scheduling on the Internet are listed at the end of this chapter. Although none is singularly dedicated to library media and block scheduling, all provide useful information.

The Internet provides a wealth of information on block scheduling. Many schools have posted their experiences with the block on their own home pages. At this time, there is no definitive assessment on student achievement and block scheduling because it is relatively new and the data are insufficient. There are numerous reports and evaluations by individual high schools and educational agencies that present data from their own surveys and draw conclusions regarding how the schedule affects student learning.

Special mention is being made of the Association for Supervision and Curriculum Development (ASCD) web site, which, among numerous valuable learning opportunities for educators, provides a forum for people to discuss important issues via e-mail. The category for block scheduling is of particular interest. Following are some excerpts from this site (date of access January 3, 1998).

The URL for this site is *http://www.ascd.org.* Once connected, select Forums. (The forums are subject to change. At the time of publication there were ten forums. Five are relevant for library media specialists investigating block scheduling.) Now you may select from a variety of educational issues.

ASCD Forums

- Web Sites/The Internet
- Block Scheduling
- Technology in Schools
- ASCD Network: Problem Based Learning
- ASCD Network: Cooperative Learning

Table 4.1
Recommended Listservs for Library Media Specialists

Listserv Name	Address	Hosted By	Members
AERA American Educational Research Association	listserv@asuvm.inre.asu.edu	AERA	2,600
BIGSIX Approach to Information Literacy Mike Eisenberg	listserv@listserv.syr.edu	Syracuse University	1,478
BLOCKLIST Block Scheduling Discussion List	listserv@tc.umn.edu	University of Minnesota	230
CALIBK12 California K–12 Librarians	listserv@sjsuvm1.sjsu.edu	——	294
ISLMANET-L Illinois School Media Association	listserv@postoffice.cso.uiuc.edu	University of Illinois, Urbana	225
K12ADMIN K–12 Educators Interested in Educational Administration	listserv@listserv.syr.edu	Syracuse University	1,149
LIBRARY Libraries & Librarians	listserv@miamiu.acs.muohio.edu	Miami University, Ohio	1,089
LM_NET School Library Media & Network Communications	listserv@listserv.syr.edu	Syracuse University	7,786
SLMS-LIST School Media Specialist List	listserv@listserv.acsu.buffalo.edu	State University of New York at Buffalo	54

Each forum contains an extensive list of subtopics. Below is a small sampling of the issues for discussion on block scheduling:

Block evaluation—2/03/98
Block scheduling—12/03/97

The School System software package—9/12/97

Block scheduling and graduation requirements—9/11/97

Foreign Language in Blocks—2/13/97

Block Scheduling Web Site—12/17/96

Block scheduling—3/10/97

Study Groups—3/11/97

Following is an electronic message that was attached to one of the topics. Readers can readily and easily create a reply screen to continue the conversation:

Reply to this Message

Posted on: December 10, 1996 at 17:28:4

Posted by: Don Ford Grosse Ile High School

Subject: Block Schedules and Foreign Language/Math

Message: Please, we are looking at block schedules and other alternative scheduling possibilities. Does anyone have any comments about extended periods and foreign language instruction? Pro & Con Our staff needs to hear from you!

Replies:

Block Scheduling Web Site—12/17/96 15:48

Foreign Language in Blocks—2/13/97 16:21

For library media specialists, there is a wealth of information to be learned from these web sites regarding how the school milieu is affected by block scheduling. Unfortunately, there is very little information that specifically addresses the library media program. One has to look between the lines for the impact on the library media program on a wide variety of information, such as resource-based learning, cooperative and group projects, differentiated instruction, study halls, flexible scheduling, student responsibilities, and freedom to move about the campus. These and many other topics have a great impact on how library media specialists will design programs to be more responsive to the needs of teachers and students under block scheduling.

Comprehensive Professional Development

Professional development opportunities for block scheduling are available for library media specialists, but we may have to work a little harder to find them. Networking with area library media specialists and lobbying for regional presenters is an effective way to have shared professional development for the library media specialists in your area. You may be able to convince your administration that it is most cost-effective for you to travel to a distant conference than to have a presenter come to your school for a limited number of people.

At the beginning of this chapter, I wrote that library media specialists should avail themselves of as many workshops and learning sessions as possible, even when the topic is not specific to libraries or technology. I have become enthused about learning outside my area of expertise, mainly because there is always an important part of the workshop that does relate to the library media center. This new knowledge offers me another view from which to evaluate the library media program I administer.

As high school reform sweeps our nation, two observations are made: (1) teacher learning must be the heart of any effort to improve education in our society, and (2) conventional professional development is inadequate when it is faddish, superficial, and aimed at the "one-shot workshop" (Sykes 1996, p. 465). The anticipated reform resulting from the adaptation of block scheduling has heightened the awareness of and promoted the need for teacher professional development from school boards, teachers, administrators, parents, community members, and even students. "How is the traditional teacher going to change his or her instructional methodology to maximize the time in the block for student learning and achievement?" is a question asked again and again by the interested parties.

All teachers will benefit from professional development, but everyone will not need the same training. Some teachers will be experienced with cooperative learning, while others will need help with time management. Once the school has adopted the block, identifying and supporting ongoing professional development is critical to the continued success of the block (Shortt 1997, p. 11). At East Lyme High School, appropriate professional development was the key to our success with the block schedule. In the transition year, we had national speakers conduct workshops on models for teaching in the block and instructional strategies in the block schedule for the entire faculty. Our professional development has continued in many directions, with excellent workshops on curriculum integration, teaching strategies, and instructional technologies. Are we finished? Absolutely not! If anything, these workshops have created an appetite to learn more and to reflect on our own practice of teaching in the block.

A recent study (Tanner 1996) surveyed the perceived professional development needs of twelve faculties that teach in alternative-day block-scheduled high schools in Virginia. The teachers said they needed professional development in the following areas (in this order)

- Cooperative learning
- Strategies to promote creative problem solving
- Incorporating the use of instructional technology in the classroom
- Strategies to manage students

It is of interest to note how much importance teachers place on their need to know how to use instructional technology in order to be successful with block scheduling. This is an area where library media specialists can have a major impact. It also places an increased pressure on us to be knowledgeable and comfortable not only as users but as instructors with current and multidimensional technologies.

INSTRUCTIONAL TECHNOLOGY AND PROFESSIONAL DEVELOPMENT

Technology is critical to the success of school reform, yet teachers, on the whole, are not prepared to maximize this investment to its fullest potential for student learning. As administrations have worked to obtain enough computers to give students equitable access, they have not focused on the primary promoters of the new technology: classroom teachers. "Teachers, long the neglected stepchildren of the movement to computerize the nation's schools, are beginning to get invited to the party" (Cwiklik 1997, p. R8).

How teachers learn to use computers is very important. It has been found that staff best learn how to use educational technology when they have a presentation with theory and information, are provided a demonstration, have sufficient practice time with feedback and coaching, and then have follow-up over time after they try their new skills in the classroom (Bradshaw 1997, p. 88). The library media specialist has the flexibility to support the teacher in the critical time of demonstration, practice, and follow-up to ensure that the teacher is using the computer properly and to its greatest functionality.

Susan Bastian, director of Teaching Matters, a New York group that trains teachers to use information technology, says that if the role of the computer is not clear, the teacher will resist computer training. "By and large, teachers resent it terribly" (Cwiklik 1997, p. R8). The most effective kind of professional development for technology is peer-to-peer because it has the least psychological barriers, says David Aylward, head of the McGuffey Project, a Washington organization trying to establish a national mentor network. Library media specialists are in the ideal position to be that peer to instruct, support, and encourage teachers to try the unlimited possibilities of educational technology in a nonthreatening environment.

A statement by the dean of libraries at Purdue University, Emily R. Mobley, is applicable to the role of the library media specialist as a provider of technology professional development. Pronouncing the highlights of the year for the academic library, Dean Mobley states: "The goal of having a technically able, information proficient staff to support user needs in an increasingly electronic environment is being met with the introduction of a very pro-active staff development program introduced during the year. It is unique to the nation and will no doubt become a model for emulation by others" (1996–97, p. 1).

Supporting information technology users is a goal for all providers of information services in all types of libraries. In the schools, however, we are overwhelmed with the sheer numbers of computers, the age of our patrons, the veteran staffs, and the tremendous pressure for successful school reform. The library media specialist can learn from and with the computer teacher in the building or district. One of the benefits of being a member of the East Lyme High School faculty has been my professional relationship and personal friendship with our computer coordinator, Sandra Austin. Having Sandy as my partner in technology has supported me in many roles: as a user, a provider of professional development, a grant writer, a troubleshooter, an instructor, and a planner for future technologies. The encouragement we give each other benefits the entire school community for our advancements, procurements, and uses of educational technology. The technology has given us a forum to grow professionally individually and together.

One recent successful professional development activity we conducted was to create learning packets for local area network (LAN) access, the Windows environment, Internet, and PowerPoint. We determined that each of these technologies was essential for staff who teach in the block. Teachers were encouraged to work alone, in pairs, or be part of a large class for instruction. The day was divided into four blocks with a set schedule. We created a "learning spa" of technology instruction, a great deal of fun, and healthy refreshments for the staff. Two other teachers got caught up in the planning and offered their help throughout the day, so that all teachers felt comfortable with their experimentations with technology. Several weeks later, we continued to hear from the teachers how successful this day was. In an efficient and fun way, over seventy-five teachers received training in the basics. The result is that they now, in designing more engaging learning activities for their students in the block, have high expectations of their students and require final products that demonstrate not only their content knowledge but a sophisticated level of technology skill. In other words, "If I can do it, my students can do even more!"

TIME AND CULTURE

There is much written about the conflict between the need for professional development and the time it takes from the teacher day. Most states have a mandatory continuing education requirement for teachers, and a minimal number of days are provided in the school calendar. With major school reform, this time requirement is not sufficient. Yet "perhaps the most formidable challenge to institutionalizing effective professional development time may be the prevailing school culture that considers a teacher's proper place during school hours to be in front of the class. . . . It is a culture that does not place a premium on teacher learning" (Abdal-Haqq 1996, p. 3).

Flexibility is important to take advantage of professional development opportunities. In our transition summer before block scheduling, my high school faculty was given the option to move a professional day from the coming school year to the day after school ended so that we could participate in a workshop on teaching strategies. We then had the summer to reflect on what we learned and design lessons for the coming school year. This flexibility was appreciated by all, and ultimately it benefited the students, who were met in September by teachers who were confident that they could teach effectively in these new blocks of time. Compromises must be made when it comes to professional development, and teachers know that a well-designed learning opportunity will result in a multitude of future benefits to students.

BIBLIOGRAPHY

Print Sources

Abdal-Haqq, Ismat. "Making Time for Teacher Professional Development." *ERIC Digest* (October 1996): pp. 1–4. (ED400259.)

Baker, Robert C. "Block Scheduling: Impact on Library Media Programs." *Florida Media Quarterly* 21, 2 (1996): p. 10.

Bradshaw, Lynn K. "Technology-Supported Change: A Staff Development Opportunity." *NASSP Bulletin* 81, 593 (December 1997): pp. 86–92.

Cwiklik, Robert. "Those Who Can't . . . If Technology Is Going to Transform Our Schools, the Place to Start Is with the Teachers." *Wall Street Journal*, November 17, 1997, pp. R8, R14.

Galt, Joan. "Block Scheduling: Comments from Inside the Media Center." *Florida Media Quarterly* 21, 2 (1996): p. 12.

Mobley, Emily R. "The Purdue Libraries Looking Backward and Forward." In *The Libraries of Purdue University Year End Review*, pp. 1–2. West Lafayette, IN: Purdue University, 1996–97.

Rettig, Michael D., and Robert Lynn Canady. "All Around the Block Schedule." *Education Digest* 62, 6 (February 1997): pp. 30–34.

Shortt, Thomas L., and Yvonne V. Thayer. "A Vision for Block Scheduling: Where Are We Now? Where Are We Going?" *NASSP Bulletin* 81, 593 (December 1997): pp. 1–15.

Sykes, Gary. "Reform of and as Professional Development." *Phi Delta Kappan* 77, 7 (March 1996): pp. 465–476.

Tanner, Brenda Marie. *Perceived Staff Development Needs of Teachers in High Schools with Block Schedules.* Doctoral study, University of Virginia, 1996. (Dissertation Abstracts AAG9708553.)

Wilson, Suzanne, M., Penelope L. Peterson, Deborah L. Ball, and David K. Cohen. "Learning by All." *Phi Delta Kappan* 77, 7 (March 1996): pp. 468–470, 472, 474–476.

Internet Sites

ASCD Connections, Association for Supervision and Curriculum Development. *http://www.ascd.org*

Block Scheduling, College of Education, University of Minnesota. *http://carei.coled.umn.edu/bsmain.htm*

Block Scheduling Research, University of Virginia. *http://curry.edschool.virginia.edu/~dhv3v/block/research/research.html*

Peter Milbury's School Librarian Web Pages. *http://www.cusd.chico.k12.ca.us/~pmilbury/lib.html*

Tile Net—Listserv and Newsgroups. *http://www.tile.net*

Block Scheduling and Curriculum Development

5

The high school curriculum must offer substance and practicality to prepare students for an uncertain future, resisting artificiality and meeting individual needs without compromising larger goals. ("Breaking Ranks" 1996, p. 3)

Curriculum is at the core of school reform or restructuring. High school graduates face a complex world that demands that they have a comprehensive knowledge base and the skills to access and evaluate information relevant to decision making and learning. The traditional curriculum that relied on memorization of isolated facts and events is no longer appropriate or functional. Curriculum today must:

- Be responsive to the integration of concepts, disciplines, and subjects.
- Provide a solid foundation of knowledge and, equally important, teach problem-solving and decision-making skills.
- Be relevant to the student and his or her place in the twenty-first century.
- Rely on broad information and technologies for skills and content.
- Engage the student in his or her learning for long-term retention.

Gordon Cawelti, in the high school restructuring model he developed, proposes that the curriculum of the future have content standards, performance graduation expectations, use critical thinking, be interdisciplinary and integrated, provide active learning, be based in performance assessment, and have varied instructional strategies. School reorganization is one of four categories that affect the curriculum of the future, along with technology, incentives, and community. Within school reorganization, block scheduling is just one mechanism that will allow and facilitate these changes in the curriculum. Others include house plans, grouping strategies, and decentralized, shared decision making (Cawelti 1995, p. 3).

Cawelti's observations are important to place what the relationship of block scheduling is to curriculum. A school does not change to block scheduling and then make the curriculum fill the time frame of the schedule. Rather, the goals of curriculum change are facilitated and supported because the right schedule is in place to allow students to learn in a better environment. An example of letting the block schedule dictate the curriculum is when a school adapts block scheduling and unilaterally increases all former half-credit electives to full-credit courses. Did the curriculum goals and objectives of the majority of courses in the school require 100 percent more time, or did the administration see this as an easy way to make a new schedule work? If it is the latter, undoubtedly there will be problems as teachers try to make such radical adaptations to their curriculum in their formative years of block scheduling.

A more common example of a disaster in the making is the assumption that a teacher can readily adopt two lessons to the time frame of the block: "Teachers will be ineffective in the block if two formerly 45-minute long lessons are simply stacked on top of each other to form one 90-minute lesson. Concepts and activities must be reorganized within the new time frame" (Canady and Rettig 1996, p. 20). This is not to say that a school should wait until it has all its curriculum rewritten to work perfectly in a longer block of time. Curriculum documents are meant to be living, responsive, and changeable in response to research, the influence of national and state standards, frameworks, and guidelines, initiatives such as technology and school-to-career goals, and other educational factors.

An example of thoughtful planning for broad-based curriculum goals is found at the Lab School, an experimental after-school and summer supplement to middle school public education, located in Chappaqua, New York. Its academic goals should be considered when writing and evaluating curriculum:

- Provide practice in intellectual inquiry.
- Delve into complex and demanding topics.
- Create a curriculum designed around problems and questions they present.
- Create a curriculum that integrates modes of thinking from the various disciplines.
- Experiment with assessment techniques (Cardellichio 1997, p. 786).

Finally, many states and high schools in reform are considering replacing the Carnegie units with graduation standards. Minnesota will be the first state to do so on a wide scale beginning in the year 2000 (Monson

1997, p. 22). Of the ten Minnesota graduation standards, I have noted three standards with an asterisk that the library media center program can support through the curriculum:

1. Read, view, and listen to complex information in the English language.*
2. Write and speak effectively in the English language.
3. Use and interpret the arts.
4. Solve problems by applying mathematics.
5. Conduct research and communicate findings.*
6. Understand and apply scientific concepts.
7. Understand interactions between people and cultures.
8. Use information to make decisions.*
9. Manage resources for a household, community, or government.
10. Communicate in another language.

CURRICULUM MODEL

There are as many models for writing curriculum as there are school districts. Each district must decide what is important for student learning and achievement. At East Lyme High School, there were broad curricular goals in place prior to adapting block scheduling. It was determined the goals could be better achieved in a reorganization plan that included block scheduling. At the time we moved to the block, a different management structure was piloted to support the goals of the curriculum and ensure that the block was the correct format for meeting the goals. Individual and isolated department heads who did not function as a team were replaced by curriculum instructional leaders, who were charged with, among other tasks, ensuring that the curriculum was relevant and responsive to the needs of all students. As we used the block to provide the appropriate learning environment, we simultaneously rewrote the curriculum to include for each department a philosophy statement, program goals, and student outcomes and examined each course to ensure that it had all three components. If it did not, it was either redesigned or removed from the curriculum.

The curriculum for each course now has these components:

- A course description
- Two or three objectives for each unit
- Suggested instructional methodologies
- Suggested activities
- Materials and technology required
- Assessment strategies

Each course as well must have a technology objective, a school-to-career objective, and a required activity of research or a major writing paper. These three requirements have had a major influence on the writing and technology skills of our students. The format of the curriculum model provides flexibility for change and creativity, and it grounds each course in the broad department philosophy, goals, and student outcomes.

The library media program and computing services went through the same curriculum model for each department. Following are the library media philosophy, program goals, and student outcomes.

FRANCES HART EWERS LIBRARY MEDIA CENTER

Philosophy

The Library Media program supports student learning by providing up-to-date technology, multimedia, and print materials. By the end of 12th grade, students will know how to find and utilize information and technology for acquiring content knowledge, communicating information and ideas, and solving problems. Life long reading skills for all students will be reinforced through quality literature.

Program Goals

- The Library will provide a wide range of educational technologies for students to conduct research, communicate information and ideas, secure materials through resource sharing, create original works, organize data, and solve problems.
- Students will apply the skills necessary to locate, evaluate, interpret, and synthesize information from print, nonprint, and electronic sources.
- Students will use technology to enhance essential skills and facilitate learning in content areas.
- The Library and its materials will support instructional and curriculum changes due to block scheduling.
- The Library and its materials will support interdisciplinary teaching.
- The Library will support the East Lyme Technology Plan, "Target on Technology."
- The Library will offer professional development opportunities to the staff to refine their information and educational technology skills in areas of changing curricula and personal growth.
- The Library will provide and continually update a diverse collection of materials that represents various viewpoints on current and historical issues and provide quality literature for personal and required reading.
- The Library will provide materials and opportunities to support the school to career initiative.
- The Library will support the building requirement of a major paper for each course.

Student Outcomes

- Students will define their information needs and identify effective courses of action to conduct research, solve complex problems, and pursue personal interests.
- Students will apply principles of organized information systems to learning endeavors.
- Students will demonstrate a command of information skills and strategies to locate and use effectively print, nonprint, and electronic resources to solve problems, conduct research, and pursue personal interests.
- Students will apply evaluative criteria to the selection, interpretation, analysis, reorganization, and synthesis of information from a variety of sources and formats.
- Students will use appropriate technologies to create written, visual, oral, and multimedia products to communicate ideas, information, or conclusions to others.
- Students will evaluate the effectiveness and efficiency of their own choices and use of information and technology for problem solving and communication.
- Students will read quality literature that will reinforce reading practice and vocabulary, as well as establish a life long habit of reading for information and pleasure.
- Students will demonstrate the responsible and legal use of information resources, computers, and other technologies, recognizing the attendant social, economic, and ethical issues.
- Students will use career information to assist them in their school to career choices and transition.

THE LIBRARY MEDIA SPECIALIST AND CURRICULUM

Perhaps because I have shared responsibilities of being a curriculum instructional leader for several departments, including the library media center, with also being the library media specialist, curriculum development is a high priority for me. Understanding the components of the curriculum model is necessary in working with teachers. Having clearly identified program goals and student outcomes for the library media program helps me articulate how teaching information literacy is appropriate in the context of the broader unit objectives of the subject content. With the restructuring of our school and having the elongated block, many teachers plan with me and my staff for ways they can make adjustments to or design new activities around their unit objectives. Often a teacher will have one or two activities in mind, and I am able to verify that we have the materials and technology to support those activities or can suggest modification or new activities that will be more successful for students and simultaneously have information literacy outcomes.

Is the activity designed for preinformation, such as fact finding about apartheid before reading the novel, *Cry, the Beloved Country*? Is it a culminating activity whereby students draw conclusions or solve a problem after they have found a plethora of information from both outside and inside the library media center? A few teachers will "bond" to the library media center for an entire semester or year for several unit objectives that have multiple activities for each objective. Knowing where the assignment fits on the curriculum model is vital.

When the library media center is identified as being critical to the success of student learning and achievement, especially if teachers promote resource-based learning, "a solid relationship between proximity and use, the [library media] center's close coordination with the instructional program can promote increased usage of the curriculum-related materials." Further the "benefits of the library media program cannot be realized unless there is a concerted effort to integrate the classroom with the media center" (Thompson 1991, p. 26). The block schedule reorganized the school day so that students now have the time seamlessly to move their learning from the classroom to the library media center for sustained learning.

The library media specialist should serve on the building or district curriculum committee (or both) to be a viable member of the curriculum team, along with the teacher, curriculum instructional leader or department head, and principal. At Archbishop Chapell High School in Louisiana, a three-times-recognized Blue Ribbon School, the library media specialist describes her role in curriculum:

As head librarian I serve . . . as a member of the school's advisory board, composed of academic department chairs. By serving on the board, I become familiar with the activities of every academic department and can easily foster library support and cooperation schoolwide. During the past school year the department chairs met on a regular basis to discuss issues dealing with writing across the curriculum, problem-solving, and basic thinking skills. (Thibodeaux 1997, p. 12)

Her involvement guaranteed that the resources of the library media center—both staff and materials—were available to support the new directions of the curriculum.

At a time when the entire school is evaluating the curriculum, the library media specialist can seize the opportunity to promote changes in the information and technology skills curriculum that he or she may have been wanting to make but could not do in the traditional school. It is an exciting time for all as teachers share ideas. In my school, teachers from diverse departments now get together and freely offer suggestions and support to one another. As the library media specialist, I found a new role as facilitator. From our position, we have an excellent overview of the curriculum and the exciting activities students are doing throughout the school.

RESOURCE-BASED LEARNING

Resource-based learning promotes learning by discovery. Instead of the teacher's drawing the conclusion for the student, the student gathers information, tries out several hypotheses, and then draws conclusions based on the evidence. Resource-based learning is an educational model that actively involves students, teachers, and the library media specialist in the meaningful use of appropriate print, nonprint, and human resources. It requires the library media specialist to assist teachers in integrating the use of the library media center resources into their classroom instruction (*Resource-Based Learning* 1994).

The library media center becomes even more essential to high schools that restructure and adopt block scheduling. The classroom does not provide the wide variety of resources that students must have to learn and so is no longer the only place of learning. In public education, where we are striving to meet the basics with limited budgets, the ideal classroom that is the sole center of learning does not exist. Even in the most heavily endowed schools, where there is a wide variety of technology in the classrooms, there is still the need for an inclusive library media center.

Let's attempt to define the terms *resource-based learning* and *information literacy*. There are many definitions in the literature. I have selected two that are clear and strongly correlate to each other:

Resource Based Learning is a method that allows students to learn from their own confrontation with information sources. (*Learning* 1994)

Information Literacy . . . is an individual's ability to recognize a need for information, identify and locate appropriate information sources, know how to gain access to the information contained in those sources, evaluate the quality of information obtained, organize the information, and use the information effectively. (Hancock 1993)

Information literacy supports the student who is self-directing his or her learning from a variety of sources. Students have to be information literate to maximize the ideas from the content (resources) and apply it to their learning. The library media specialist may plan with the classroom teacher to team-teach lessons and to purchase a variety of appropriate materials that tie directly into unit outcomes (Dalbotten 1990). One successful example of this kind of collaboration is the lesson, "Paragons and Paladins," which was awarded a Connecticut Celebration of Excellence award in 1997. Edythe Rose, an English teacher at East Lyme High School, and I collaborated to create a culminating exercise that demonstrated students' knowledge of mini-epic. Using library resources, performance assessment was done through writing and dramatization. She taught the students the subject content, while I taught information literacy skills. It was a unit that proved very beneficial for the students and fun for all. (This lesson is contained in Chapter Thirteen.)

Hilda K.Weisburg and Ruth Toor (1994) have researched the effectiveness of teaching information literacy. Their "information curriculum" has ten core concepts that deal with organization, resources, the assessment of information, thinking, and reading:

Concept 1: A shared pool of materials benefits everyone.

Concept 2: Library materials are arranged by subject.

Concept 3: Reference materials are available for all subjects.

Concept 4: Recognition of the arrangement of resource speeds access to its information.

Concept 5: Indexes are the major key to locating information.

Concept 6: Not all information is an important consideration.

Concept 7: Timeliness of information is an important consideration.

Concept 8: Information may carry bias.

Concept 9: Research requires thinking and communicating.

Concept 10: Voluntary reading is a basis for building knowledge. (p. 64)

Block scheduling will increase students' use of the library dramatically. Where in the past I may have seen a particular student at most twice a day, now I may see him or her three or four times in a day. The manner in which the library media specialist instructs information skills also needs to adapt. The concepts of the information curriculum seem very appropriate for a block-scheduled library media center whereby we do not spend time instructing about individual books or resources but rather cluster common traits or important attributes about sources and technology. The library media specialist then develops instruction that helps students readily recognize and understand these traits or attributes that will be transferable to a variety of sources. Teachers are requiring students to synthesize information in ways that they never had time to in the traditional period of 45 minutes of class. So accurate to what I witness now when students visit the library media center in the block schedule, Weisburg and Toor (1994, p. 63) say that students will learn to make choices, recognizing that when dealing with complex issues:

• There is no one right answer.

• There is no one correct route to finding information.

• Analysis is more important than rote memory.

• Their own purpose defines the value of a specific piece of information.

• Information needs change during a research project.

SCHOOL TO CAREER

Information literacy skills are critical as we prepare students for their school-to-career transition. Most of today's innovative curriculums also emphasize application to the world outside school (Brandt 1996, p. 3). In the world of work, information is a commodity, and those who have knowledge will be most valuable workers. Employees must be able to explore, connect, and apply knowledge. Washington and Oregon have integrated information literacy skills into their state curriculum guides (Hancock 1996, p. 6).

Finally, do not overlook Mike Eisenberg's Big Six Skills information problem solving in the block-scheduled environment. The Big Six Skills integrates what were once isolated library or technology skills into a problem-solving curriculum based in a process framework. An active listserv exists for the exchange of ideas and discussion.

LEARNING ACTIVITIES AND LESSON PLANS

Activities that the teacher designs to reinforce learning are perhaps the area of curriculum most affected by the block schedule and new instructional methodologies. The amount of sustained class time helps to create the right environment for meaningful, active learning. As more and more is understood about the human brain, we discover that the brain is a social organ and we learn from each other, the brain seeks connections to what it already knows, and every brain is unique in its organization (Scherer 1997). All of these facts are significant to how activities should be constructed so that each student can maximize his or her potential to learn.

It is recommended that in a block of 90 minutes, the teacher plan for a minimum of three activities. Through research projects, collaborative activities, oral presentations, use of technologies, and critiquing of one another's work, students engage more actively and socially than they do by reading or listening (Wyatt 1996, p. 16). The library media center is an extension of the classroom with its collection of materials that relate to the curriculum, the multimedia, and technologies. The library media specialist has an important role in planning with teachers meaningful activities that are driven by content material, with the objectives of the daily lesson dictating the activities (Brett 1996, p. 34). The restructured high school will rely heavily on the resources of the library media center to provide the materials and technology support needed for students to learn. The library media center strives now and in the future to provide "the right resource at the right time to the right person" (Farmer 1997, p. 17).

In the time that East Lyme High School has been a block-scheduled school, the quality of learning activities in the library media center has been exceptional. No longer do we have the "country report," whereby students take an almanac, an encyclopedia, and a book and write a summary of facts about the country. Today students contrast information and draw inferences about the government and economic policies, relate historical events to current events, and understand literature through the history and culture of a country. The lessons set out in Table 5.1 could not be accomplished without the sustained research time afforded by the block schedule. (These lesson plans are set out in Chapter Thirteen.)

Table 5.1
Example Lessons

Title	Teachers/Authors	Purpose of Lesson
Paragons and Paladins: A Search for Perfection Without and Within	Edythe S. Rose and Marie K. Shaw	English, Grade 12: Writing, information literacy, research, literature, understanding the ideals of a society.
River Valley Civilizations	Alice Pembrook and Marie Shaw	World History, Grade 9: Students learn how to evaluate the available sources on a topic and compile a research bibliography for both print and technology before taking notes.
Journeys: The Cultural Mosaic	Karen Libby, Deborah Bergeron, Ruth Bley, and Claire Hanlon	American Studies, Grade 11: The overview of the unit lesson and one of six supportive activities from an interdisciplinary unit of social studies and literature is provided.
Freshman Academy	Marie Shaw	Library Orientation, Grade 9: This introductory and hands-on lesson to the LMC is repeated many times in groups of 12 students for the entire 9th grade class during first quarter. Students use resources and organize material for a speech.
World Literature	Michael Landow	English, Grade 10: This year-long thematic approach to world literature engages students in the nonfiction, novels, short stories, poetry, and drama of a foreign country.

BIBLIOGRAPHY

Print Sources

Bleakley, Ann. *Resource-Based Learning Activities: Information Literacy for High School Students*. Chicago: American Library Association, 1994.

Brandt, Ron. "Overview: Starting Over." *Educational Leadership* 53, 8 (May 1996): p. 3.

"Breaking Ranks for High School Reform." *Education Digest* 62, 2 (October 1996).

Breivik, Patricia Senn, and J. A. Senn. *Information Literacy: Educating Children for the 21st Century*. New York: Scholastic 1994.

Brett, Monroe. "Teaching Block-Scheduled Class Periods." *Education Digest* 62, 1 (September 1996): pp. 34–37.

Canady, Robert Lynn, and Michael D. Rettig. *Teaching in the Block: Strategies for Engaging Active Learners*. Princeton, NJ: Eye on Education, 1996.

Cardellichio, Thomas. "The Lab School: A Vehicle for Curriculum Change and Professional Development." *Phi Delta Kappan* 78, 10 (June 1997): pp. 785–788.

Cawelti, Gordon. "High School Restructuring: What Are the Critical Elements?" *NASSP Bulletin* 79, 569 (March 1995): pp. 1–15.

Dalbotten, Mary, and Joan Wallin. *Classroom Instructional Design: Tools for Teacher/ Media Specialist Interaction*. St. Paul, MN: Minnesota State Department of Education, 1990. (ERIC ED337128.)

Farmer, Lesley. "Crystal Ball Gazing into Library Land." *Book Report* 16, 3 (November–December 1997).

Hancock, Vicki E. *Information Literacy for Lifelong Learning*. ERIC Digest, EDO-IR-93-1 (May 1993): pp. 1–2.

Hancock, Virginia. *Learning How to Learn: Information Literacy as a Curriculum Priority*. Alexandria, VA: ASCD Networks, 1996.

Kirk, Joyce. "Information Skills and Educational Perspective for Tomorrow." ERIC Abstract, ED359981, 1987.

Learning for the Future: Developing Information Services in Australian Schools. ERIC Abstract, ED377826, 1994.

Monson, Robert J. "Redefining the Comprehensive High School: The Multiple Pathways Model." *NASSP Bulletin* 81, 588 (April 1997): pp. 19–27.

Resource-Based Learning: An Educational Model. Manitoba, Canada: Manitoba Department of Education, 1994. (ERIC Doc. ED372736.)

Scherer, Marge. "Perspectives/How Do Children Learn?" *Educational Leadership* 54, 6 (March 1997): p. 5.

Thibodeaux, Annette. "The Library in an Award-Winning School." *Book Report* 16, 3 (November–December 1997): pp. 11–12.

Thompson, James C. "Resource-Based Learning Can Be the Backbone of Reform, Improvement." *NASSP Bulletin* 75, 535 (May 1991): pp. 24–28.

Weisberg, Hilda, and Ruth Toor. "The Information Curriculum: Teaching Concepts for the Virtual Library Environment." *School Library Media Annual* 12 (1994): pp. 63–69.

Weisberg, Hilda, and Ruth Toor. "Resource Based Instruction." *Emergency Librarian* 23, 2 (November–December 1995): pp. 8–10.

Wyatt, Linda D. "More Time, More Training: What Staff Development Do Teachers Need for Effective Instruction in Block Scheduling?" *School Administrator* 53, 8 (September 1996): pp. 16–18.

Internet Sites

Big Six Skills Listserv. Subscribe to *LISTSERV@listserv.SYR.EDU*. In the body of
message type SUBSCRIBE Big6 yourfirstname yourlastname

ERIC Lesson Plans. *http://ericir.syr.edu/Virtual/Lessons*

Internet School Library Media Center, James Madison University. Select Unit/Lesson Plans Page. *http://falcon.jmu.edu/~ramseyil/*

Oregon Department of Education. *http://www.ode.state.or.us/*

Washington Department of Education—Information Literacy Guides. *http://www.ospi.wednet.edu/*

Yale–New Haven Teachers Institute. Select Curricular Resources. *http://www.yale.edu/ynhti/*

Of Practical Consideration: Staffing, Collection Development, and Budget

6

BLOCK SCHEDULING AND THE STAFF

With reform will come an assessment of personnel and the functions they perform. "Working cooperatively with other professionals in the school, the library media specialist can affect the educational process and bring about changes in the roles of the various professionals and the students in the school. Restructuring begins when someone wants things to be different and seeks out others who want to work for the same goals" (Wright 1993, p. 34).

There is no question that block scheduling will affect the library media staff. There will be a shift in purpose from the library media center's being a support facility for traditional instruction to its being an exciting, essential place of learning where students explore ideas and solve complex issues. All library media specialists surveyed reported a dramatic increase in facility use with block scheduling. "Staffing is crucial. . . . When you increase the number of classes, you need the manpower to work with them" (Keenan 1997, p. 7).

At the onset of planning for change, each school must examine how the facility is used and think creatively about the future. Library media programs have been serving and supporting instruction effectively for years under traditional schedules. Often it is the media center staff who have initiated instructional change by promoting new technologies and information sources. If you are in the planning stage, it is helpful to survey teachers to learn what they perceive are the most valuable services of the library media staff prior to block scheduling. Figure 6.1 shows a sample survey. You can add to the checklist other services that you and your staff offer that you think are valuable to the faculty. It will be revealing to see if

Figure 6.1
Survey for Teachers About the Library Media Center

Block scheduling will bring many changes to our school, including to the Lib
Media Center! As we plan to support you in block scheduling, it would be v
helpful for us to know what services we now provide that you value the mos
Please rank order with #1 being of the highest priority to you and #11 being
lowest:

_____ Introductory lessons with your students before research
projects

_____ Technology support with the Internet and other computers

_____ Interlibrary loan

_____ Helping your students when they come individually with their
research

_____ Providing assistance with on-line searches

_____ Monitoring students during study hall

_____ Planning lessons with you for library research

_____ Offering professional development workshops

_____ Ordering books, magazines, software, videos

_____ Providing help with computer and audiovisual equipment

_____ Organizing and locating materials for you and your students your perceptions are the same as those of your users. A teacher who collaborates with you on designing lessons in the traditional schedule will depend on your help even more under the block schedule.

It would be helpful to survey the administration about what they perceive the changes will be for the library media staff with block scheduling. Arrange for a short informative meeting with each administrator in your school with some focus questions such as these:

- What are the most valuable contributions of the library media staff to the education of the students?
- Which duties currently performed by library media staff have the most impact on the positive functioning of the school?
- What changes in duties do you envision for the staff that will support block scheduling in the school?

The information learned from the faculty and administration will help you prioritize how you allocate staff time and responsibilities and could be used to justify a case for the expenditure of additional staff and materials.

From your discussion with the administrators, you may learn, for example, that your support in professional development activities for teachers is the service most valued. If so, you will want to shift time and funds toward this important endeavor. You may need to develop a short list of other schools or service centers in your geographic area that offer information and technology workshops. Rather than spending the time to prepare and deliver numerous workshops, you may find it a better use of staff time to locate an affordable workshop each month for faculty.

The information you gain from the surveys and meetings will help you define the mission of your library. If your school recently participated in an accreditation process, the mission may already be defined. Locate it, and see if it is still applicable. Read it again, and see if it meets the needs for a block-scheduled high school that is making an educational shift to resource-based learning with authentic and experiential lessons.

PROJECTING STAFF NEEDS

In preparing for the changes block scheduling will bring, examine the job descriptions of the library media staff. What are the duties of professional, paraprofessional, and clerical support staff? How do district support staff interface with the high school? In some districts, audiovisual services are centralized; in others, there is central processing. Have a clear understanding of who does what as you project staffing needs for block scheduling.

A simple analysis of how each staff member allocates his or her time is revealing. Do tell the staff that this is not a evaluative exercise but rather a constructive means for determining how their time will best be used to meet the new goals of the library program with block scheduling. Complete an analysis for your own time spent, and share all the results with your staff to help prepare them for the changes anticipated with block scheduling. There are many ways in which you can gather these data, one as simple as keeping a log per person for each half-hour or hour of the workday. Ask each staff member to keep this journal for five days. At the end of the week, average the amount of time each person spent doing the major tasks related to his or her job.

You may find, for example, that the circulation clerk spends 25 percent of the time related to the function of retrieving overdue books (notices, phone calls, etc.). With block scheduling, circulation will increase; thus, you may discover during this transition time that you will need to place

Figure 6.2
Professional Allocation of Time

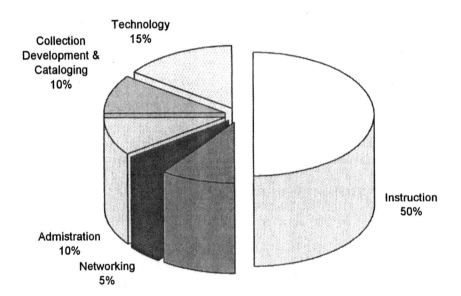

Figure 6.3
Paraprofessional Allocation of Time

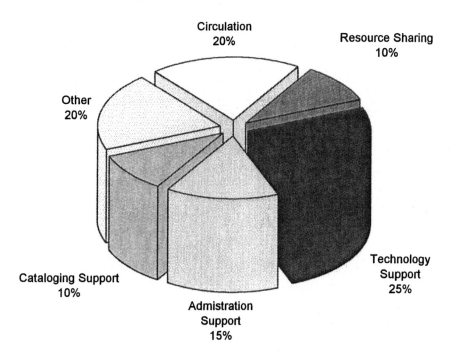

Circulation
20%

Resource Sharing
10%

Other
20%

Technology
Support
25%

Cataloging Support
10%

Admistration
Support
15%

more staff time on retrieving overdue items or lobby for a change in the school accountability policy. Or you may find that the professionals are spending too much of their time performing clerical tasks. If so, you may determine that the professional's time must be redirected.

You can draw pie or bar graphs of your results to show staff. Sometimes a picture is worth a thousand words, and by visually demonstrating how library media staff time is spent, you will be more convincing in your presentation to initiate needed changes. Figures 6.2 through 6.4 show an example of how each level of staff may have spent their time during the five-day period.

In anticipating the block schedule, the library media specialist and the administration decide if the existing level of staffing is adequate in order to be successful with resource-based learning. Knowing the talents and strengths of the existing staff, the amount of time each person allocates for major tasks and responsibilities, and anticipating the demands that will result from block scheduling will help you determine if you can do with no changes. In the survey of our participants, almost 30 percent of the schools

Figure 6.4
Clerical Assistant Allocation of Time

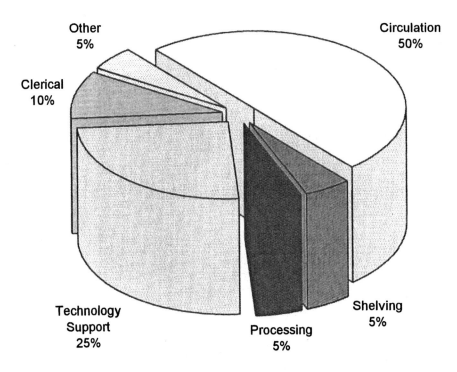

increased the staff in preparation of block scheduling (see Table 6.1). A few schools did increase professional staff for the anticipated increase of services and instruction the block would demand. A recent article published in the *San Francisco Chronicle* quotes a sample number of library media specialists to students by state. The ratios vary from a respectable 1 library media specialist per 476 students in Kansas to the totally unsatisfactory ratio of 1 library media specialist to 6,179 students in California (Asimov 1997, pp. 4–5). For schools that have an unsatisfactory ratio of students to professional staff, a high priority should be placed on obtaining an increase in professional staff for the increased demand on services that block scheduling will have.

Respondents indicated the need for technical support personnel who could troubleshoot and solve small but consistently time-consuming problems, such as printing problems, circulation-associated issues, minor repairs, audiovisual support, and processing.

The ten responding library media specialists to my survey were asked if the current staffing was adequate for the challenges of a block-scheduled

Table 6.1
Survey of Staff Changes Due to Block Scheduling

High School	Increase in Staff Due to Block Schedule
Centralia Regional High School	No increase
Duncanville Ninth Grade School	15 percent professional staff
East Lyme High School	50 percent increase in professional staff (first two years) Year three: Replaced part-time professional position with a full-time paraprofessional
Edward Little High School	No increase
Evergreen High School	100 percent decrease in professional staff 200 percent increase in paraprofessional staff
Harrisburg High School	No increase
Kingswood Regional High School	No increase
Scotland High School	No increase
Shaw High School	No increase
Vines High School	No increase, but added a technology assistant for the building
West Brunswick High School	No increase

school. For the most part, the schools that added additional staff are now satisfied with the level of support (see Table 6.2).

Library media specialists prefer to have paraprofessional assistance in a block-scheduled school.

Technology and Staffing

I don't think any library media specialist would disagree that technology is a mixed blessing. It has certainly augmented the availability and access of information, but it comes with a personnel cost for inputting data, helping users with search strategies, and troubleshooting problems. It behooves the library media specialist to form a team approach with other members of the faculty for technology support.

Many schools have developed full television and audio centers either as part of or separate from the library media center. Technology education has expanded its role into communications. Once a department that was

Table 6.2
Survey to Determine if Staff Positions Are Sufficient
for Block Scheduling

High School	Is Current Staffing Adequate?
Centralia Regional High School	Yes—but we could use another paraprofessional
Duncanville Ninth Grade School	Yes
East Lyme High School	Yes
Edward Little High School	Yes
Evergreen High School	Yes
Harrisburg High School	Yes
Kingswood Regional High School	No—need paraprofessional help
Scotland High School	No—need full time computer staff member
Shaw High School	No—there is a need for paraprofessional assistance
Vines High School	Yes—added a fourth person who deals with "anything that plugs in"
West Brunswick High School	Yes

fairly isolated from the rest of the school offering materials shops, it is now an exciting place that can support interactive television, video production, editing, the creation of films, digitized imaging, and other innovative technologies.

In a school that has a technology education department with communications goals, the library media specialist and teachers should collaboratively plan how together they can support the faculty and students in the creation of visual and audio projects. Determine which hardware and software resources can be shared. Services that were traditionally offered from the audiovisual department may now be more appropriately placed in technology education, which has the ability to offer courses to train hundreds of students each year in the art of filmmaking, video production, graphics, computerized design, and so forth. If your school has this kind of model, planning and policy should clarify and facilitate the relationship between the library media and technology education departments and the services they perform.

Similar relationships can occur with other support departments of the school. What computing services are offered? Does the library media center house the computer lab? Computer services will naturally keep expanding, and even more quickly under block scheduling. The computer coordinator is the professional who institutes instructional change with technology; he or she helps faculty teach more effectively with educational technologies. The computer coordinator also has an important role in designing curriculum that uses that latest technologies so that students are prepared for school-to-career transitions. The computer department and the library media department should work in harmony to offer technology services.

The Role of the Library Media Specialist

Once block scheduling is initiated, there will be little to time to think back on how things were once done. Yet reflection is very important to help us analyze how well we are doing, and it promotes assessment that can result in positive change. Below are some of my findings from talking with media specialists who now work in schools with block scheduling:

School Media Specialist as Consultant

Teachers will seek out the library media specialist to consult about new lesson design. Working with teachers to develop lessons, being a point person to try ideas out, and letting teachers know the realm of possibilities with the kinds of information available in the library are all important functions for the library media specialist. Teachers must also be made knowledgeable of new materials and services, as well as older materials and traditional services. A donation of World War II magazines from a community member that had been on the shelf for years may now be the primary source material for authentic research about this important event. The *increased demand* of so many teachers at the onset of block scheduling will prove challenging.

Library Media Specialist as a Curriculum Leader

Curriculum development has always been an important function for library media specialists to be involved in. In planning how the staff time will be used, there should be a regular, important allocation for curriculum development. This could be in the form of attending a department meeting or district curriculum council meeting, setting a goal of meeting with two teachers a week for 30 minutes on revisions of lessons, dropping off articles or notes to teachers highlighting something new, and so forth. In a recent article a former high school principal (Hartzell 1997, pp. 24–29) chastises library media specialists for not sharing their wealth of knowledge about information technology innovations, problem solving, curriculum, and fiscal management with other educational professionals outside the library. He recommends that library media specialists broaden their leadership role by joining and participating in organizations that have influence and power with teachers, administrators, accrediting agencies, and legislatures—for example:

National Education Association

National Association of Secondary School Principals

American Association of School Administrators

Association for Supervision and Curriculum Development

National Council of Teachers of English

National Council of Teachers of Mathematics

National Staff Development Council

Being a Member of a Larger Community

The need to network with other professionals and organizations is extremely important in block scheduling because the curriculum or course activities will change substantially. Student research now may require interviews, interlibrary loans, and visits as the nature of their information needs changes in resource-based learning. The library media staff must also support networking with local and global communities over the Internet and other online resources.

Professional Development

Faculty continually seek professional development activities that reinforce technology integration and instructional methodology for teaching in the block. The computer coordinator and I offer professional development to our faculty both after school and on professional development days, in the areas of Internet access and evaluation, network access, and software applications.

Acquisitions and Cataloging

The increased purchase of books and materials will have an impact on the selection and cataloging of resources. It may be difficult to find competent catalogers, especially if the support staff has not had formal training. If your library is located near a college or university, you may inquire if there are catalogers who would like to work part time or contractually for your library. There are independent cataloging services and librarians who have formed their own cataloging services businesses. Determine if there is a cost savings to contract out the cataloging versus hiring staff permanently. Do not overlook the ability to copy or extract MARC records from statewide databases. A tremendous savings of cataloging time can be had by duplicating existing records. The bottom line is that more resources in resource-based learning does require more staffing (outsourced or insourced) for selection, processing, and cataloging.

Paraprofessional Staff, Volunteers, and Supervising Faculty

The results of my surveys indicate the importance of paraprofessional staff. The advances of technology and the increased use of the library media center in block scheduling require that the library media specialist have adequate support staff.

Paraprofessional responsibilities will grow with block scheduling. In our school circulation doubled in the first year of block scheduling. This meant an impact on support staff for circulation-related duties, shelving, and processing. Interlibrary loan, for the most part, can be accomplished by paraprofessionals. With block scheduling, the movement of materials and technology increases, and paraprofessional staff are essential to keeping the collection and equipment in operational condition.

Student helpers can contribute greatly to the library media program. High school students often look for ways to perform community service, and the library is an excellent place to offer them this opportunity. Offer work in the library for credit, such as independent study, or, if your community college offers a library assistant degree, arrangements could be made to offer that course to your students that would involve completing authentic tasks. Outstanding students in the business program may want to exercise their skills in office practice in the library, and credit could be offered them for this school-to-career experience. Supervision of volunteers and students is always an issue, and with the block schedule, the professional will have even less time to do so. Students can work directly with paraprofessional staff if their tasks are well defined.

Some schools assign a duty period to faculty to the library or computer labs to help with supervision of students. This can be very successful if the teachers feel comfortable with the assignment and have the training they need to help users. There must be clear expectations from the media or computer professional to the teachers so that there is no ambiguity. Agreement may be made that when the teacher's assistance is not required, he or she may use the time to work one on one with individual students whom they teach for support or remediation.

Evaluating the Library Media Staff

Evaluation and review are important components of the staffing cycle. How can the staff be assured that their goals are also the goals needed for the success of block scheduling in the library media program? How do you convince staff that the new demands of block scheduling are really worth it?

Students will be the first to let us know if we are doing our job correctly. I found that as the demands for information increased on the students, they became more dependent on the library staff to help them. Sharing the positive experiences of the students with staff is an excellent place to start. Ask the student to tell the person who helped how she or he was crucial to the success of the project. We all appreciate hearing firsthand how we can positively affect students. If there is a formal, annual review for staff, be sure to include a statement about their contributions to making block scheduling successful.

Second, just as teachers need professional development with new technologies, so do the support staff. Look for opportunities that provide paraprofessional staff in-service training. Computer training should be ongoing and can be obtained through adult education courses, a community college, or even with the vendor of a product or service. Regional workshops can be held for a technology, such as learning the Internet. The level of service will increase when the paraprofessional is confident and competent with new technologies.

Periodic staff meetings can set direction and reflect on accomplishments. Weekly meetings are an ideal, but with the hectic pace of most library media programs, this cannot be done. Even once a month it would be beneficial to review the successes of the month, discuss what could have been done better, and outline your goals for the coming few weeks. Share the goals of the principal for school reform with your staff. Plan a "histograph" of the typical things that have to be accomplished each year so staff can anticipate certain tasks or events on their planning calendars.

Block scheduling will challenge every staff member. Library media specialists will find their knowledge and skills of management, planning, instruction, human development, learning theory, professional development, technology, and curriculum challenged and used every day. The job you had will never be the same again. However, you now possess an exciting and enviable place on the faculty to facilitate authentic resource-based learning. High school restructuring through block scheduling has created the need for the library media specialist to acquire and promote information technologies. Along with the library media specialists need to be a talented staff of paraprofessionals who are committed to providing a full complement of services and support.

COLLECTION DEVELOPMENT

"Does block scheduling increase the demand for learning resources?" "Absolutely!" replies Cynthia Tobojka of Wareham High School. "The schedule effects every aspect of the collection." She states that the collection must support a greater range of topics, including "areas that students didn't get into before" (Keenan 1997, p. 7).

How does the library media specialist ensure that a collection that has been carefully developed to correlate with and support the curriculum of the traditional high school meet the needs of students and teachers in the new environment of block scheduling? In our transition year, when I was researching the impact of block scheduling on the library media center, I was told repeatedly to plan for my budget to be inadequate for the changes. However, no one told me *what* I would be purchasing if I was fortunate to acquire the extra funding—just that I would need more. In this section I share my observations and experiences with collection development under the block and why resource-based learning requires the right materials in a supportive library media center.

The first year of block scheduling will be one of trial by fire for everyone involved. Teachers should be encouraged to experiment, but experimentation can be costly in terms of purchasing materials when it is unsuccessful and the acquisition has been made. It goes against the frugal grain of the library media specialist to acquire items that may have a very specific utility or a one-time use. If your library media center has a resource-sharing system in place with other libraries, you can try many new books out by borrowing them before you commit to a purchase.

Departmental Acquisitions

In my collection areas that needed immediate relief due to the block were reference, sociological and historical materials, science, biography, math, and online resources. Depending on the innovations and change that your faculty institutes, your priorities will naturally vary. Here is my rationale for acquisitions during the first years of the block.

English Department

The block schedule has allowed our English Department to examine the goals and delivery of its curriculum thoroughly. After study it was determined this department would retain the curriculum goals and objectives, but radically change the format and activities by instituting English course electives. In the past, the offerings were English I through IV as full-credit courses. Now we are offering electives on Shakespeare, allusion, the mystery, and other specific genres or topics in half-credit courses. Our English teachers have moved away from the annual literary criticism paper and now teach literature by making interdisciplinary connections with either social issues or historical events.

Literary criticism is now used as a reference for students to determine the merits of the interpretation of a work; it is not the sole source of a research paper. English students are using the library media center even more than they were before, but the research and writing activities require collaboration, synthesis of concepts, acknowledgment of differences of opinion, and so forth. With these dynamic changes came the need for the library media center collection to reach out well beyond the 800s to a wide variety of material. Keeping open dialogues with individual English teachers and the curriculum instructional leader for this department has been critical to our success in having the right materials available and for me knowing how to focus acquisitions.

Reference

The reference collection was one that I had been particularly proud of prior to block scheduling. Major investments had been made in the science, music, and art encyclopedias. Our high school owns the updated version of an unabridged, multivolume music encyclopedia, as well as an extensive collection of literary criticism and authorship. All of these resources are still important for us, but not in the same way that they had been in the past. I quickly discovered that these were not the reference materials that would repeatedly serve our students in the block for the kinds of activities they needed information. The following attributes should be sought in selecting reference materials for resource-based learning:

• Primary source material
• Colorful pictures that are usable for scanning or other duplication
• Summarizes the topic in one or two pages
• Chronological format
• Multivolume that are thematic or chronological so that many students can use several books of the set at one time

The reference collection was infused with many new materials, and now our students rely on it as an important place to begin their research. By having a variety of resources that work well, we are able to reinforce and model good research practice that begins with using reference material. No longer do we rely on encyclopedias to initiate research. In fact, even the CD-ROM encyclopedias are not as necessary to students; I suspect many students have them at home. Students are confident they will find a reference book that will give them much more thorough information than the encyclopedia.

I found it important to spend the time with sales representatives for the extensive purchasing I have made in the reference area. The cost necessitates that the library media specialist is comfortable that the books will address the new activities of the curriculum and that students will find them easy to use. A few of the areas of reference that have proved invaluable to our students under block scheduling are biography; surveys of world and American literature; geographical and topographical works; chronologies; studies of the culture, government, and history of Americana; and medical resources, including alternative and holistic medicine.

Sociological and Historical Material

One of the most delightful surprises to me, perhaps because this was my area of study in my undergraduate work, was the tremendous increase in student research that now requires information about patterns of social evolution and history. These needs occur not only from the social studies projects but throughout the curriculum. In science, math, and family and consumer science, among other areas, teachers are asking students to understand the background of the issues they are studying. The following areas are in great demand:

- Opposing viewpoints or books that put forth divergent opinions on an issue
- Statistical material that is attractively visual and easy to read, such as pie or bar graphs
- Women's and children issues
- Lifestyles, clothing, music, and sports of any era
- Specific events (e.g., prohibition, the Progressive Era)
- Full documents, speeches, and acts of legislation that can be interpreted
- Summaries of major trials and court cases
- Prints or sets of authentic posters and documents that serve as primary source visuals

Teachers are requiring their students to use the higher-order thinking skills of Bloom's Taxonomy to interpret and synthesize data into meaningful knowledge and understanding of relationships. They are also acknowledging the multiple intelligences theory of Gardner and designing activities that have objectives that can be accomplished by many different approaches. The research students now do is laced with questions such as these: "What were the contributions of . . . ?" "What if . . . chose to do . . . differently?" "If you were . . . how would you react to . . . ?" Sociological and historical materials have the information to help students make the connections between the evolution of a concept and its current importance or relevance.

Biographies

Similar to sociological and historical material, the importance of individuals has found its way into curriculum in a way that it had not before block scheduling. Biographical research is now assigned in *all* curricula areas—for example, "What were the contributions of women mathematicians, chemists, and physicians ten, fifty, and one hundred years ago?" and, "Tell me about the rulers of the Greek and Roman civilizations." Although there has been an increase in the number of biographies and autobiographies circulated, more important for research, there continues to be a need for collected biographies that in a chapter summarize the contributions of an individual. No longer can I count on students' asking only about presidents and other famous people. I am learning new names regularly and finding their contributions fascinating.

Science

In this area, we have always enjoyed a strong collection development policy, but what I discovered with the institution of block scheduling was that students needed current research that supports their own laboratory work. There are many more questions being asked about the latest discoveries in genetic research, alternative healing and medicine, and environmental impact. The block schedule now gives laboratory time to every science class, not just selected areas, and thus the students are highly engaged in benchwork in the room. There is also a regular pathway of students from their laboratories to the library to substantiate research, and for this we have heavily relied on our "virtual library" with the online periodical resources. For scientific and local topics, I have found the need to keep an active "vertical file" of pamphlets, clippings, and interesting articles that are brought to my attention. Although much of the material that in the past I would have clipped for the file is now obtainable online, in the science area there is a need to keep it active, especially for local issues. Interestingly, the research shows that when surveyed, half of the school media specialists said that vertical files could not be replaced by technology (Savich 1993).

Math

The Math Department has metamorphosed from a department that came to the library media center once a year to pick up overhead projectors to one that now uses it for student research. Much discussion and professional development revolved around teaching mathematics in the block schedule, and it was this content area that was one of the main reasons for our school's selecting the alternate-day block schedule.

Mathematics students now manipulate information and data through problem solving. Areas of collection development that have had to be expanded have been in the history of algebra, geometry, and calculus, as well as biographies of mathematicians. Many math students are now researching daily stock information, company portfolios, and historical business data. Our reference books are being used by mathematics students as they gather information on population, the environment, and a variety of other topics for graphing and other methods of comparison and analysis.

Virtual Libraries

In other chapters in the book I speak to the need for dependable and extensive electronic digital online resources, which we can consider our virtual library because it leaves behind no visual collection that requires cataloging, circulation, storage, and handling. Linda Schamber (1996) states that "there is a shift in library philosophy of ownership of locally stored resources to provision of electronically stored resources, and the need for rethinking collection development policy." As high school library media centers invest in CD-ROM and online resources, there will be a reduced effect on the acquisition of print materials and collection development. Funds that ten years ago would have gone to printed books now are siphoned to the virtual library. Can we be assured that the information that was located and useful two years ago can be accessed today when one does not own the "hard" copy? Laverna M. Saunders (1995) writes, "The evolution of virtual libraries challenges the concept of what libraries are and should or can be. Printed materials such as books will always be a part of library collections, but the shift toward networked and local electronic resources presents exciting possibilities for reengineering collection development and acquisitions processes" (p. 45).

The success we had in meeting our students' information needs during the first year of the block was due in part to the fact that we had a strong virtual library in place that consisted of an online magazine database and an online newspaper database. We were just experimenting with the Internet in 1994–95 so could not consider it a viable research tool. The online magazine and newspaper access continues to be the workhorse of our collection because of the timeliness, points of view, and depth of the collection. There was confidence in the library media center's ability to support the new research activities that would be generated under the block because of our track record in providing students a wide variety of information from our electronic, virtual library.

As schools rely on electronic databases, research is being done about the reliability and access of information from these sources. Patricia Hare (1997), a library media specialist in a block-scheduled high school in Cincinnati, published the results of a study she conducted with tenth-grade students. She reports that using a variety of online and CD-ROM sources, the average increase in the number of resources found when the groups used technology was 359 percent. This translates to over five times more resources found with online and CD-ROM technology than with traditional research.

In an electronic posting on LM_NET, results of a survey of popularity of online databases were shared (McBride 1997). The Electric Library was chosen as the first pick for its ease of use and its hits for topics. The library media specialist will have to evaluate current online subscriptions regularly to determine the best for research.

The Internet is a very important resource to have in every classroom for its extensive array of information; however, it cannot replace a strong library collection of materials. After their initial romance with the Internet, many students go back to traditional print resources in the library because they are not satisfied with the amount or authenticity of information they are finding. Although the Internet can be the source for many queries, it cannot replace the wide repertoire of books, periodicals, multimedia, and local and archival material found in the media center.

Steps the Library Media Specialist Can Take

We all strive to make the collection a usable resource to students and teachers, regardless of whether our school is on a block schedule. When a school does adopt the block, the importance of the library media center dramatically increases. I have taken the following steps to ensure that the collection is growing to meet the demands of new learning and information activities:

1. *Regularly meet with individual teachers or small groups to tour the appropriate sections of the collection that correspond with their curriculum activity.* Often it is a comfort to teachers to know in advance what the books look like that their students will use and that there are appropriate numbers for the class size. You could do this formally by scheduling departments, grade-level teams, or other configurations. I prefer to work with an individual teacher at the time we are planning their lesson in the library media center. There is no need to take more than just a few minutes if you highlight new resources. Sometimes just one or two items will stimulate a creative approach to a lesson.

2. *Work individually with teachers to plan one unit of study.* The investment of your time will pay great dividends to the students, as they will have a realistic project that will meet the learning objectives of their teacher. Particularly for new teachers (and in block scheduling, all teachers feel like new teachers), the learning process of putting a research project together will establish a pattern for further activities. I find that a well-constructed first-quarter project will encourage the teacher to design other activities for the remainder of the year.

3. *Survey teachers as to what they will need in the coming year.* This can be done in many ways (conference, paper survey, etc.). It is critical to know what teachers are planning for activities. You may postpone purchases in order to obtain what the teachers tell you they will need in order to teach in the block (Baker 1996, p. 10).

4. *Consider an online, full-text, periodical service.* Periodical literature is current, and students can retrieve the articles immediately.

5. *Analyze what kinds of materials circulate.* If you have an automated circulation system, track the areas of the collection by call number that circulated the most. At a glance, I realized that there was a great demand in our first year (and it continues to prove true) in our sociological and historical materials.

6. *Keep your scheduling book of classes that used the library the first year of block scheduling.* What kinds of assignments took place, and were they successful? How did they differ from what students traditionally used the library for? If the senior English paper was still assigned, did the approach or requirements of the paper change? If you have old copies of assignments, compare them to the new

Figure 6.5
Teacher Request Form for Resource Materials

It's Time to Order Books and Materials

for the Library Media Center

Your input is always very valuable, and with the block schedule, there are changes in the curriculum. Please use this form to tell me what you need so I can try to purchase materials that will be useful to your students.

Name_____

Courses Taught or Will Teach:_____

_____

Suggestions for the library media center next year:

Topic	Specifics	Format	Quantity
History	Social life in America, 1890	Books	4-5

_____

_____

_____

_____

Specific Titles to Purchase:_____

_____

_____

ones, and make note of the important differences and what the teachers expect the library to offer. There is great demand for pictures, primary source letters and speeches, and documentary and archival material. Look for those subtle (and not so subtle) changes in requirements that result in the use of different types of research materials. In my school, it is very common now to have the teacher require multiple types of sources, such as a reference, an electronic, two books, an interview, a visual, and so forth.

7. *Look to nontraditional vendors of materials.* Prior to the block, I did not haunt used book dealers as I do today. For example, our need for different kinds of materials (copyrighted material of the 1940s through 1970s) that reflect social and cultural norms has challenged me to go beyond the new book market. Donations are always appreciated, but I look at them from a different perspective. Sound selection policies are still in place, but there is a need to broaden the kinds of materials that the collection has to offer. Our community members have responded by donating extensive collections of the periodicals *Life* and *American Heritage Magazine*.

8. *Look at the research.* Many studies have been conducted on collection development, and I have found that my school library collection is not that different from other schools. An example of an interesting study is the one conducted by the Louisiana Public Schools, published in 1993. It concludes that high schools have collections that are, on average, 24.6 years old.

9. *Develop a survey form to get feedback from teachers as to what kinds of materials they want to have purchase.* Use broad categories, such as biographies and time period. Figure 6.5 contains a sample form.

Collection development must respond to the needs of the students and teachers. The restructured high school redefines what those curriculum and instructional needs will be. The library media specialist has to be positioned to hear these new needs and directions the curriculum and teacher expectations are taking in order to purchase appropriate materials in print, digital, and electronic formats.

I recommend the acquisition of the third edition of G. Edward Evans's *Developing Library and Information Center Collections*. It is written for all types of libraries and thoroughly examines all the components of solid collection development, including assessment techniques, policies, and the selection process. There are new sections in this edition on electronic materials. This is an excellent reference to have as you make philosophical and practical decisions about the future of the library media center collection.

BUDGET FOR THE BLOCK

A close analysis of the total school budget must be made before adopting a block schedule. A school that is having a problem with the block may discover a year or two later that it cannot meet its goals for restructuring because it is not properly funded. Shortt and Thayer (1997) warn, among other issues, that "ignoring or neglecting to budget additional funds for increased educational and personnel needs" (p. 7) will surely fuel the fire for those who are against the change to the new schedule when classes are overcrowded and/or materials and technology are in short supply.

In the reform process (Pogrow 1996, pp. 656–663) we are forewarned about the myths versus the realities. Two myths indicate that successful reform requires high quality and appropriate quantity of staff and materials, both which are budgetary considerations:

Myth: You can change instruction through advocacy, in-service, and training.

Reality: Large-scale reform requires highly specific, systematic, and structural methodologies with supporting materials of tremendously high quality.

Myth: You can reform education by disseminating knowledge and leaving it up to practitioners to apply that knowledge.

Reality: Reform requires technology, methodology, structure, and materials.

Robert L. Canady and Michael D. Rettig (1997) have emphasized the importance of the budget for the library media center: "It is reported in all types of block schedules, additional staff and materials are needed in the media center because, with expanded time periods, teachers spend more time with whole class groups in the media center. (Note: In the 4/4 plan fewer textbooks are required; that may be a source of some money that can be transferred to the media budget.)"

There is never enough to go around! In our underfunded environment, school media specialists have become masters of ingenuity in being able to stretch the dollar. An important reference for all readers is the annual series in *School Library Journal* that tracks library media spending across the nation (Miller and Shontz 1997, pp. 28–37). In 1995–96 library media specialists overall were given a materials budget that was, after inflation, $600 less than two years before. High school library media specialists spend only one dollar more per student than do those in lower grades. These deplorable numbers are self-defeating in schools that are on the brink of school reform and cannot continue if reform is to be successful.

Some of my suggestions for fiscal management under the block schedule are common sense, and you have been doing them for years. The fact is, however, that block scheduling will tax library media center resources even more and you will have to be creative to get the most out of your budget. There is no doubt that block scheduling puts a strain on already lean budgets. To have a whole school change its instructional methodology from lecture to resource-based learning all at once can require a significant cost, depending on the level of services at the onset of block scheduling.

Savings can be realized when a shift is made from ordering large quantities of textbooks. In the traditional classroom, the textbook *was* the curriculum, and it was imperative for each student to have a copy. There will still be courses that require textbooks with block scheduling. For example, advanced placement or college credit courses often must use a prescribed textbook, and it is mandatory that the book continue to be the basis for the curriculum. In preparation for block scheduling, each department must critically examine the resources it uses and determine as best it can what additional materials they will need.

Often block scheduling drives major changes in the curriculum. Suddenly teachers will be able to teach how they always wished they could but were unable to because of the limitations of the eight-period day schedule. Teachers should be encouraged to plan creatively for new instructional methodologies based on the curriculum goals and objectives, not on the format of the textbooks or the other materials. The textbook may become just another resource, and only a few copies need to be purchased for a classroom. Contemporary research articles are more appropriate as the basis for class discussion than an outdated textbook chapter. The budgetary analysis for these changes for more primary and secondary source materials should be carefully done.

Teachers should be encouraged to experiment during the first years of the block. One school gave a small budget to each teacher to purchase materials and supplies, such as paper, markers, and pamphlets. Most high school academic classrooms have not been traditionally equipped for creating projects, and it is important to have these small yet essential materials available for all students. The person who orders routine school supplies will need to be alerted to include in the order items such as colored pencils, construction paper, scissors, crayons, markers, and other items that have not routinely been part of a high school supply order.

A school that is committed to block scheduling must use a new rubric for fiscal planning. Flexibility will be key to being able to allocate resources for maximum benefit and for interdisciplinary instruction. A department that has clear curriculum goals and objectives will be able to articulate to the administration its fiscal needs successfully.

The Library Media Budget

The library media specialist must be an early advocate of a fiscal study of the school's resources. Be knowledgeable of the savings that will result by changing to the block in some areas and predict where costs will be greater, such as in the library media program. Depending on which block schedule your school adopts, there may be savings realized that could be channeled into the media center budget. The obvious example is the 4 × 4 schedule, which often has half the number of students taking the same course at any one time. For example, only half of the ninth-grade students will have English in a semester; thus the need is to purchase only *half* the previous number of classroom support materials. Textbooks are a significant expense for any high school, and if the amount needed can be reduced, substantial moneys would be freed for other uses.

The library media specialists who participated in the surveys for this book indicated a wide range of financial support for their programs for the transition to block scheduling, as Table 6.3 shows. Disappointingly, some schools indicated that there were no additional funds given for block scheduling. Where budgets were increased, library media specialists spent their funds in different ways, it did not all go for books or collection development. Some schools needed to increase the print collection; others had a greater need for technology. (See Table 6.4.)

When the library media specialist is a member of the planning committee, he or she can advocate for the funds that are necessary to bring the library media center to where it can support resource-based learning. Schamber (1996) states, "The challenges of integrating electronic resources and technologies . . . are many. . . . there are large-scale management issues to consider such as budget. Some of the biggest problems, not surprisingly, stem from simultaneous decreases in funding and increases in operating costs" (p. 1). The argument stands that no matter what kind of schedule the school adopts, the library media center must fully fund its operational budget.

Table 6.3
Changed Financial Support for Resources

High School	Budget Changes Due to Block Scheduling (Excluding Staff)
Centralia Regional High School	No increase (but an adequate budget)
Duncanville Ninth Grade School	25 percent increase
East Lyme High School	25 percent increase
Edward Little High School	No increase
Evergreen High School	No increase
Harrisburg High School	No increase for block (increased for other reasons)
Kingswood Regional High School	No increase
Shaw High School	Anticipate an increase after first year
Vines High School	100 percent increase
West Brunswick High School	50 percent increase

Table 6.4
Use of Increased Budget for Resources

High School	If Increased, How Was It Utilized?
Centralia Regional High School	No increase (but an adequate budget)
Duncanville Ninth Grade School	12 percent increase for books, 13 percent increase for software
East Lyme High School	25 percent increase for books, 100 percent increase in technology
Edward Little High School	No increase, but a significant transfer of funds from books to software
Evergreen High School	No increase
Harrisburg High School	20 percent increase for technology
Kingswood Regional High School	No increase
Shaw High School	No change, but anticipate an increase after first year
Vines High School	500 percent increase for books, 100 percent increase for software/online, 100 percent increase for hardware
West Brunswick High School	50 percent increase for books

Sound fiscal planning continues to be important, and phases already established for replacement or growth should not be abandoned (Buckingham 1991). However, you may find that the current implementation schedule you have may need modification. For example, I have a multi-year plan to upgrade and expand our fiction collection, an important goal outside of resource-based learning. Due to block scheduling, I have had to purchase books in areas that I did not anticipate four years ago, so I will meet my goal for the fiction collection later than I had originally anticipated. I have not been able to purchase as many hardcover fiction as I would have liked, but by purchasing paperbacks and by resource sharing, our students are able to acquire any fiction book that they want.

Areas to Examine

When planning for the block, examine these fiscal areas.

Staffing

Staffing is always the most expensive item, but without adequate and knowledgeable staff, the library media center will not deliver instructional and support services to students. Assess existing staff and their duties. Is the staff based on a traditional model whereby people are not cross-trained? Has the support staff been given sufficient training in technology? A needs assessment of what staff should be able to do compared to what the existing staff does now will be very helpful. Paraprofessionals under the direction of certified personnel can be effectively used to assist with technology support, resource sharing, and other processes, such as ordering materials and reviewing data input for initial cataloging. Outsourcing—the hiring of experts on a consulting or per task assignment—may be a way to save the expense of hiring staff, particularly for cataloging and network or computer maintenance and support.

Professional Development

This is an area that should be budgeted for. Do not rely on a district committee's anticipating your and your staff's needs. Create long-range professional development goals with each staff member. What is it that they now do very well? What is it that they need to learn for the library media center of the twenty-first century? Examine strengths and weaknesses, and then develop a plan to meet their professional needs. If you determine that there will be greater use of technology with block scheduling, it is important for all staff to be proficient. Look to the services of your local educational regional support office, the state library, and the state department of education for workshops. Local area businesses may be interested in forming liaisons with the schools. Develop a relationship with your public library, and determine if there are joint opportunities for professional development among the two library staffs. The planning committee for block scheduling may be able to find the funds for the professional development the library media staff will need in order to deploy and assist teachers and students with technology and instructional methodology.

Books

Most schools participating in the survey for this book found an immediate increase in circulation of books with block scheduling (see Table 6.5). The library media specialist should immediately develop and promote a plan (if one is not already in place) for increasing the book budget incrementally over a short period of time to reach the anticipated demand. Although it may be too soon for a definitive conclusion, we have found that the number of books missing in inventory has increased significantly, with the areas of loss in the categories of the most active research. It is wise to anticipate the need to replace a higher number of unaccountably missing volumes once you begin block scheduling.

The Virtual Library

Saunders (1995) states, "Libraries today include the costs of network memberships, document delivery, CD-ROM and on-line full-text electronic indexes, licensing fees, and in some cases, even OCLC cataloging as

Table 6.5
Changes in Circulation with Block Scheduling

High School	Change in Circulation
Centralia Regional High School	25 percent increase
Duncanville Ninth Grade School	No change
East Lyme High School	100 percent increase
Edward Little High School	10 percent increase
Evergreen High School	15 percent decrease (large increase in on-line offerings)
Harrisburg High School	10 percent increase
Kingswood Regional High School	25 percent increase
Scotland High School	25 percent increase
Shaw High School	25 percent increase
Vines High School	over 100 percent increase
West Brunswick High School	10 percent increase

elements of their materials budgets" (p. 44). It can be difficult to quantify the projected use of online resources that charge per document delivery fee, such as the archival services of other state and national newspapers located on the Internet. I suggest that you budget twice the amount you have spent in the past for document delivery for the first year of block scheduling. That amount was about right for my school. Network subscription costs can actually be reduced if you are able to obtain membership through a state or regional cooperative group.

Library media specialists can increase their fiscal power by obtaining federal and state funding for online access and networking. At this writing the Universal Service Fund (USF) holds promise for reduced telecommunications costs for computer and videoconferencing transmissions. Be knowledgeable of legislation that offers reduced online access and telecommunications costs.

Membership and Dues

Be aware of local and regional opportunities that will maximize the budget. In Connecticut, school, public, and academic libraries cooperatively bid for book vendor discounts, which are substantial. Library supply, computer software, and CD-ROM companies also discount this same cooperative because they are guaranteed a large volume of business with competitive pricing. The small membership fee the school pays is recovered many times over through the discounted savings. Most states have cooperatives through the state library or state department of education.

Technology

Technology planning is essential to the acquisition of computer software and hardware. In the plan, there should be a phased-in acquisition and budgeting process. No school can acquire the technology it needs from the regular operating budget, which usually is 85 percent of staff-related costs. The remaining 15 percent cannot acquire technology in the numbers and standards that students and teachers need today. Be involved in district and building decisions that maximize licensing for software and networking services. Hardware and maintenance are very difficult because there is not a clear determination in the purchase versus leasing argument. Learn what options you have. Some technology experts and visionaries opt for leasing because it frees the school from the expense of capital investment, usually keeps maintenance to a minimum, and keeps hardware current.

When developing a technology plan, it is important to create a technical structure, which consists of hardware, software, telecommunications, and other components of an information system. Simultaneously a social structure made up of alliances among people who will fund, maintain, and use the information system should be established (Rux 1996, p. 21). Without both structures to support each other, the hardware may be acquired, but the ongoing use of it as an educational tool may be compromised without the support of those to maintain it and share ideas for maximizing its potential.

Another avenue to explore is having all departments contribute to the expense of operating the computers in the library media center. Unexpectedly, I discovered that with the acquisition of an LAN in the library media center, the associated printing expenses were astronomical, and I had not planned for them. At the same time a computer was dispersed into each classroom. A proposal was made that each department would have to contribute an associated cost for each computer in its department; the English Department has twelve computers, for example, and thus would be assessed a $50 fee per computer, for a total of $600. That money would go foremost for the printing and maintenance of its own computers, but a portion of it would help support the printing in the library media center since students are now printing English papers from our LAN.

Supplies

With resource-based learning there is a great need for supplies. We found that students were asked to do collages and pictorial representations, and initially the library media center was not prepared to support them in this until we made a request to the community for magazine donations. There was also an increase in the use of sound recordings for music to accompany performances and presentations. It may be as simple as having a discussion with your Music Department to determine how it can render support to students for their projects, or you may need to establish a clearinghouse of where to find music in the building or community. We found that there are many individuals with extensive collections who were delighted to let students borrow a sound recording.

Art supplies are increasingly in demand, and I found that the department stores occasionally have great discounts on basic supplies. A small reserve fund for these kinds of purchases will facilitate project design for many students, who will be grateful that the library media center came through for them one more time. Look at district bids for reduced costs.

Interlibrary Loan and Resource Sharing

Belonging to an interlibrary loan network can be an effective means of savings. Students borrow over 1,000 books through interlibrary loan through our school library media center. Using the cost of $40 for the average price of a nonfiction adult book, a convincing argument can be made for interlibrary loan support to the administration.

Alternative Sources of Funding

It was rare until a short time ago that library media centers could obtain additional funding from sources other than the local parent-teacher organization or a community benevolent group. Today there is strong support for technology and infrastructure from the state and federal government, and updated information is located on government and department home pages. One source you may consider checking regularly for new sources of funding is:

Office of Educational Research and Improvement (Library Programs)
U.S. Department of Education
555 New Jersey Avenue, NW
Washington, D.C. 20208-5571

These journals may be useful:

- *Electronic Learning*
- *Media and Methods*
- *Technology and Learning*
- *T.H.E. Journal*
- *Educational Funding*

Innovations

This may be hard to determine at the onset, but with block scheduling, there will be much innovation and excitement. There is a need to have discretionary funds available to try new ideas. For example, you may need to increase your budget for faxing and phone calls because students may be encouraged to pursue research leads and need to use these facilities. Teachers and students alike will be trying new approaches to the curriculum, and they will come to the library media center with unique requests.

BIBLIOGRAPHY

Print Sources

Asimov, Nanette. "Outdated Books Fill Libraries at Many Schools and California Has Few Librarians for Students." *San Francisco Chronicle*, December 16, 1997.

Baker, Robert C. "Block Scheduling: Impact on Library Media Programs." *Florida Media Quarterly* 21, 2 (1996): pp. 7–10, 12–13.

Baker, Sharon L., ed. "Twenty-Eight Quick Recipes for Stretching Your Popular Adult Materials Budget." *RQ* 34, 3 (Spring 1995): pp. 282–285. (ERIC EJ503465.)

Buckingham, Betty Jo. *Planning for School Library Media Center Budget*. Des Moines, IA: Iowa State Department of Education, 1991. (ERIC ED343605.)

Canady, Robert Lynn, and Michael D. Rettig. "Block Scheduling: What Have We Learned, What's Next." Handout, ASCD Conference, Baltimore, MD, March 1997.

Evans, G. Edward. *Developing Library and Information Center Collections*. 3d edition. Englewood, CO: Libraries Unlimited, 1995.

Hare, Patricia J. "Technology Helps Students Do More Research Better and Faster." *Book Report* 15, 4 (January–February 1997): pp. 23–24.

Hartzell, Gary N. "The Invisible School Librarian." *School Library Journal* 43, 11 (November 1997): pp. 24–29.

Keenan, John. "Block Scheduling and the LMC." *Media Forum* 19, 1 (January 1997): pp. 7–8.

LeLoup, Dennis. "Finding Funds to Go High-Tech." *Book Report* 14, 4 (January–February 1996): pp. 19–20.

McBride, Kay. "Summary of On-Line Databases." *kmcbride@pisd.isd.tenet.edu*. October 29, 1997.

Miller, Marilyn L., and Marilyn L. Shontz. "Small Change: School Library Media Center Expenditures, 1995–96." *School Library Journal* 43, 10 (October 1997): pp. 28–37.

Perritt, Patsy H. *Louisiana Public School Library Collection Assessment*. Baton Rouge: Louisiana Library Association, 1993. (ERIC ED382191.)

Pogrow, Stanley. "Reforming the Wannabe Reformers: Why Education Reforms Almost Always End Up Making Things Worse." *Phi Delta Kappan* 77, 10 (June 1996): pp. 656–663.

Rux, Paul. "Wasting Money." *Book Report* 14, 4 (January–February 1996): p. 21.

Saunders, Laverna M. "Transforming Acquisitions to Support Virtual Libraries." *Information Technology and Libraries* 14, 1 (March 1995): pp. 41–46.

Savich, Chanelle McMillan. "The State of the Vertical File in DuPage County, Illinois, Public High School Libraries." 1993. (ERIC ED375853.)

Schamber, Linda. "Library Collection Development in an Electronic Age." *ERIC Digest* (1996): pp. 1–3. (ED392467.)

Shortt, Thomas L., and Yvonne V. Thayer. "A Vision for Block Scheduling: Where Are We Now? Where Are We Going?" *NAASP Bulletin* (December 1997).

Wright, Kieth. *The Challenge of Technology: Action Strategies for the School Library Media Specialist*. Chicago: American Library Association, 1993.

Resource Sharing

7

Resource-based learning requires that the local library media collection expand to meet the information needs of students and teachers. In these exciting times, there is tremendous growth in online information technology, and the library media specialist is increasingly faced with difficult decisions of collection development. The high expectations for resource-based learning only add to the complexity.

Fortunately, interlibrary loan between and among libraries can offer an option. Not only are school libraries struggling for adequate funding, but public and university libraries have similar concerns. Ever resourceful, librarians have been experts at sharing and established a model many years ago that can be capitalized on today by library media specialists who, with block scheduling, find their program and collection in great demand.

There are four models of cooperation established by Michael Sinclair in "A Topology of Library Cooperatives" (Evans 1995, p. 429), which we should consider for resource sharing. The first is the *exchange model*, whereby two libraries simply exchange materials. Next is the *pooling model*, which has more than two libraries contributing to a common pool and drawing the resources from it. OCLC started as a pool. The third model is the *dual service model* of two or more participating libraries that use the facilities of one of the libraries, such as a computer system, for a common output. The last type of cooperative activity is the *service center model*, whereby many libraries establish a unique organization to input and process materials for the individual libraries. Most school libraries will find that they use many of these types of cooperatives. The exchange model can be as basic as one high school media specialist's relying on his or her professional relationship with a neighboring media specialist for an impromptu telephone interlibrary loan request. The pooling model and service center model are found at the state library or regional educational cooperative level that provides numerous types of libraries various levels of resource-sharing services.

Although collection development philosophies of school, public, university, special, and state libraries differ, there is a large enough sphere of shared interest that interlibrary loan practices make sense for all types of libraries. In most states, interlibrary loan has been encouraged and practiced among the public libraries for many years. Public libraries that have branches or are in close geographic proximity have developed logical clusters for borrowing purposes. On a larger scale, policies for interlibrary loan for public libraries are often directed by a larger entity, such as the state library, where guidelines are established for types of items to be loaned, length of loan, responsibility for the loan, and a delivery mechanism.

Schools have not had this kind of support or direction for interlibrary loan. When it happened, it usually occurred not by state or even local district policy, but because the library media specialist knew that he or she could maximize the success of finding information or reading selections for students by looking elsewhere. In most cases, the library media specialist has been an independent broker with interlibrary loan; that is, it was up to this person to find partners, establish policies, find a delivery system that works, and find time to fit it in with all the other demands of the position.

The technologies we now have for shared data retrieval and online public access catalogs (PACs) are often designed for resource sharing. The proliferation of large, automated local, state, and regional databases available through telecommunications has made interlibrary loan increasingly accessible to library media centers (Wright 1993, p. 74). As more and more schools participate in shared public access catalogs or statewide databases, the rate of interlibrary loan transactions is bound to increase and will benefit block-scheduled schools at a time when increased information demands are being placed on them.

Where does the library media specialist begin, and how does he or she keep it manageable? How many times can he or she be told, "It's too late. I don't need the book any more; the assignment was due last week," before interlibrary loan is relegated to failure? Interestingly, the responding blocked school libraries that responded to the survey reported on later in this chapter found that interlibrary loan did not require large amounts of staff time.

ANTICIPATING THE CURRICULUM SCHEDULE

It is important to be familiar with the curricular offerings and sequencing of courses. Schools using the accelerated block may offer a course or area of study for only one semester. This shortens the window of time that the library media specialist has to acquire necessary books from other locations. More than ever before, the library media specialist must initiate the conversations with classroom teachers and curriculum leaders to anticipate when large library research projects and activities will be conducted. The senior English paper that was always assigned in the early spring may now be written in autumn. Are we prepared with the right books and materials early in the year? Knowing what to anticipate the first year of the block schedule will contribute to its positive impact on student learning.

The library media specialist may want to have the person responsible for scheduling, such as the registrar, run an extra copy of the master schedule for the library for the purpose of tracking the curriculum offerings in the school. In this way, he or she can initiate conversations with teachers to plan research projects and not be constantly responding to the fires when classes arrive and the collection does not support the activities.

COMMUNICATION

Curriculum instructional leaders or department chairs can help you anticipate peak times of activity. Ask them in September to create a quick time line of the major projects their teachers anticipate giving for the year. Of course, teachers may have to adjust and modify their plans as the year progresses; however, with your data from past years, you will have a fairly good idea of how to plan interlibrary loan services for the coming year.

A simple form, as in Figure 7.1, can be a communications device between you, the curriculum instructional leader, and a teacher. With this information, you could initiate interlibrary loan requests even before the students come to the library to do their research, thus having a wider variety of materials available on the first day. While I do not do this routinely, there are certain assignments, such as historical biographical research, whereby students have to read books that are of a minimum length and have to have an accompanying critical analysis that I will order books ahead. As midterm and final examinations become more performance based, students are often expected to bring specific titles to the test. Ordering titles ahead of time alleviates unnecessary panic for students. Students appreciate having the selection already in the library media center, and I will continue to do this "preordering" until I can build up our own collection in this area. Once the student has selected a book from the arrivals, we ask that they give us another five minutes to create a short record for the book and enter it under their name in the computer system.

The form in Figure 7.1 can be used as a communications device between you and teachers for the purpose of planning upcoming library research activities. You may distribute it to teachers at the beginning of the year or periodically offer it, such as at the beginning of each marking period. This

Figure 7.1
Planning Ahead for Research Activities

Library Research Assignment
Teacher:_____
Course:_____
Level of Course:_____
Date(s) of Library Research:
Research Topics:
Student Expectations/Project Description:
Support Needed From Library Staff:

form will help the teacher articulate student outcomes to you and at the same time give you an opportunity to plan ahead for resources, both staff and materials, that will be required. By communicating well ahead of the project, you will have an allowance of time if resource sharing is needed to have the appropriate materials available by the dates of research.

SURVEY RESULTS

Our survey participants were quizzed about resource sharing. On average, there was an increase in circulation of approximately 25 percent in the first year of block scheduling. Of the ten schools asked, only three had an increase in the budget for purchasing books. For the majority of school libraries, the budgets will remain static or see a very moderate growth. At the same time as many high schools are moving to the block schedule, student enrollment is increasing. The dilemma is how to offer a higher level of information service with a static budget that must also stretch to cover a larger student population. Resource sharing can be part of the solution.

All but one of the library media specialists surveyed responded that they participate in resource sharing with other libraries. Clearly in order to be successful with the block, library media specialists must network and share with other institutions. There was a wide disparity among the schools in the number of interlibrary loan books borrowed for students. At the high end was East Lyme High School, which realized approximately 10 percent of its circulation from interlibrary loans. Most of the other

Table 7.1
Number of Books Borrowed Last Year through Interlibrary Loan

High School	How Many Books Were Borrowed Last Year with ILL
Centralia Regional High School	75
East Lyme High School	1,100
Easton High School	300
Edward Little High School	43
Evergreen High School	25
Harrisburg High School	2
Kingswood Regional High School	100
West Brunswick High School	—
Vines High School	400

schools borrowed a much smaller number of books. Not surprisingly, there was a high correlation between online catalogs or OCLC connectivity and the number of books borrowed.

Of the surveyed libraries, those that process a high number of interlibrary loans per year (see Table 7.1) belong to an online consortium for data retrieval, have a statewide catalog as a CD-ROM product, or have OCLC access. Convenience of transportation of materials was also a key factor in whether a high school media center promoted interlibrary loan to its students and teachers.

RESOURCE-SHARING PARTNERS

Look to state departments of education and state libraries to determine if there already exist procedures and polices that support interlibrary loan between schools and other libraries. Most state libraries either have established or are in the process of creating a statewide database. If your school belongs to a regional support center or a learning consortium, determine if resource sharing is already being done by members of the group, and if so, how your school can participate. Established regional nonprofit cooperatives may exist that your school may join.

Lesley Farmer (1997), in her futuristic article about high school library services, contends that librarians will work together "so students experience a seamless service continuum" between public and school libraries (p. 17). She also writes about the importance of all types of agencies, from social and health nonprofits to government and business, to be partners with students through the high school library media center for the sharing of materials, information, and talent.

The survey participants revealed that they share resources with many different types of libraries, shown in Table 7.2.

Local Public Library

An informal partnership with the town or local library that serves the public is invaluable for resource sharing. For almost any major assignment, it is inevitable that the reference librarians at the public library will be trying to obtain materials for some of your students. Why not work together? Respondents to the survey who offer interlibrary loan to their students agreed that a strong working relationship with the local public library was essential to their success.

Automation expedites the success of resource sharing. A few years ago, automation was seen as affordable only by large libraries. Today, even the smallest elementary school is automated or is making plans to do so. The key to resource sharing is being able to view the status of the collections of other libraries remotely. The more access that students have to viewing

Table 7.2
Resources Borrowed From

High School	Type of Library Borrowed From
Centralia Regional High School	Schools
East Lyme High School	Schools Public libraries Colleges and universities State library service centers Special libraries (superior court library)
Easton High School	Schools Public libraries Colleges and universities State library OCLC
Edward Little High School	Colleges and universities State library
Evergreen High School	Schools
Harrisburg High School	Colleges and universities
Kingswood Regional High School	Schools Public libraries Colleges and universities
West Brunswick High School	Informal phone calls
Vines High School	Schools Public libraries Colleges and universities State library OCLC

the holdings of other libraries, the more effective interlibrary loan can be as a viable alternative to collection development.

A model partnership has developed between East Lyme High School and East Lyme Public Library, which serves a community of 15,000 with a collection of over 75,000 items. It is located approximately three miles from the high school. Both libraries belong to the same automated consortium, thus sharing the same computer at a remote site with seventeen other libraries. For a high school planning to automate or in need of a major upgrade to existing automation, the schools and public library could consider a shared system, as in our model.

From the high school public access terminals, students can obtain active status of East Lyme Public Library books, and patrons at the public library can obtain active status of the high school books. A school courier travels between the libraries each day, facilitating delivery of materials. Often a student can request a book at the school from the public library in the morning, and before he or she leaves for the day, the book is at the high school. Materials are returned in a similar fashion, thus helping students return public library loans initiated through either interlibrary loan or individual patron borrowing.

Among the benefits of the partnership are these:

- Students have access to a larger realm of materials in a timely fashion.
- Community members have access to high school materials.
- Local tax support for libraries is enhanced by all parties' having shared access.
- Daily communication between libraries encourages joint projects and sharing of ideas and resources.
- Future telecommunication upgrades may be shared if feasible.

Summer Reading

An aside to this cooperative spirit is our summer reading program. For many years, our school had a summer reading requirement, but we did little to help students obtain the books. It was summer, and school was closed. A few summers ago, we tried an experiment that has been highly successful. In June, once inventory is complete (and we now begin inventory with the fiction and paperbacks so there is time to do this), we take all the titles from the summer reading list (usually upward of 200) and pull them from our shelves. The books are checked out to the local public library for the summer and not due back until mid-September. The public library creates a special display for the summer reading books, making it easy for students to find them. The books that are owned by the high school are quickly classified as interlibrary loans by the public library, so they are circulated through the public library, subject to its circulation policy.

Students and parents are overwhelmingly pleased with this arrangement. The books that the high school wants its students to read are available to students during the summer, not locked up in our building. The public library staff, who can now put a book in a student's hands, are much more supportive of our program than when they were continually frustrated by not having the titles for their patrons.

Area High Schools

In some areas of the country, local high schools are no more than a few miles from each other. In New England, for example, each school district is independent of each other, thus having no directive to work together. Library media specialists, however, need to form alliances with each and network, not only for professional growth but also to share resources. If you belong to a regional roundtable of library media specialists, suggest that resource sharing be a topic for discussion. Brainstorming ways that schools in a geographic region can share resources can bring forth great results. Examine common systems that are already in place. For example, do all the high school libraries have fax machines? Can each library supply its neighbors with its periodical collection list? Some simple resource sharing, such as faxing magazine articles, could be done first so that sharing is established and a working relationship is tested.

The problem of how to view others' collections needs to be resolved. Does your automated system offer remote dial access? If so, share that information with your neighboring schools. If you do not have this option, consider web page development and linking your database to the school site. Exchange URLs with the understanding that an interlibrary loan request from a neighboring high school will get priority attention. Another possible solution for sharing databases is to have your system managers discuss dedicated connectivity with each other. This would give libraries propriety access to viewing each others' databases with active status.

Whatever you do, set an initial goal of resource sharing that is easy and affordable within your existing parameters. One of our survey respondents from a large school district noted, "We no longer have a school library department so we media specialists (fourteen in our high school group, with two others, one parochial, one private) support one another in many ways, including exchange of materials." She describes her network for interlibrary loan as an informal arrangement whereby schools and colleges in her geographic region (which includes two states) have a tactic understanding that they can pick up the phone or fax a request for materials. These are not libraries that have shared databases, but do have the friendly and cooperative philosophy of helping each other.

As library media specialists learn they can rely on their fellow professionals for resource sharing, the need for sophisticated and technologically advanced systems can be justified. More important, the groundwork is laid for extensive sharing of materials.

Statewide Databases

Most state libraries have the automated libraries contributing to a CD-ROM or online statewide database. Here are some ways to locate URLs of the statewide databases:

- California State Library Database: *http://www.lib.state.ca.us/*
- Connecticut State Library Database: *http://www.cslnet.ctstateu.edu/rqst.htm*
- New York State Library Database: *http://unix2.nysed.gov/gpo*

- Texas State Library Database: *http://link.tsl.state.tx.us/*
- Other state library databases: *http://andromedia.einet.net/galaxy/Reference/Libraries/ State.html*

Local Colleges and Universities

Most colleges and universities have their databases linked to their home page on the Internet. It is important that a proper relationship be established with nearby institutions. Public-supported colleges and universities often are agreeable to interlibrary loan activity because of their funding status. Policy may dictate that since they are supported through state taxes, there should be resource sharing with the citizens of the state. Private institutions determine their own policies. A few of the respondents to our survey had an excellent rapport with their local college. Patricia Gautier, media specialist at Edward Little High School in Auburn, Maine, reported that Bates College is supportive in lending its materials to her students. Through personal contact by the library media specialist and an establishment of a successful record in returning their materials in a timely fashion and in good condition, many private colleges will share their materials with high schools in their communities.

Local Agencies

Agencies that address specific social, health, emotional, or economic needs can offer expertise in their field. Pamphlets are often given to schools at little or no cost. Because of the higher expectations teachers now have for students' performance, primary source material is often required. We found that telephone interviews with experts in a field can be a major contribution to a student's research. Again, most nonprofit organizations now support Internet access to their home page, and increasingly important information can be obtained through this vehicle.

Government Agencies

Government agencies should be used as resources. State clearinghouses offer free pamphlets and brochures. Ask the state government for names and contact points for historical societies (state and local). The Internet is becoming a vital link to resources. Look up state government addresses, and see what they have to offer.

Business

Businesses often desire to partner with schools, and their talent and materials can be successfully used by students. With the longer class periods that the block offers and the opportunity for learning in depth, the business community should be included in the inventory of outside partnerships. Resource sharing should not be one-dimensional; that is, it does not always consist of sharing of materials. Talent and expertise of employees are also resources that can be called on in our educational environment, and we in the schools should explore ways that we can assist the business.

DELIVERY SERVICE

One of the major problems all libraries that share resources face is responsive and economical delivery service. In Connecticut and New Hampshire, there is limited van delivery between and among public libraries, funded by the state library. This kind of delivery system exists in other states, and it is to library media specialists' advantage to learn what options are available for participation. Unfortunately, in my state there are not enough vans and drivers to make the service as expedient as we would wish or to have direct delivery to the schools. In the past year, it took an average of eight days for a book to be shipped from one public library to another in our state, which is one of the smallest in size in the country and can be traveled from east to west in approximately 2 hours. In this age of digitized information transfer, we in the library community have to do better for our users in moving our print resources from one institution to another.

In order for East Lyme High School to benefit from state delivery service, we had to ask the local public library if we could channel our books through it. Agreement was made. Next we had to think of a way to move our items to and from the public library. The solution we found was to have the school district courier put the public library as an extra "school" or drop. Fortunately, the public library is located between our middle school and an elementary school. The courier each morning drops off the books the high school has for the statewide delivery service. Because the van does not arrive until later in the day, our courier makes a second stop at the public library to bring to us any items that arrived from the van. Although there is a short lag time, this system works with minimal impact on the staffs of both the public and school library. Cooperation has been the key for being able to offer students a full range of interlibrary loan services.

A second benefit of having the courier make two stops at the public library each day is that the cooperative sharing between the two libraries has strengthened and grown. We work with each other as partners, which ultimately benefits all citizens of the town.

Respondents to the survey offered some other ideas for delivery service besides an in-district courier or participating in state library van delivery service. These include using the U.S. postal service, the library media specialist's dropping off the books to the lending library, using instructional aides to pick up books from lending libraries, and using existing interdistrict delivery service or pony service (an established interschool mail system for many purposes, now including interlibrary loan). One city and school system in Texas resolved the problem of delivery by jointly hiring their own driver, and they anticipate resource sharing will increase in the future.

STUDENT RESPONSIBILITIES

Students must understand that when they request a book from another library, they are entering into a unique relationship with that lending library. One or two errant students can ruin the good faith and rapport established with lending libraries. The need to have a large selection of materials for students to meet the demands block scheduling will bring cannot be jeopardized by one or two individuals.

In the first year of block scheduling at East Lyme High School, I discovered that our library was establishing a reputation with one library as not getting the interlibrary loan materials back in a timely manner, and its interlibrary loan librarian decided that no longer would it lend to us. I had been relying on the standard overdue process we use for our own books for interlibrary loan material and found that students who ignored returning our books were just as likely to ignore returning an interlibrary loan book as well. We brainstormed, and came up with the following solutions that have made a positive difference:

- Interlibrary loan items are "fast-added" into the computer system, with a printout of the item made. Student must sign their name on this hard copy when they pick up the book as an acknowledgment of their receipt.
- A sleeve is created that we tape to the front of the book. When the student picks up the book, the staff member reiterates when the book is due.
- The standard lending period in our state for interlibrary loan material is six weeks. It usually takes one week for the item to arrive. We let the student have the book for only two weeks, thus giving us headway time of two weeks to retrieve the book and one week for its return.
- One staff member is assigned to interlibrary loan. She files the patron receipt by due date, thus being able to see at a glance what items are coming due. She does not rely on the computer-generated overdue slips; rather she locates the students from class, calls home, or does whatever else she must to make personal contact with the student long before the book is due to the lending library.
- These books are considered school accountabilities, and students know when they sign for it, they are responsible for its return in good condition. A $30.00 default is the price we tell students they must pay if the book is damaged (or more if the library gives us a higher charge).
- Telephone calls to the lending library are important if it appears we are having a problem returning a book. Good communication helps keep the channels open.

We have been able to borrow over 1,000 books annually for our students over the past few years with a 100 percent return rate because our policy is strict. We reestablished our credibility with the lending libraries and are considered a member in good standing in our interlibrary loan network.

IMPACT ON STAFF

Library media centers in block-scheduled schools will see a significant increase in usage, and it will be apparent that the print and nonprint collections need to be expanded to accommodate new teacher-designed projects (Baker 1995). Resource sharing, if there is support within a network of libraries and efficient delivery service, can be an essential part of the solution to collection development. When the library media specialist decides to maximize this option, staff allocation has to be addressed. Just as the block schedule will increase circulation of in-house materials, it will cause the number of interlibrary loans to escalate. Determine if the results of resource sharing warrant the time spent by staff, who will have to complete the following steps for each book:

1. Offer selection guidance and consultation to the student.
2. Verify the availability of the item and its circulation status.
3. Initiate the request by e-mail, fax, telephone, or written form.

Table 7.3
Time Allocated for Interlibrary Loan

High School	Impact on Staff Time
Centralia Regional High School	Minimal time and training
East Lyme High School	60 to 90 minutes per day; initial training was extensive
Easton High School	Student aides do most of the work
Edward Little High School	Minimal impact
Evergreen High School	Minimal impact
Harrisburg High School	Minimal impact
Kingswood Regional High School	Minimal impact—depends upon the number of requests
West Brunswick High School	——
Vines High School	2 hours per week; training of staff was initially important

4. Periodically check on the delivery of the item, even if just to make sure the system is working.
5. When the item arrives, charge the book to the student.
6. Notify the student.
7. Follow up on late or overdue books.
8. Ship the book back to the lending library.

Staff time is always at a premium, and the block schedule will draw on the talents of the staff in many ways. Evaluation should be ongoing of the quality and quantity of information received through interlibrary loan versus the amount of staff time it takes. Table 7.3 shows how much time survey participants allocated for interlibrary loan.

IN CONCLUSION

Block scheduling will create a tremendous demand on the existing collection, and without significant, immediate funding, students may not be successful in locating the wide variety of information they need. A solution is to look to neighboring libraries whose collections can augment resource-based learning for students. Your library media collection too has its own unique characteristics and can provide resources for people in your community or state. The technologies today are highly developed for locating the holders of titles; there is a need for cooperation and communication among libraries and other institutions to provide effective and efficient physical access to materials (Schamber 1996). If your library media center is not a member of an active resource-sharing consortium, establishing partnerships for borrowing and lending of materials should be given a high priority as you plan for the implementation of the block.

BIBLIOGRAPHY

Print Sources

Baker, Sharon L., ed. "Twenty-Eight Quick Recipes for Stretching Your Popular Adult Materials Budget." *RQ* 34, 3 (Spring 1995): pp. 282–285. (ERIC EJ503465.)

Evans, G. Edward. *Developing Library and Information Center Collections*. 3d ed. Englewood, CO: Libraries Unlimited, 1995.

Farmer, Lesley. "Crystal Ball Gazing into Library Land." *The Book Report* 16, 3 (November–December 1997): pp. 16–17.

Schamber, Linda. "Library Collection Development in an Electronic Age." *ERIC Digest* (1996): pp. 1–4. (ED392467.)

Wright, Kieth. *The Challenge of Technology: Action Strategies for the School Library Media Specialist*. Chicago: American Library Association, 1993.

Technology in a Block-Scheduled High School

8

Library media centers traditionally have been the hubs or centers of technology in the school. As high schools restructure, technology is deemed a critical factor for educational reform. It is physically located throughout the school, and it has the potential to transform student learning and accomplishment into the next decade (Mehlinger 1996, p. 402). Technology is much more than the hardware and software that is acquired, and it can have anywhere from a negligible impact to a very positive influence on how and what students learn.

The explosion of information from technologies can be confusing for students. "Technology . . . expedites our ability to access, share, manipulate, and display information, [but] it provides little or no guidance regarding the quality, relevance, or timeliness of the information it processes. Teachers must take this responsibility and help students develop their own information discrimination skills" (Mergendoller 1997, p. 15). The library media specialist continues to be a leader of technology in the school for acquisition, policy, training, instruction, curriculum content, and evaluation.

THE "GOOD OLD DAYS"

Twenty-five years ago a "high-tech" facility offered Beta video, 16-mm, overhead, and filmstrip projectors. Sound equipment consisted of reel-to-reel, cassette, and record players. A few wealthy districts had labor-intensive, centralized dial-access configurations that the media specialist operated to transmit video programs to the classrooms. Cameras were limited for slide reproduction. Multimedia projects were often no more sophisticated than a coordinated slide show accompanied by music or a brief narrative. Microforms were of limited quantity, and often the readers did not have hard-copy capability. Other than an occasional mimeograph machine that happened to be located in the library, these were the technologies of the 1960s and 1970s. Were library media specialists challenged with these devices? Of course they were! Audiovisual departments were developed to train and support teachers and students in the creation of projects and presentations, schedule equipment, and coordinate supplies and inventories.

Although we still use some of these traditional technologies, they take minimal time and attention. The working vocabulary of the library staff now includes words such as *routers, fiber, T-1, multiplexer, laservideo,* and a host of abbreviations such as *LCD, PPP, LAN, OPAC,* and *ISDN* that could challenge a linguist! Media specialists are conversing with vendors, computer and support personnel, and their own professional peers in a language that they themselves would have thought as foreign just a few years ago (Mather 1997, p. 1).

Digitized information as we know it today had no bearing or impact on us twenty-five years ago because the personal computer had not been developed for the mass market. Computers did exist, but they were used almost exclusively for mathematical functions. In the library field, the MARC record was just beginning to be realized at universities and large public libraries as a useful means of creating information in a retrieval fashion for a large database. *MARC* was not a term most library media specialists were familiar with, and even if they had heard of it, they did not have to learn how to use the MARC record, for the standard of the day was the traditional paper and file card catalog.

BLOCK SCHEDULING AND TECHNOLOGY

Every public, academic, special, and school library media center should regularly assess the technology needs of its patrons. Library media centers should lead in the selection and evaluation of information technologies for students and teachers. High schools that are on block scheduling are being challenged to provide the best information to their students through technology simultaneously as the school community undergoes the most radical change in over a century in how it delivers curriculum and instruction.

Many of the concerns that blocked schools have with technology are the same as for nonblocked schools. The primary difference is the intensive and supportive role that library media programs have to provide immediate and appropriate information and technology to a blocked school that has changed to resource-based learning.

A high school that is block scheduled will be even more eager to have advanced, current information and presentation technologies for its students as teachers adapt divergent instructional techniques and modify the curriculum. Teachers will depend on more performance-based assessments of their students, and in order for students to demonstrate their knowledge and skills, they will need to have flexible access to multimedia and online resources.

Technology integration throughout the curriculum must occur to achieve the goals of block-scheduled schools. To integrate technology successfully, active involvement and support must be shown by the board of education, the administration, and the teachers ("Integrating" 1994). The goals of these three groups must be in alignment for not only positive school change through block scheduling but also for technology advancement.

In order for students to meet the new requirements of a resource-based learning classroom, there must be a wide range of information technologies readily accessible. It was very gratifying to read the following comments from the editors of my school newspaper shortly after the school acquired a significant increase in technology in the library media center:

On behalf of all of ELHS [East Lyme High School], the Viking Saga wishes to express thanks for the technological advancements in the library. More than ever before, students can make use of their library to be productive and successful, and this surely deserves appreciation. (*Viking Saga* 1997, p. 8)

This one paragraph did more for me than any ceremony or award. I knew that the intense lobbying efforts I made the previous spring with the administration were right on target by the comments of the students printed in the schoolwide newspaper.

DIGITAL LITERACY

One of the most thought-provoking articles I came upon in doing research for this book records a conversation with Paul Gilster, author of *Digital Literacy* (1997): digital literacy is "the ability to understand information and—more important—to evaluate and integrate information in multiple formats" (Pool 1997, p. 6). A student today has to be able to select and evaluate information from multimedia and then be able to integrate it into his or her knowledge base. How does one authenticate information from the Internet when the responsibility for and the ownership of the information may be vague at best? Gilster insists that the Internet user has the right to question the creator of a web site, and if the author does not respond, the user should be guarded about the validity of the information found on the site.

Library media specialists have the skills needed to select and evaluate information, and it is our responsibility to help students and teachers become digitally literate. We cannot control every search that is done, nor would we want to, but we can teach how to do a well-constructed search and evaluate a site so the user has confidence in the information obtained.

SURVEY RESPONSES

The library media specialists who participated in the surveys for this book all reported an immediate, renewed focus on the library media program with block scheduling. Not only were the materials of the library media center being maximized in their use with significant increased circulation, but the online and technology budgets increased to keep up with an accelerated demand by students and staff. Following are the answers to two questions asked about technology and the role it has in a block-scheduled high school:

What technologies have you acquired or increased because of block scheduling?

Online resources, towers, computers, fiber optic connection, video editing equipment, more televisions and VCRs, more overheads, LCD and projection equipment, multimedia access, presentation software.

I can't say we acquired anything because of block scheduling, but [we are using] more of the unique qualities technology brings to research and education [with the block].

We are trying to strive [with block] toward a more technology-driven media center.

With block scheduling we need the options of distance learning and video production classes.

Internet, periodical indexes, LAN.

Our district put in a computer network, the Internet, and Electric Library.

Hard to say if block scheduling is the reason or if my involvement on Technology Planning Committee but we have increased our Internet computers from 1 to 14, on-line catalog. . . . Definite block scheduling impact has increased the need for presentation software and hardware. Students have to create interesting and informative presentations. Current information is available online, but must be infused with evaluation skills—there is a great need for checking relevance and authority.

As a direct result of block scheduling, we acquired full-text on-line periodical database, increased Internet connections from 1 to 8, established LAN, acquired PowerPoint presentation software for LAN, wired a computer in every classroom to a wide area network. For the LMC a scanner, digital camera, and video converter were purchased to help students create presentations or products which are now required in the block.

Does block scheduling require more technology?

The answer to this question was emphatically yes. When asked what technology these libraries still need, school media specialists said:

> We can never have enough computers. Our goal for this year is to triple our current number. This, however, isn't a result of block scheduling. It is something that would have been needed regardless.

> We need hardware! We also need to phase out some of the older technologies like overhead projectors and replace them with LCD units.

> Additional networking to all classrooms, additional computers to match the networking. We need to give students more access and experience in finding, using, evaluating information from a variety of sources.

> We need to upgrade our computers so they can all run multimedia applications. We want to have cable and satellite drops in every room. This would provide extra resources for teachers in their classrooms. We always seem to need overheads. Laserdiscs are popular in Science and History areas.

> We need many more word processing computers in the library and in the whole school. . . . Some students still do not have computers at home, but they are required to have assignments word-processed.

> More computers both to run existing programs and to get others.

> CD-ROM network. We are running standalones—too many students—too few stations. Information is needed and cannot be accessed because of large numbers of students using the LMC.

> We need to significantly increase the number of computers in the LMC as well as find affordable on-line databases for newspaper and archival information. More sophisticated video production equipment and videoconferencing access need to be acquired.

Are nonblocked schools less supportive to their teachers and students? Of course not! However, schools that are on the block have recently undertaken an intense study that sets forth goals and action plans to improve learning. The changes in instructional practice and the delivery of curriculum that the educational community wants to achieve with block scheduling cannot occur without the support of a wide variety of information and presentation technologies.

TECHNOLOGY PLANNING AT THE LOCAL LEVEL

At the same time that many high school communities are determining if block scheduling is the right choice for them, school districts have systematically been developing technology plans. These plans have many purposes, and the following important steps should occur:

1. Technology plans are used as a self-assessment as to where a district currently is.
2. The planning process provides an opportunity for districts to determine where they should be.
3. A process is defined that will guide the district for achieving its technology goals.
4. Fiscal planning for technology over multiple years results from the planning process.
5. An assessment component is developed that will monitor all attributes of the plan.

Technology plans should be districtwide, but individual schools must be able to focus on plans that they can accomplish with building funds and staff. Some district plans focus on common goals and objectives and then append building-level plans. This is acceptable as long as there is consistency among the building plans and they support the district plan. Another approach is to have one technology plan that is districtwide, and then schools in the district must formulate their own processes, which become action plans to accomplish the district plan. Whichever approach your school district takes, the following components should be present in the technology plan:

- Executive summary
- Committee members
- Introduction
- Vision statement
- Mission statement
- Goals and objectives
- Demographics
- Priorities and time line
- Curriculum

- Instruction
- Professional development
- Staffing
- Hardware and software configurations (including infrastrucure and maintenance)
- Links to the community
- Management
- Budget
- Assessment and monitoring of the plan
- Appendixes and bibliography (Mather 1997, pp. 8–11)

Sample technology plans can be obtained from the state department of education and state libraries. The web site "Education Technology at State Departments of Education" lets the user easily find the technology plans, technology content standards, and educational standards of each state. This site should be used not only to keep abreast of the local technology planning of your state, but also to compare and contrast the standards and plans of other states that may be at different stages.

Know what level of technology your program is at and where you ultimately want to be. What kind of service do you provide students with today? What are students capable of doing when they leave school? Will they have the technology skills required to be successful in higher education or on the job? What are the critical elements for a library media center to be a technology center for the school and larger community? Is it having an automated card catalog?

From an American Library Association conference roundtable on writing technology plans for public libraries, the following recommendations were made (Simmons 1996). The same questions are appropriate to local school libraries that are converting to block scheduling (my comments are in italics):

A. Community Assessment—what does the public want? *What do the students and teachers need from the library media center with differentiated instruction and resource-based learning that result from block scheduling?*
B. Self-awareness: what do we have right now and what do we need? Elements to consider:
   1. Computer capacity (how many, how old, and what software?)
   2. Staff knowledge of computers/software/Internet
   3. Space in the library for workstations
   4. Electrical/air conditioning
   5. Staff training needs
C. Identify potential partners in assimilating new technologies:
   1. Volunteer groups
   2. Computer clubs

3. Business groups

4. Schools, Chamber of Commerce (*public libraries*)

D. Pick one or two technologies and project *how these will change the level of technology service you can offer in the block schedule.*

E. Have a ballpark figure ready for the total cost.

F. Get at least two (*adhere to school district policy*) bids on the hardware.

G. Write it down, write it down, write it down and distribute it to many groups.

H. Plan for staff, self, *teacher training, student training.*

I. Communicate with your staff (*library staff, teachers, administrators*) of your plans for adopting new technology.

J. Celebrate your success and *have open house demonstrations on the new technology you acquire.*

TECHNOLOGY PLANNING AT THE STATE LEVEL

Library media specialists who are in districts developing or modifying technology plans should also look to state libraries for recommendations for technology. There is much overlap between public and school libraries and what they need for technology for the future.

An example of leadership in technology planning from the state library occurred in Connecticut. A gubernatorial commission was formed in 1993 to examine the future of the library in Connecticut. Technology and networking was one area of examination, and the resulting six recommendations that came from this Blue Ribbon Commission in April 1996 have guided all libraries, including school media programs, in developing local technology plans.

**Networking and Technology Recommendations of the Governor's
Blue Ribbon Commission on the Future of the Library**

- The State Library shall develop a Connecticut Library Network (CLN) which will assure Connecticut's ability to fully participate in the programs, resources, and services of the emerging National Information Infrastructure. The CLN is a telecommunications infrastructure which will link the State's library resources in a single network.

- The State of Connecticut should provide at least $1.6 million in additional funds to bring public and other state funded libraries to "network readiness."

- The State of Connecticut . . . shall continue to support the recommendations of the Connecticut Preservation Task Force by providing the necessary funding for both existing and developing technologies for preserving library and archival materials.

- Ongoing financial support for the CLN should come, at least in part, from the technology providers who will benefit from the existence and use of the network.

- The Connecticut State Library shall participate in the development of state information policies ensuring that library users are better served.

- The Blue Ribbon Commission endorses the recommendations, expanded to include libraries, of the Joint Committee on Educational Technology.

- The Connecticut State Library shall aggressively support legislation that is proactive in providing access, by all Connecticut residents, to state government information and telecommunications. Support, as it is relevant to libraries, should be given to future legislation that addresses satellite, multimedia, and other technological advances in communication and information.

Concurrently collaboration between the Connecticut Department of Education and the Department of Higher Education resulted in recommendations for educational technology for all students, kindergarten through higher education. The Joint Committee on Educational Technology (JCET) worked with the Blue Ribbon Commission, for it was evident that educational technology could not be exclusive of library technology.

Joint Committee on Educational Technology, Long Range Plan for Educational Technology in Connecticut: Goals and Objectives

- Every learner and educator will have equitable access to learning opportunities through a wide range of information resources and educational technologies, regardless of economic status, geographic location, or special needs.

- Every student will demonstrate competency in the skills necessary for using technology: to locate, acquire, evaluate, and apply information, to communicate, and to enhance thinking skills and problem solving.

- Every educator will have the opportunity and support to develop, maintain, and broaden skills in the effective application of educational technology.

- All pre-service educators will achieve competence in the effective integration of educational technology as part of their preparation.

- All schools, colleges, universities, and other institutions with an educational or training function will use educational technology as a means of accomplishing their missions.

- The State will create a publicly supported integrated system that will provide educators with information and technical assistance on how to use technology to achieve learning objectives, how to manage learning environments, and how to plan for, acquire, and manage educational technology resources.

- The State will support a statewide electronic networking system through which all educators and learners will have the ability to access a statewide network of databases and information resources and communicate with other educators and learners.

- The State will support the development and implementation of distance learning networks to deliver education, utilizing voice, video, and data communication.

- The State will provide funding to plan for, pilot, and sustain equitable access and use of educational technology throughout Connecticut.
- The Departments of Education and Higher Education, in conjunction with the JCET, will periodically assess and report on the progress of the State in achieving the goals of this plan.

Every library media specialist must know what his or her state is now providing or what the state intends to provide and position the school accordingly to benefit from state resources.

The Connecticut State Board of Education has authored a position paper on educational technology. Following are excerpts (in italics) from this paper, with my comments suggesting that block scheduling can be part of the solution for fulfilling the technology education for students.

"Educational technology is a key factor in improving educational achievement and equity and producing a competent and technologically literate work force to promote economic growth." The block schedule more closely models the world of work, giving students sustained, longer periods of time to accomplish a task. The methodology that students use in the block to learn, such as collaboration, research, extending writing, and oral presentations, are also task expectations of employers. Access to educational technology that is current and comprehensive must be had by all students.

"All Connecticut's schools and institutions of learning must be transformed." This is exactly what block scheduling does. Change for the sake of change is frivolous, but students must have an environment that is conducive to learning. Practice in using worldwide resources on the Internet and communications are extremely important in our global society. Just as no longer can a 45-minute lecture cover all that students need to know, so it is true that we must expand our horizons in the arts, sciences, literature, and economics.

"The role of the teacher must be redefined." Teachers today must be facilitators and guides. So is the library media specialist who has the skills to decipher a wide variety of electronic information systems for users. Not only is the access of information important, but also the library media specialist must partner with classroom teachers to help students evaluate the information they obtain from unlimited sources.

"Educators must become fluent in the use of technology and telecommunications." The block schedule accelerates the importance of having a wide variety of technologies, and the library media specialist has a critical role in making sure that users are proficient in all the features and functions of the technologies.

"Students must learn to use technology resources to enhance the quality and scope of their learning experience." This gets to the heart of why a school would change to the block schedule. Student-centered learning engages the learner by actively doing rather than passively receiving. The block

gives the time in the classroom for teachers to facilitate student-centered activities. Educational technology supports these curriculum and instructional changes, and the library media specialist has an active role in helping the teacher select, instruct, and evaluate the appropriate technological system to accomplish the learning task.

"[The] state must take a leadership role in ensuring that there is equity and access." Just as the state has its responsibility to schools, so does the library media specialist have a responsibility to ensure that all students have access to information technology. Resource-based learning in the block schedule increases the need for all students to have access to computers and technologies throughout the day.

"Statewide integrated network." Chapter Seven discusses the benefits to a block-scheduled school of belonging to a statewide network. It is much too expensive and limiting not to use the greatest number of sources at a subsidized cost.

A useful book that documents the most recent educational technology and telecommunications planning for each state is an annual, *Educational Telecommunications: The State-by-State Analysis*. Descriptions include recent developments, statewide and local planning, names of key planners, and if there are statewide and local networks and funding initiatives. Monitor the progress in your own state, and compare technology and telecommunications developments across the nation.

TECHNOLOGY AT THE NATIONAL LEVEL

The U.S. Department of Education promotes the use of technology in schools and libraries through many initiatives and legislative acts. Library media specialists, with the help of district computer or administrative staff, may find that there are grants or funds available to the school that will help with the acquisition of technology or training of personnel. Educational technology is an important federal priority. Visit the U.S. Department of Education Web site for information on the latest technology initiatives of the federal government. Among the current list of programs are these:

- Technology Innovation Challenge Grants
- Getting America's Students Ready for the 21st Century
- Federal Technology Resources for Math and Science
- The Future of Networking Technologies for Learning
- Resource Guide to Federal Funding for Technology in Education
- Star Schools

Two programs merit special attention in this chapter.

Technology Literacy Challenge Fund: Elementary and Secondary Education Act, 1996

This fund was established as part of Title III of the Elementary and Secondary Education Act as a step to ensure that local districts have the opportunity to integrate technology into their educational programs. It provides resources to speed the implementation of statewide strategies designed to enable all schools to integrate technology fully into school curricula. A key purpose of the program is to assist school systems that have the highest numbers or percentages of children in poverty and demonstrate the greatest need for technology. This grant program will provide school districts, especially those with high rates of poverty, funds that will help them to meet their professional development needs, highlight and disseminate best practices, and strengthen interdistrict coordination each year.

The Technology Literacy Challenge Fund has these goals:

- All teachers in the nation will have the training and support they need to help students learn using computers and the information superhighway.
- All teachers and students will have modern multimedia computers in their classrooms.
- Every classroom will be connected to the information superhighway.
- Effective software and online learning resources will be an integral part of every school's curriculum.

Universal Service Fund

The Federal Communications Commission has ruled that schools and libraries will be eligible to receive discounts on telecommunications services, internal connections, and Internet access for each year beginning in 1998:

- *Telecommunications services:* Schools and libraries are given maximum flexibility to choose among different types of commercially available telecommunication services for both voice and data. Examples include regular telephone lines for teachers to receive phone calls in the classroom and direct connections such as frame relay and T1.
- *Internet access:* Internet services are eligible for discounts.
- *Internal connections to bring technology into the learning environment:* Basic installation and maintenance of a network infrastructure are eligible for discounts. Examples of eligible technologies necessary for establishing a network include routers, hubs, network file servers, wireless LANs, and software needed for operation of file servers. Personal computers used solely as switches for file servers are eligible (personal computers for teachers and students are not covered).

The discounts will range from 20 to 90 percent, and about one-third of all schools will be eligible for discounts of 80 to 90 percent. There is up to $2.25 billion per year available from the Universal Service Fund, and schools and libraries will have their discounts determined based on the level of eligibility in the federal free and reduced lunch program.

THE FUTURE OF TECHNOLOGY

It is presumptuous for anyone to try to look into the crystal ball and declare what technology will look like in ten or twenty years and how we in education will be using it. I defer to two authors, Paul Gilster and Howard Mehlinger. Gilster states:

In the near term—the next five years—I see a backlash against technology. A lot of people are upset about the state our schools are in. They say, "you know, we spent X many millions on computers. Where are the results?" . . . A backlash might be productive because it will make us reexamine how we use technology in the classroom.
Ideally, technology sets up wonderful possibilities for multimedia projects. . . . Within ten years, we're going to have very broad bandwidths and thus much faster connections. A school's best teachers can become available to anybody on the Net. [Gilster] sees great potential for distance learning or distributed education through the Internet and videoconferencing. (Pool 1997, p. 11)

Mehlinger has these predictions:

I can say with confidence that schools should expect more *integration, interaction, and intelligence* from future technology. Voice, data, and images will be brought together in one package, such as the desktop video. Technology will become more interactive. Teachers and students will see each other simultaneously, thereby making distance learning more like face-to-face classroom interaction. Technology will have greater intelligence . . . with more features and greater capacity. It will have the ability to learn from the user, so it can customize its services to fit the user's learning style and interests. It will provide knowledge databases that will be valued by a user and alert him or her to its availability. (Mehlinger 1996, pp. 405–406)

BIBLIOGRAPHY

Print Sources

Connecticut. Governor's Blue Ribbon Commission on the Future of the Library. *Final Report*. April 1996.
Connecticut. Joint Committee on Educational Technology. *Long Range Plan for Educational Technology in Connecticut*. Hartford, CT, 1994.
Connecticut. State Board of Education. Position statement on educational technology. Hartford, CT, January 8, 1997.

Educational Telecommunications: The State-by-State Analysis, 1996–97. Syracuse, NY: Hezel Associates, 1997.

E-Rate—Questions and Answers. *http://www.ed.gov/Technology*

"Integrating Technology in Secondary Schools." ERIC *Curriculum Report* 23, 4 (March 1994). (ED369150.)

Mather, Becky R. *Creating a Local Area Network in the School Library Media Center.* Westport, CT: Greenwood Press, 1997.

Mehlinger, Howard D. "School Reform in the Information Age." *Phi Delta Kappan* 77, 6 (February 1996): pp. 400–407.

Mergendoller, John R. "Technology and Learning: The Research." *Education Digest* 62, 8 (April 1997): pp. 12–15.

Pool, Carolyn R. "A New Digital Literacy: A Conversation with Paul Gilster." *Educational Leadership* 55, 3 (November 1997): pp. 6–11.

Riley, Richard M. Letter from *rwlette.html* at *www.ed.gov*

Simmons, Dave. "Writing Public Library Technology Plans." *dsimm@winslo.ohio. gov.* American Library Association 1996 Conference.

Viking Saga (East Lyme High School). October 14, 1997.

Internet Sites

Apple Education WorldWide. *http://education.apple.com*

California Instructional Technology Clearinghouse. *http://clearinghouse.k12.ca.us*

Connecticut State Board of Education, Position Statement on Educational Technology. *http://www.state.ct.us/sde/tech/sbe.htm*

Department of Education. Select Technology. *http://www.ed.gov*

Federal Communications Commission. *http://www.fcc.gov*

Grants—Education, Goals 2000. *http://www.nekesc.k12.ks.us/grants.html*

Schools and Libraries Corporation, Universal Service Fund Information. *http://www.slcfund.org/*

Software Publisher's Association—Education Market Section. *http://www.spa.org/project/spa_edu.htm*

State Departments of Education—State Technology Plans and Educational Standards for Connecticut. *http://www.state.ct.us/sde/tech/tech.htm*

Technology and Learning Magazine Online. *http://www.Techlearning.com*

U.S. Department of Education Technology Initiatives and Planning. *http://www.wssd.k12.pa.us/tech.plan.html*

The Internet, Multimedia, and Block Scheduling

9

No other invention since television has had such a global impact on communication and information as the Internet. When history reviews the last decade of the twentieth century, the Internet will be noted as an important influencing force on society. Equitable access to information became, in the 1990s, a championed right for all people. In the educational environment, the Internet is changing the role of teachers to be facilitators of information. Students must be able to evaluate information quickly for its quality, accuracy, depth, validity, and readability.

THE INTERNET IS HERE!

Library media specialists have had to become proficient Internet users, trainers, and guides in a very short amount of time. The Internet has dramatically changed how students do research. Collection development philosophies and guidelines that were once sacred to acquisition policy are under constant review and evaluation. A title that the library media center acquired in print for many years may be obtained in a digitized format on the Internet and may never be purchased again in book format. What the library shelves look like may be changing as online access technologies take a larger share of the budget because they can satisfy so many information requests.

At the same time that the Internet has grown from being a new, frivolous toy to an essential reference and communication tool, high schools have been under scrutiny to assess if the traditional schedule meets the needs of students, the future workforce. It is hard to say if the availability of the Internet, development of quick and user-friendly products, the affordable pricing, and the development of LANs has created a market for the Internet in high schools. Or did the need to restructure the high school environment encourage teachers and administrators to examine the Internet as a device that would help meet new educational goals?

Teachers agree that the traditional textbook can no longer keep pace with the knowledge explosion and changing world conditions. Online searching that the Internet provides involves problem-solving activities, and problem solving promotes the use of higher-order thinking skills (Crane and Markowitz 1994, pp. 41, 43). A noticeable benefit since my school adopted block scheduling is that we now can provide the time for sustained activities, such as online searching on the Internet, that will result with students using information creatively and extensively. No longer does the library media specialist "serve" information as if he or she were in a fast food restaurant. Students have the time to select their information more thoughtfully from both print and digitized sources.

LESSON PLANS ON THE INTERNET

Lesson plans are prolific on the Internet for teachers to download, adapt in full, or modify. When a school changes to block scheduling, teachers must carefully examine how they teach and the traditional content of their lessons. No one advocates throwing the baby out with the bath water; however, teachers will need resources for new ideas and instructional methodology that uses the time provided in the block.

The Internet provides numerous sites for lesson plan exchange. The quality of the lessons can be very good, and the choices of curriculum and content are growing. Recently I was asked to help a teacher find lesson plans on Shakespeare suitable for a senior level. To my surprise, not only did I discover web sites devoted to Shakespeare and the teaching of his literature, but also that the ERIC Virtual Lessons had improved significantly. In addition, the Yale–New Haven Teachers Institute offers detailed, thorough, and excellent lesson plans that teachers can use as is or adapt.

THE LEADERSHIP OF THE SCHOOL MEDIA SPECIALIST

If block scheduling has the predicted impact on the library media program of significantly increasing its use and the Internet is exploding right in front of you, do you run for cover or jump in and become an information technology leader? Block scheduling encourages resource-based learning, and one of the most intriguing, challenging, and pervasive resources that the world has ever encountered is the Internet.

Glenda C. Rakes (1996) contrasts the traditional learning model with a resource-based environment. In this new environment, students develop the ability to:

- Gather and organize facts.
- Distinguish between fact and fiction, primary and secondary sources, correlations and causations, and direct statement and implied meaning.
- Recognize bias.
- Make systematic comparisons.
- Form and defend an opinion.
- Identify and develop alternative solutions.
- Solve problems independently.
- Use responsible behavior. (p. 53)

Many of these skills are intrinsic to the training of library media specialists. As technology leaders in our school, we must make the opportunities to share our knowledge of the Internet with other teachers so that they can expect their students to use the information they obtain on the Internet in a responsible and worthwhile manner.

Rakes (1996) offers guidelines for creating lessons using the Internet as a resource. The library media specialist can offer professional development and leadership as he or she guides a teacher through these important strategies:

1. Select a question or problem and determine the suitability of using the Internet for the solution.
2. Define specific instructional objectives for the search. Tell students exactly what product they should have at the end of the project, what process they are to use to obtain the necessary information, and how much time they have to complete the project.
3. Select appropriate Internet sites for conducting the research.
4. Introduce the process of Internet searching.
5. Present the problem, the question, or the puzzling situation to the students in writing. Provide students with a way to record their data.
6. Collect, evaluate, and organize data.
7. Develop an answer to a question or problem. Students should summarize, interpret, infer from, and analyze the information they have recorded and then use the information to support their conclusions.
8. Analyze the search process with students. What techniques worked well for them, and which techniques were less efficient?
9. Evaluate and assess the student product. (pp. 55–56)

The collaboration between the library media specialist and the faculty on making the Internet a viable resource for research and problem solving will result in students' using the Internet fully for their learning. Teachers who are confident and knowledgeable of Internet technology will begin to incorporate it into their course expectations. Working as a team with teachers, the library media specialist can share his or her knowledge of Internet accessibility, lesson design, and how to evaluate resources of the Internet. Teachers, with proper professional development and leadership, will have high expectations for the kind of material and the critical thinking activities their students can perform using the Internet.

INTERNET TRAINING FOR STAFF

East Lyme High School has traditionally dedicated one of its three professional development days to technology. Over the past few years Sandra Austin, the computer coordinator, and I have offered a wide variety of Internet workshops. In addition to the professional development days, we offered after-school sessions that were tailored to our audience and fun too. Our workshops always have a theme. Two of our favorites revolved around relaxation and fun. In our first year of the block, in order to "cruise" the Internet, we designed a theme of a cruise ship and had our travelers come aboard for a wide variety of searching activities. It was so popular that three years later people are still asking when we will do it again. Recently we offered another technology professional development day that included the Internet. This time we turned the school into a "learning spa," and in comfortable clothes and at their own "workout" pace, teachers developed their strength with technology.

We find that there is always great enthusiasm to try the Internet. Many teachers request and require the help of the library or computer staff to guide them through the plethora of resources. The cumulative effect of these activities helps position many of our faculty to be skilled Internet users who create high expectations of their students as users.

MULTIMEDIA

Increasingly, people are required to communicate and express their ideas using a wide variety of media. Before computerization, thoughts were exchanged either orally or in writing, with visuals being reserved primarily for entertainment. This is not the expectation today. In both education and business, ideas must be communicated through computerized multimedia devices.

Block scheduling can be a catalyst for teachers to change how they traditionally assess student performance and knowledge. Certainly teachers will retain formal testing devices for some assessments, but they should be encouraged to try more authentic means for measuring long-lasting understanding and comprehension. Multimedia support all aspects of curriculum and instruction, including assessment. Students now have time during class to demonstrate their knowledge and skills, and often they do this through multimedia presentations.

Multimedia use and production encourage creativity and resourcefulness. Multimedia require the simultaneous use of at least two different pieces of hardware working together to accomplish one common product. Multimedia combine and organize sound, video, and data. Often a computer is the controlling element between data entry and a visual-audio output. The tremendous development of computers for speed and functionality in the past ten years has resulted in similar advances in multimedia.

Library media centers strive to offer teachers and students the following multimedia equipment:

- Computers with CD-ROM capability and/or hypercard extensions
- Scanners
- Digitized cameras
- Video recorders and converters
- Laservideo disk
- Video and computer large screen projectors
- Projection devices, such as LTD viewers
- Electronic keyboarding and other sound devices
- Color printers and copiers
- Editing equipment
- Compact disk-interactive and CDTV players
- Slide and filmstrip projectors

THE IMPORTANCE OF MULTIMEDIA

Stanley Chodorow, recently a provost at the University of Pennsylvania, cited the Internet and multimedia as leading advances for the humanities and medicine. Multimedia packages can manipulate massive amounts of information and will change traditional teaching and learning (Chodorow 1995). Multimedia are used for researching information. They can be an instructional methodology, help people learn new ideas and concepts, and provide the format for succinct and interesting presentations.

Multimedia allow students to express their knowledge and skills using a variety of intelligences. Research shows that people learn best and can express their knowledge and understandings in the intelligences that are unique to them. It is important for teachers to provide appropriate opportunities for students to achieve and demonstrate their abilities. Having sustained blocks of time for learning and information communication technology are two important steps for improving student achievement. Multimedia can support multiple intelligence theory by providing a means for students and teachers to approach a concept or discipline in a variety of ways—in other words, to personalize their learning. Gardner (1995) suggests that teachers often try to condense too much material into a course, only to have students walk away with a superficial understanding of key concepts. Teachers should approach a topic from numerous perspectives because students learn in many ways. He notes that "understanding can be demonstrated in more than one way, a pluralistic approach opens up the possbility that students can display their new understandings . . . in ways that are comfortable for them and accessible to others" (208). In commenting on the need to make learning meaningful for each child, he says, "Materials that are worth knowing are presented in ways that afford each child the maximum opportunity to master those materials and to show others (and themselves) what they have learned and understood."

There is a very important role for multimedia in education, and it is even more criticial in a block-scheduled school because the members of this institution have already determined that resource-based learning and performance assessment are essential components of education.

The results of using multimedia can be artistic and meaningful. Students can be challenged to be creative when they have to make decisions about visuals, audio, and text. An exceptional feature of using multimedia is the capacity to try numerous formats and sequences before making a final selection. An artist using traditional materials may have made a handful of attempts to get the picture right, but with the technology now available, any user can bring his or her work through a very complex evolution to the final product without recreating the entire work again and again.

THE LIBRARY MEDIA PROGRAM AND MULTIMEDIA

It is appropriate that the library media center be a location in the school where students and teachers find the equipment, supplies, and assistance they need to make their projects. Block-scheduled high schools have a great need for students to have a place to design, experiment, and produce. Since my school has gone to block scheduling, I am finding myself demonstrating "old" processes to students that have not been used in a long time. For example, laminating student projects had not been done in my school for years, but now I have several teachers who are assigning projects such as collaborative newspapers who want their students' work preserved as it is shared among the class for discussion and assessment. Suddenly the library media center became the supportive place where students could have their project laminated. Interestingly, once students committed to having the project preserved in such a manner, their pride in their work increased exponentially. Color copies have to be just right, grammar and spelling corrected, and the content verified.

In lieu of the new emphasis on multimedia with block scheduling, it makes sense to revive the multimedia room of the high school media center (McLellan 1992). This would not exclusively be a technology room, but a place where students can create objects, use photography, laminate, and have the space to plan, design, and lay out their work. In some schools that have the luxury of space, departments may have their own multimedia project room. It makes sense to centralize a multimedia room in the library media center to allow for shared use of equipment and supplies and maximum access to students. Not only is centralizing multimedia supplies, equipment, and technology in the library media center economical; it gives unlimited access to students throughout the day and after school. Schools that have fragmented approaches to the equipment—that is, it is scattered among two or three departments—often discourage their students from experimenting and gaining confidence in using the equipment. If a student has to go to two or three locations to complete a project, often he or she will give up or lose interest. Creating a complete multimedia station in the library media center will encourage the greatest number of students to try their hand and be creative.

The library media specialist should always be aware of how the media are being used. Is a teacher in need of support when using combinations of equipment in the classroom for instruction? At a basic level, we can ensure that "all systems are go" and that the equipment is functional and easy for teachers to use. More important, we can share our expertise with teachers in how to evaluate the content of the multimedia and, knowing the curriculum, whether it is appropriate to use multimedia at a certain juncture of a lesson. (For sample lesson plans that integrate multimedia to stimulate student motivation, see Mendrinos 1994, chap. 7).

In the library media center we rely more and more on multimedia as research and information devices. When students combine sound with a CD-ROM to learn about an event in American history, we, as media specialists, help them obtain the best and most appropriate information. A recent study found that middle school students placed a greater trust in information that comes from video and sound sources (Small and Ferreira 1994, p. 104). Because of this perception the authors urge school media specialists to address literacy as a broader issue than the printed word. We have an important role to teach students how to validate and evaluate information that they retrieve through multimedia sources.

COMMON CONCERNS

There are several concerns that teachers rightfully have, and the library media specialist can help ensure that students use multimedia wisely (Mergendoller 1997, pp. 14–15). The first concern is the amount of time it takes to create a multimedia presentation versus writing a research paper. We have all felt sincere dismay for the student who spends hours and hours creating a presentation, only to discover that he missed the objectives of the lesson. Similarly, we also see the student who passes off that scanned picture in just a matter of moments and thinks he or she has created a work of art worthy of the teacher's praise. As multimedia presentations become de rigeur with block scheduling, we can help students plan their activities and monitor their progress through the development of the project. We can also serve as communicators between students and teachers during the creation of the presentation to ensure that each party is confident that the work is on target.

A second legitimate concern has to do with assessment of the multimedia project and the artistic talents of the student. Rubrics must be developed and shared with students so that they know just how their artistic talent will be assessed, *as well as* their originality, thinking, knowledge of content, and understanding. Teachers may need support on how to devise the rubric and ultimately judge the presentation. "Technology must be seen as a means to the end, rather than an end unto itself" (Mergendoller 1997, p. 15).

A third issue surrounds copyright infringement and multimedia. How do we obtain permission to use copyrighted works or parts of a work in a multimedia presentation? With the ease of scanning, duplication of sound, digital formats, and video, do we have a responsibility to teach students that this presentation they are creating belongs, in part, to others? Carol Simpson (1997) reminds us that there are four tests that apply to all copyrighted materials used in schools:

1. The purpose and character of the use
2. The nature of the copyrighted work
3. The amount of and substantiality of the portion used in relation to the copyrighted work as a whole
4. The effect of the use upon the potential market for and value of the copyrighted work. (pp. 25–26, 65)

These multimedia guidelines should be followed when creating a presentation:

- Materials used in multimedia works created by students and teachers must be properly cited as being taken from the works of others.

- Students and teachers *may* use copyrighted material in multimedia presentations if quantity limits are observed.
- Students and teachers *may* use copyrighted material in multimedia presentations if they support direct instruction.
- Students and teachers *may* keep the multimedia presentations they create for class, though teachers face a two-year limit.
- Specific limits are established for the amount of material that may be used in multimedia presentations, based on the original medium. (Simpson 1997, pp. 25, 65)

STAFF TRAINING

One of the more challenging goals of the library media specialist is to be one step ahead of high school students when it comes to technology. Today many children have some or all of the component pieces of a multimedia station right in their own homes, and they are accomplished users.

Training on the uses of each type of equipment, and then training on the totality of the multimedia station, is essential to the success of its use to students and staff. The library staff are often the first contact teachers and students have with multimedia equipment and design, and we must be given the proper training. Reading each instruction manual is a must with the complicated and multidimensional equipment we are now expected to be experts with.

One technique I have successfully used is to identify the key functions of the equipment. I then write a one-page instructional table that step by step lets the user successfully master the basics of the equipment. These instructions are posted next to the piece of equipment or are packaged with the new unit. Most users look for these instructions. When their confidence is higher, they are offered the instruction manual for the "bells and whistles" at a later date. Sometimes I ask one or two of my librarian assistants to write the directions and then to teach the other assistants. When they feel the bugs have been worked out, I sit down and follow their instructions. This is not only a time-saving technique for me, but it also gives me the opportunity to praise the thought process and work of my assistants. We have done this now very successfully for developing basic instructions for the scanner, the video/computer projector, and devising a technique to make printing efficient and relatively problem-free on the library LAN.

I also try to attend workshops on multimedia topics such as hypermedia and presentation software. Do not hesitate to have the vendor who sold you equipment demonstrate its features to you, your staff, and the faculty if appropriate. If there is a perceived need to have staff development on, for example, scanners, ask the building professional development committee to schedule such a session or find an outlet where it can be given.

Take each piece one step at a time, and network with other library media specialists and computer coordinators when you have questions.

PRESENTATIONS

If asked a few years ago if the library media specialist had a key role in helping students design their presentations, I most likely would have answered that we primarily provide the information and it is up to the student to decide how to present it. This is not my response today.

In the block schedule, students are required to demonstrate their knowledge and skills in a wide variety of creative means. Often teachers encourage students to select a means of presentation that best suits their learning styles and talents. One student in the class may write a song, another could design a three-dimensional object, and a third may choose to pen a letter. The library media center must be ready to support all of these presentations and more.

Presentation software, such as PowerPoint, has great potential for student assessments. It is easy to use, and its format supports the organization of ideas and thoughts. Because technology is infused in the classrooms, presentation software will naturally function as a means for students to convey their knowledge and understanding of concepts and ideas.

More complex authoring tools for multimedia abound. Until a few years ago, hypercard was the primary means to create individual multimedia presentations. It took a fair amount of software knowledge to maximize the benefits of hypercard. Today there are numerous convenient and extensive packages that are very user friendly and allow the student or teacher to demonstrate unlimited creativity. A few of the recommended authoring tools specifically for high school students are Digital Trainer 4.1, Director 6, and SuperLink (Sealey 1997, pp. 16–17). Each has sophisticated editing and graphical interface capability that older students can appreciate and maximize for their presentations.

BIBLIOGRAPHY

Print Sources

Chodorow, Stanley. "Educators Must Take the Electronic Revolution Seriously." Alan Gregg Memorial Lecture, given at the 106th Annual Meeting of the Association of American Medical Colleges, Washington, DC, October 22–November 2, 1995.

Crane, Beverly, and Nancy Lourie Markowitz. "A Model for Teaching Critical Thinking Through Online Searching." *Reference Librarian* 44 (1994): pp. 41–49.

Gardner, Howard. "Reflections on Multiple Intelligences: Myths and Messages." *Phi Delta Kappan* 77, 3 (November 1995): pp. 202–209.

Lanham, Richard. *The Electronic Word*. Chicago: University of Chicago Press, 1993.

McLellan, Francis R. "Systematic Collective Action to Improve Media Services in a High School Library." Ed.D. practicum, Nova University, 1992. (ERIC ED352043.)

Mendrinos, Roxanne. *Building Information Literacy Using High Technology: A Guide for Schools and Libraries*. Englewood, CO: Libraries Unlimited, 1994.

Mergendoller, John R. "Technology and Learning: The Research." *Education Digest* 62, 8 (April 1997): pp. 12–15.

Rakes, Glenda C. "Using the Internet as a Tool in a Resource-Based Learning Environment." *Educational Technology* 36, 5 (September–October 1996): pp. 52–56.

Sealey, Mark. "Multimedia Authoring 1997." *Technology & Learning* 18, 3 (October 1997): pp. 12–17.

Simpson, Carol. "How Much, How Many, and When? Copyright and Multimedia." *Book Report* 16, 1 (May–June 1997): pp. 25–26, 65.

Small, Ruth V., and Sueli M. Ferreira. "Multimedia Technology and the Changing Nature of Research in the School Library." *Reference Librarian* 44 (1994): pp. 95–105.

Internet Sites

AskERIC Lesson Plans. *http://ericir.syr.edu/Virtual/Lessons*

Association for Supervision and Curriculum Development. *http://www.ascd.org/*

Classroom Connect. Select ClassroomWeb, Thousands of Schools Online. *http://www.classroom.net/*

Curry School of Education, University of Virginia. *http://curry.edschool.virginia.edu/*

Gateway to Educational Materials. *http://geminfo.org*

Internet Connections: Integrated Interdisciplinary Educator. *http://www.mcrel.org/connect/integ.html*

Logging into a MOO. Select MOO: The Virtual Classroom. *http://ccat.sas.upenn.edu/jod/teachdemo/moo.html*

New Tools for Teaching by James J. O'Donnell. *http://ccat.sas.upenn.edu/jod/teachdemo/teachdemo.html*

Online Schools and Classes. *http://www.geocities.com/Athens/8259/skonet.html*

Portland State University, College of Liberal Arts and Sciences. Select Courses in CLAS that have WWW pages. *http://clas.www.pdx.edu/*

School Librarian Links. *http://www.yab.com/~cyberian/*

Webucation 101: A Basic Course on Teaching Through the Internet. *http://home.san.rr.com/webucation/education/index.html*

World Lecture Hall. *http://www.utexas.edu/world/lecture*

Yale–New Haven Teachers Institute. *http://www.yale.edu/ynhti*

Distance Education

10

A significant benefit of block scheduling is the potential to offer students an increased number of courses and learning opportunities. A school that has seven periods a day cumulatively offers a student twenty-eight credits over four years. Most block schedules offer eight courses per year, or thirty-two credits over four years. It is pragmatic for school administrators and curriculum specialists to determine new and creative means for students to participate in additional courses.

Most schools cannot incur significant staff increases, even when they change to the block. In many districts that adopt the 4 × 4 model, teachers are required to teach an additional course per year, or three per semester. This staffing model can be controversial. Financial support for education continues to be level or even unstable in many communities. With school enrollments rising for at least the next decade, reflecting the rising birthrates of the early 1990s, there is concern of a teacher shortage (Kronholz 1997, p. B1). At the same time, the teaching staff has become older, thus projecting an acute need for teachers in the future.

Many high schools find that they are able to support only the traditional curriculum at a time when they are offering students many more opportunities for learning. Study halls and dismissing students early are not the solutions when a reason for changing to block scheduling is to increase student achievement. Distance learning can provide an option for many districts.

Distance learning takes place when the students and teacher are not physically in the same classroom or space. The teacher could be five miles or five hundred miles away from students, yet they are together electronically by being able to see and hear each other throughout the lesson. Using a fax machine, telephone, and overhead projection device at each site, participants can quickly become comfortable in a virtual electronic classroom that uses multimedia for distance learning, has distributed learning environments, and employs synchronous and asynchronous interactive learning throughout the course (Wilson 1997).

There are numerous reasons for schools to share resources through distance learning, including the need to expand course offerings with the opportunities that block scheduling brings. How often are courses dropped because fewer than the number of students required by board policy enroll in the course? This does not mean that the course is frivolous; it may indicate that it is at a specific level or has a limited appeal. To these few students, however, it may be the most important course in their schedule. If more than one school can sponsor the course together, then the chances of cumulatively having a satisfactory enrollment increases. This is just the right scenario for distance learning, when there are small groups of students from more than one school who are interested in a subject that normally would not be provided in the existing program of studies.

FORMING A LOCAL CONSORTIUM

Once the commitment has been made to explore distance-learning education, how do schools make the connections, and what are the various technologies available? What is affordable? Each school should look to their region and the state and learn if there are schools successfully using distance learning. If so, it may be as simple as joining an existing consortium. If a group already exists, policy, funding, scheduling, and technology issues have already been determined. Be sure that the courses and curriculum being offered meet the needs of your students and that your school philosophically can support the goals of the entity.

East Lyme High School is a member of the Southeastern Connecticut IN-TV, formed in 1995 for the primary purpose of expanding opportunities for students of ethnically diverse backgrounds to learn together. Three suburban high schools joined with an urban high school so that students in each environment would be able to meet and get to know each other through a common denominator of academics. All four schools are located in a 10-mile radius, thus making it convenient for face-to-face activities and field trips as well. At the time, the affordable technology for distance education was cable television, and this mandated that the schools belong to the same cable franchise. By supporting our distance-learning goals, the cable provider had an opportunity to demonstrate its support for education by working closely with the planning group and providing hardware and dedicated channels to the high schools.

Connecticut supported the effort through a series of grants. Initially we were given a small planning grant that allowed representatives from each district to come together and form a steering committee that weighed the merits of the proposed consortium. Policies and curriculum were decided, and this steering committee continues to guide the project at monthly meetings.

Implementation grants from the state support the capital investment of equipment for each school and provide the salary for a part-time coordinator for the project and some of the teaching staff. The coordinator deals with policy and hardware issues and works with the cable company. It has been very important to have this project adopted by the state department of education for its continued leadership and financial support.

The decision was made that each of the four schools would be responsible for offering one course; it would have to plan the curriculum and provide the staffing resources (if feasible). This model has proved successful. Not only are academic courses regularly scheduled, but the consortium has sponsored enrichment activities, such as guest authors and musicians. The courses offered currently by the IN-TV consortium are Multicultural Literature, Immigration and Multiculture, Maritime Studies, and Conflict Resolution.

Each school determined who on the staff would offer primary support for distance learning. Some schools designated the task to the video production teachers in technology education. In each of the schools, the library media specialists support distance learning by serving on the steering committee and acting as liaisons with the faculties in their buildings.

If your school is looking at videoconferencing for distance learning, there is no need to be restrained by a geographic boundary. Many universities offer courses over a wide spectrum of topics for a diverse level of students. State departments of education may offer courses at a reduced registration rate for schools in their jurisdictions. In the Internet bibliography at the end of this chapter, there are suggested sites to contact for more information for locating providers of distance education.

THE ELECTRONIC FIELD TRIP

One lament associated with block scheduling that is heard throughout my school is the dilemma of the field trip. Students who miss a whole day of school for a field trip have to make up a large amount of work in other classes. Teachers who lose students to field trips are justified in expecting the student to maintain his or her place in the class, but with block scheduling, we are now asking that students make up the work of 90-minute classes enriched with activity. We are discovering that faced with this problem, more and more students are opting *not* to participate in field trips for this reason.

An excellent compromise solution is the electronic field trip through distance learning. A number of organizations today, such as the Smithsonian

Museums and NASA, offer electronic field trips for classes throughout the world. Guides or docents lead the viewers to galleries of interesting memorabilia or demonstrate scientific equipment. These trips are efficient in that they usually are no longer than an hour and are extremely cost-effective—not only in dollars but in regaining classroom time that would have been missed with travel.

It is also possible for teachers to arrange unique field trips for their own students with outside experts. An e-mail recently came to me from the coordinator of the IN-TV consortium:

Lisa [Maritime Studies teacher] has arranged for a videoconferencing session with the crew of the NR1 on Tuesday, December 2nd from 9:30–10:30 A.M. Lisa's Maritime class will be on-line and she has room for an additional class from each one of the schools.

This opportunity enabled students to talk directly with members of Robert Ballard's Jason Project crew regarding the important recovery work they are doing in the ocean. It is just one example of how distance education can be used to enrich the curriculum in block scheduling.

SCHEDULING ISSUES

Regardless of whether a school is blocked, a synchronous-learning virtual classroom must be in harmony with the schedule of other sites in order to meet and share in real time. If there are not teachers and students present on the other end of the line, not much is going to happen.

Our consortium presently has one member on a traditional seven-period schedule, and three schools on the A/B block, so concern was raised about how the schools could schedule common time for distance education courses. We found that with backing the distance-learning class up against a study hall, adjustments could be made throughout the year for unforeseen events such as snow days. The students in the three other schools would have to have a flexible period opposite block 1 in case one school is on A and the other schools are now on B because of a disruption. For the school that is still on the traditional schedule of short periods, a solution for the students in that school to be participants in the class would be to have a double period for this course in their schedule and be allowed to go to a study hall or volunteer in a school service on the off days. Here is a student's schedule in a traditional school that uses distance education with block-scheduled schools:

Period 1   English
Period 2   Precalculus
Period 3   Conflict Resolution (distance learning)

Period 4   Conflict Resolution (distance learning)
Period 5   French III
Period 6   Chemistry
Period 7   Psychology

If your school has done away with study halls with block scheduling, look for other opportunities where student time can be flexible. Is administrative time set aside each day? Are students required to participate in community service, and if so, can that time be backed up to distance-learning courses? Do seniors have an independent study or project period, and can that also be distance-learning course time? Look for the opportunities where a student does not have to be rigidly scheduled. The more flexible time that is available to students, the more students will successfully participate in the virtual classroom.

The IN-TV consortium does not have all the answers, but we have examined and continue to discuss the issues surrounding scheduling. When the consortium began, three of the schools were on traditional schedules, and one school was on the A/B block schedule. No one school had a duplicate bell schedule of another; that is, there were variations among the schools with the starting and ending times, the length of the periods, and so forth. The blocked school had to make the most significant modifications in order for students to enroll in the courses. The other schools did not have 90-minute periods, only 45-minute periods, and so the distance-learning classes could not be broadcast more than the minimum. Lunch time was not necessarily the best time to attract students to a distance-learning course, but for the blocked school, it came earlier in the day than the other schools, and it was closest to the other schools' schedule.

It would be great to report that we have resolved the issues that surround the schedule. We have not. Enrollment is not as high as we would like it to be, and it may be simply a factor of too much, too soon. Two of the schools are beginning their first year of the block. Our starting and ending times of blocks are not coordinated. Unfortunately for distance learning, the schedule of courses is not built around this learning modality; rather, we try to fit it in after student schedules have been established for the coming year. In order to get maximum benefit from our local distance-learning consortium, the members will have to work at making the courses more enticing to students so that they will place secondary emphasis on their scheduling concerns. The curriculum obtained from distance learning has to be the primary force for having students enroll, and yet it has to be unique enough so that students do not decide they can get something comparable in the regular classroom format. Here is how distance learning works on an A/B schedule:

Day 1	Day 2
American Studies	Geometry
Biology	English
Maritime Studies (Distance Learning)	Study hall
(If course is offered for less than 85 minutes, students will have to use the remainder of the time for projects and work related to the course.)	
Spanish III	Chorus

If a school is on the 4 × 4 schedule, the distance-learning course would be every day. Depending on the schedules of the other virtual classrooms, students may also have to be online for part of the block and work independently when the schedules of the other schools change. Another option is for distance-learning courses to only meet online for a fraction of the days in a semester or year for specific activities.

AVAILABLE SYSTEMS

Advanced telecommunications and cable have given educators a reason to look again at distance learning. The systems available are cable television, videoconferencing, and satellite technology.

Cable Television

Local cable providers offer a dedicated educational channel to each school in the consortium. Often as a requirement of cable licensure, the company must offer each school its channel at no or little cost. The process is simple, and once the hardware is purchased, there is little or no expense for broadcast time. Each participating school utilizes the educational-community service channel designated by the local cable franchise. Courses are broadcast from one school site to the other member schools. Cable distance education is interactive in that the students in the receiving schools can respond to the teacher by broadcasting their responses from their schools via their own dedicated channel. These channels, one per school, can be viewed by any cable subscriber if they are not scrambled. The transmission is synchronous; it takes place in real time but in different classrooms throughout a cable region.

The equipment needed, in addition to specific work done by the cable company, includes a dedicated classroom equipped with two video cameras and a television for each channel or school in the consortium. One video camera is set on the teacher at the front of the room for lecture purposes, and the other camera is filming the students. Of course, the teacher is encouraged to be mobile and teach among the students in the room. The teacher controls the cameras with a remote and selects the broadcast view. A television monitor is used for the broadcasting school to view itself. The other televisions are tuned in to a channel of each of the other member schools. All students in the participating sites will, both visually and audibly, simultaneously and in real time, learn from the teacher and each other as content and ideas are shared. Figure 10.1 shows how this works.

Advantages

- In a cable franchise area, because of the proximity they have to each other, the planners and users of the distance-learning classroom quickly get to know each other. Professional relationships are reinforced as the project moves forward. Because of this personal contact, flexibility and creative solutions are easier to achieve as opposed to subscribing to a distance education opportunity hosted at a remote site.
- Once the equipment is in place, there is virtually no expense for on-air transmissions, that is, little or no cost to the telephone or cable companies.
- Schools within a cable franchise can share courses, professional development, and student meetings in real time.
- Teachers and students who use the medium are close geographically and can easily meet in person. In conjunction with the on-air activity, for example, field trips can be readily arranged for all students participating in the course.
- Guest speakers can be shared between and among schools with live transmissions with follow-up receptions or activities occurring at one site.

Disadvantages

- If channels are not scrambled by the cable company, there is no privacy in the classroom or meeting; the interactive course is open to public scrutiny. A misconstrued or inappropriate message could occur that could have negative ramifications for an individual, the school, or the consortium.
- The equipment is fixed in a distance-learning classroom, therefore not allowing for flexibility in broadcasting throughout the school. While students and teachers could receive the channels of the other schools from throughout the building, in order to transmit from your building, you must be in a fixed location.
- The participants in a system that relies on cable are local to each other and not global. A secondary hook-up with a satellite dish or videoconferencing would be needed to participate with a different audience.

Videoconferencing

This form of distance learning has much more flexibility and certainly has made great inroads with businesses and higher education. A user can conference with anyone with a unit throughout the world. Instead of cable

Figure 10.1
Cable Television

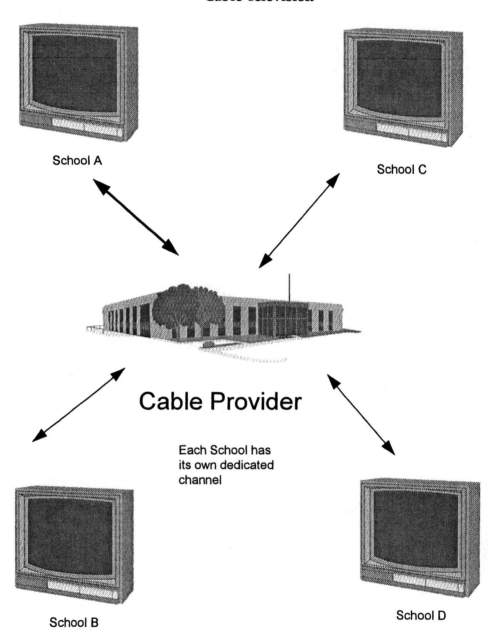

School A

School C

Cable Provider

Each School has
its own dedicated
channel

School B

School D

connections, videoconferencing uses a computer, special software that compresses the signal, one omnidirectional camera, and high-speed phone lines. There are several companies that make videoconferencing equipment, with PictureTel and VTEL/CLI holding the largest market share. The universal standard for video and audio calls is H.320, a standard that all equipment should have in order to be compatible with the majority of videoconferencing equipment on the market.

There are various types of videoconferencing equipment for a school to choose from, ranging from a unit that is suitable for a large-room presentation to the desktop environment over a personal computer. Currently ISDN lines are the most economical means of transmission, with a large group unit requiring three ISDN lines (or 384 KB) for transmission to the PC or small portable units requiring one ISDN line. The multiple ISDN lines will result in a much smoother, real-time appearance without the "tiling" or delay experienced with the single line. The future of videoconferencing transmission most likely will be through the Internet, but there are not yet adequate security measures or firewalls with the Internet to ensure privacy for users.

Videoconferencing brings flexibility into the classroom, for there are so many more end users with these systems. Videoconferencing can be used for presentations and instruction such as transmitting regularly scheduled courses. It can also be used for collaborations among students and experts, be they teachers, business, or other professionals who can add valuable insight by consulting with students about their projects and learning. Using the PC for videoconferencing has the advantage of file sharing among the individuals conferencing as they work collaboratively on a project, although with a slight sacrifice of visual clarity.

Consortiums can be established with videoconferencing as the medium. Examples of school systems that enrich their curricular offerings are Westerly High School and Block Island School in Rhode Island which, in 1997–98, videoconferenced courses in global language, business administration, and physics from the mainland to the island school.

Advantages

- There are unlimited opportunities for global educational exchanges and communication.
- There is flexibility in schedule, similar to how we currently spontaneously speak on the telephone. No third-party coordination is necessary.
- There are no geographic restrictions when setting up a consortium. Two schools from either side of the country could offer a course in partnership.
- When a school is properly wired, the infrastructure that supports data and telephone transmissions will also support videoconferencing, thus allowing videoconferences to take place throughout the school rather than in one dedicated

classroom. The future of videoconferencing over the Internet will also take advantage of an infrastructure already in place.

- The federal government will soon be subsidizing transmissions and infrastructure costs under the Universal Service Fund. Contact *http://www.slcfund.org/* for updated information, as well as your state department of education.

Disadvantages

- Telephone and carrying costs can run up to $500 a month. (The federal government is proposing discounts for schools.) Broadcast costs are approximately $25 per hour per ISDN line in the United States, and international transmissions are at least three times as much.
- Initial capital investment in equipment is expensive. However, some companies upgrade existing equipment and thus do not require a complete capital outlay to keep current.

Satellite

This is a technology that many schools have already invested in with which they receive state, university, or global programming. Many departments of education have programs that provide receiving dishes to schools, especially in rural districts. Some schools and districts have purchased their own dishes from private corporations for receiving programs. Necessary equipment includes a specialized computer to digitize the signal, satellite dish, monitor, and, if licensed to initiate programs, a video camera.

Many high schools participate in Channel One, a commercial venture that uses satellite technology to bring daily news programming into the schools. Short advertisements from business support the hardware and transmission costs.

Because this technology is primarily used for receiving programs only, a satellite dish is desirable to participate in a wide variety of advanced courses and specialized events emanating from universities and special institutions.

Advantages

- Numerous quality programs abound for the user from universities, nonprofit organizations, and other educational institutions.
- Receiving of programs is direct and simple, similar to the process used in the home.

Disadvantages

- A school cannot broadcast without an FCC license and expensive equipment (most universities or departments of education have made this investment), thus making this technology undesirable. Without broadcast capability, the course is not interactive for the students or teacher.

- The variety of transmissions will not be as spontaneous or flexible as videoconferencing because of the costs and procedures associated with renting or leasing satellite coordinates.

FLEXIBILITY

With distance education the block schedule can pose its own set of interesting dilemmas to overcome. There is no one way of creating a block schedule. Even if two high schools agree on a blocked format, such as the 4 × 4, creative rotations of blocks could make the time schedules incompatible. Reaching out to business, higher education, and other expertise for students will require flexibility. The larger amounts of classroom time with the block should help teachers and students be flexible in their ability to conference electronically rather than impede the process. However, teachers in a school that is serious about offering courses through distance learning will have to be very flexible to enable their students to benefit from the curricular and collaborative opportunities videoconferencing provides.

ROLE OF THE LIBRARY MEDIA SPECIALIST

The proliferation of technology has created many new educational settings that teachers and school media specialists are struggling to understand (Veltze and Tasher 1994, p. 115). While it may seem easy (in theory) to teach in a distance-learning classroom, problems are inevitable without face-to-face contact between teachers and students. Library media specialists can help by taking a proactive role in distance education efforts, from instructional design, to media resource development, to in-service training for staff (Schamber 1990, p. 1). In order to play this role, the library media specialist should serve on the committees that plan for and later develop policy for distance learning. The committee should be made up of representatives from all schools who participate in distance learning. Membership should include technology experts, the library media specialist, content-area teachers representing the disciplines of courses being offered, and any interested teacher who may want to teach in this format in the future. It is also important to have administrative representation on the committee.

Distance learning can be impersonal if the teachers do not have a repertoire of varied instructional methodologies they can quickly adapt when the students are not responding to the lesson. Teachers of distance-learning classrooms have to maintain all students' interest and attention because it can be a remote experience. Teachers who offer numerous consensus-building activities and promote group projects find their students can develop skills for collaboration with distant friends and partners in learning (Kerka 1996, p. 2). Increasingly these skills are needed in the global workplace (Dede 1996, pp. 197–204).

Many library media specialists are responsible for distance learning in their schools. This can be a significant responsibility depending on the equipment, the location of the room, the training of the teachers and students, and the support given by other staff in the building. If distance learning is a function of the library media center, be sure that in the planning stages provision is made for adequate support staff, training, and maintenance agreements for the hardware and related equipment and operating systems.

TRAINING

Training teachers to be comfortable in the distance education environment is an investment that will pay back great dividends. Lecturing will not engage students, but in this virtual classroom, where the teacher is miles away, can authentic experiences, such as conducting science laboratory experiments, be effective? How does the remote teacher monitor and assess students' understanding and comprehension? How does the teacher facilitate and conduct a debate where the participants are at multiple sites? And, of primary importance, what does the teacher do when there is an equipment failure?

All of these considerations and more must be carefully thought out and planned for before a teacher goes on the air. The library media specialist can facilitate training for teachers in these ways:

1. Contact other school districts in the area that are already using distance learning, and arrange to visit both the virtual classroom and the teachers using this medium. Much can be learned from colleagues, and no question is too insignificant to ask. The visits of the IN-TV planning committee were invaluable to promoting distance learning in our schools and assisting the teachers.

2. Look to higher education for guidance. Colleges and universities have been using the medium for many years and have found many innovative ways to teach students and reach out to the wider community of business leaders for consultation and integration of practical activities into the curriculum.

3. Most businesses and corporations of any size today use videoconferencing. Arrange for teacher and administrator visits to these local businesses, which will enthusiastically demonstrate how the systems work and the benefits of videoconferencing. Some corporations seek partnerships with schools for school-to-career linking activities. An example is the Bentley College/General Mills project in which, through videoconferencing, students worked with the company to design and market a new popcorn snack food (Benavides 1997).

4. Investigate courses on how to use distance learning or videoconferencing. The companies that sell the hardware have strong customer support and will help users be comfortable with the equipment. Another suggestion is to take a course

via videoconferencing on how to instruct in the virtual classroom. Texas A&M University supports the Center for Distance Learning Research on its College Station campus. Its home page on the Web offers a wide variety of support services such as the Research and Information Services Division whose purpose is to gather and distribute information on distance learning and aid in the writing of grants and contracts. In addition, the center offers courses through videoconferencing, such as Organization of Distance Learning, Television Production Techniques for Distance Learning, and Introduction to Distance Learning along with certificate training programs.

INTERNET COURSES

Schools that adopted block scheduling in the early or mid-1990s did so as they were beginning to find educational uses for the Internet. Today it is common for many colleges and universities to offer courses via the Internet. Predictably, high schools will follow this lead in the near future. As students have more productive time in the school day with the block schedule, it makes sense for schools to look at the Internet as a source of distance learning for its students who may want to participate in college or other high school courses anywhere in the world.

Courses Offered Through Higher Education

Many universities have had remote branches or learning sites for decades, serving populations of students who were not on the main campus. These satellite campuses have been the only way many students could attend college. Internet courses offer the same utility and practicality of bringing the curriculum to the students, wherever they may be.

A goal of block scheduling is to give students the opportunities to develop lifelong skills for information. Rather than the teacher's lecturing a precise quantity of information and students passively receiving it, the large amounts of sustained time the block affords almost require that teachers move away from lecture as the primary instructional method. In its place, students must learn how to obtain information on a topic so that as the knowledge base expands over time on the topic, the student will be able to grow with the information by having the ability to retrieve the appropriate sources, determine the validity of the information, and draw new conclusions and opinions.

Kimberly H. Updegrove (1995) has outlined the value of Internet courses and provides exceptional links to other Web sites that either describe the process in great technological detail or lead to unlimited course offerings. She contrasts the "changing paradigms of instruction" whereby the college or university professor is no longer an absolute authority. She views technology, and in particular the Internet, as a means for broadening communication between professor and student:

Traditional notions of academia . . . depict roles for students as subordinate sponges and professors as authoritative sages. . . .

Technological advances in methods of communication and research are beginning to change the traditional scenarios of the classroom. Specifically, the exponential growth of the Internet has promoted opportunities for new ways of teaching and learning. Professors and students are discovering the unique challenges of the Internet and its tools, and they are discovering that it is a valuable source of information that breaks down many of the barriers associated with school—geography, and time in particular. (pp. 1–2)

Networks created through the Internet are a virtual classroom where there are no walls but with teachers and students logging in at their own time and discretion. The classroom is always open and available, and the learning that occurs from sharing ideas and information can continue 24 hours a day.

The Internet Virtual Classroom

There are many ways to structure an Internet classroom. The easiest and most basic is through e-mail, next the establishment of a dedicated listserv for a course, and finally creating a virtual classroom that offers many sites and places for students to visit. (See Figures 10.2 through 10.4.)

Helpful Web sites and online journal articles and papers are available for downloading regarding curriculum and instruction, Internet style. For example, James J. O'Donnell, professor of classical studies at the University of Pennsylvania, has many helpful suggestions on how to set up a virtual classroom and instruct a course via the Internet. (See Internet Bibliography, Chapter Nine, "New Tools for Teaching.")

An example of where to find courses over the Internet is the site World Lecture Hall. The University of Texas coordinates a listing of hundreds of courses by subject area that are offered in universities throughout the world. In searching the Library and Information Science category, I found a dozen courses covering a variety of topics. For example, there is an Internet Resources course offered by the School of Library and Information Science at the University of South Florida. A detailed course syllabus is provided, along with registration information. There are no mandatory on-site meetings, and the Internet-based course does not meet at one specific time. Lessons and class participation via e-mail and the Web occur throughout the week as required. Major projects of the course are monitoring a library-related listserv and summarizing the discussion for the class, intensive use of the Internet for specific queries, building a Web page, and participation in the class listserv.

Many block-scheduled schools have eliminated study halls at a time when they are increasing the number of courses a student must take in a school year. Particularly for school districts that are overcrowded or can-

Figure 10.2
Internet Classroom Using E-mail

Student PC

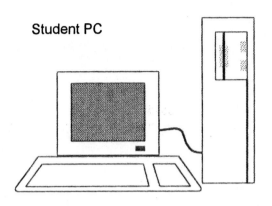

Student Obtains Lessons
Via E-Mail

E-Mail Server

Figure 10.3
Internet Classroom Using a Listserv

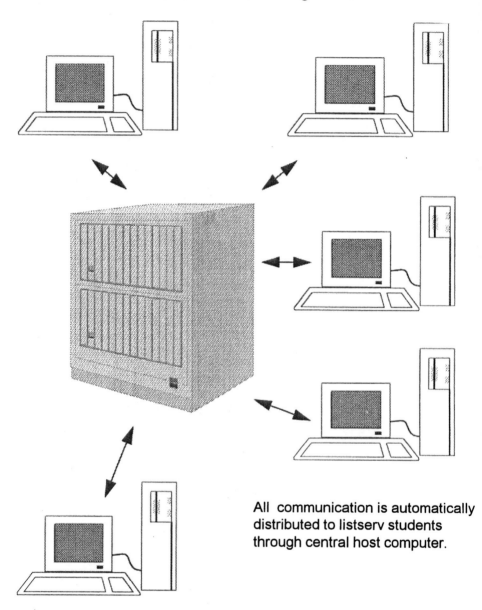

All communication is automatically distributed to listserv students through central host computer.

Figure 10.4
The Virtual Classroom

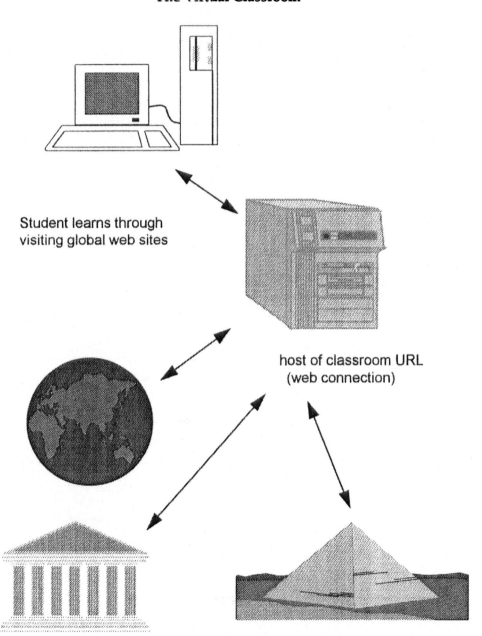

Student learns through
visiting global web sites

host of classroom URL
(web connection)

not find resources to increase staffing, an agreement with universities to enroll students in their Internet courses makes a lot of sense. Not unlike advanced placement courses, students will participate in higher-level curriculum and have their imaginations stretch and soar as they learn from the professor and other members of the course electronically.

High School Courses

Interestingly, but not suprisingly, there are numerous courses offered via the Internet sponsored and accredited by universities but few high school courses offered than are not *commercially* founded. Companies such as the Virginia Internet High School, Babbage Net School, and Web-Study encourage high school students to take courses that include textbook readings or CD-ROM material. The student submits the required work to the commercial school via e-mail and is assessed. There is creative use of linking Internet resources such as online libraries, periodicals, and reference materials for the student. It is discouraging that when we know that information exponentially increases each year, high school students are not given similar opportunities to learn in a structured way using the Internet.

This seems to be an area ripe for development because the virtual classroom proves itself to be an authentic way for students to learn and teachers to instruct. Internet classes provide flexibility that other forms of distance learning do not. Downloading e-mail or information from a listserv can be done at any time and is not dependent on synchronized schedules. For students who are capable of independent study, a course from the Internet or augmented with an online program of study has great potential merit. There are a few universities that offer accredited high school courses on the Internet. Stanford, Indiana University, and Texas Tech University either offer to help and support high school students or sponsor courses.

Will block scheduling create a need for high schools to share their best curriculum and sponsor students remotely? The need to have all students engaged in enriched learning experiences is the reason many schools moved to block scheduling. It is interesting to think in these terms, and predictably, if the universities find continued success with their virtual classrooms, secondary education will not be far behind in adopting this model.

WHERE DO YOU LOCATE THE VIRTUAL CLASSROOM?

It would be a mistake to leave the impression that distance learning should be one stationary room in the school. Schools changed to the block schedule because teachers and administrators wanted to change the way students traditionally learned from lecture to resource-based learning. If there is only one place in the school where students and teachers can contact the outside for information and consultation, it will be too difficult to arrange for the room, and teachers won't use it.

In the ideal environment, there will be videoconferencing available from the school LAN. Until the Internet replaces ISDN lines as the telecommunications for distance learning, schools will want to consider having multiple places in the building where portable, mobile videoconferencing units can be transported easily. We can learn from the business community that when there is only one videoconference room, people will become discouraged and not use it. When managers and scientists can videoconference from their offices and labs, it becomes a viable technology that has endless uses for communication and learning.

THE FUTURE

Distributed education or distance learning will become more and more attractive to users from all types of geographic considerations as its interfaces become easily accessible to the school, corporate, and home environments. "More than distance, it is increasingly the time demands and constraints that shape many programs. . . . Learners will increasingly want and need education and training on demand" (Watabe, Hamalainen, and Whinston 1995, p. 141).

Wilson (1997, pp. 13–14) states that an effective interactive multimedia distance-learning environment will have these features:

- Delivery on standards-based multimedia PCs equipped for live video and audio interactions and connected to a robust multicasting network

- A mix of synchronous and asynchronous activity

- Compatibility with industry-standard authoring tools for multimedia courseware, including audio and video clips, animation, and simulation exercises

- Use of professional-quality software tools (for computer-assisted design, symbolic math, spreadsheets, word processing)

- Small-group discussions

- Question-and-answer tools to verify content retention

- Collaborative software for application sharing over the network

- Floor control to allow classroom coordination for both instructor-led and student-centered learning

- Course administration tools for scheduling, registration, and resource management

The future is today. In a recent edition of my local newspaper was a picture that caught my attention of a teacher, student, and the Florida commissioner of education standing near a computer. The caption states that officials have "launched the first online high school, which will allow students from Orange and Alachua counties to take classes by computers. Officials hope to have *all* Florida classes online in the next three years" (*The Day* 1997). This is a very ambitious goal, and one that is supportive in the block-scheduled environment whereby students are encouraged to enroll in many courses for their own knowledge, enrichment, and career choice.

BIBLIOGRAPHY

Print Sources

Benavides, Lisa. "Bentley Students Popping with Ideas." *Boston Business Journal* 16, 52 (February 7, 1996): p. 6.

The Day, New London, CT, December 3, 1997.

Dede, C. "Emerging Technologies in Distance Education for Business." *Journal of Education for Business* 71, 4 (March–April 1996): pp. 197–204.

Gilbertson, Denny, and Jamie Poindexter. "Distance Education Classroom Design: Tips for Designing a Conference and Distance Education Classroom at County Extension Facilities." Madison: University of Wisconsin, June 10, 1997. Online. Internet. October 18, 1997. *http://www.uwex.edu/disted/rooms/county.htm*

John, Jim. "NR1." E-mail. November 25, 1997. *jjohn@ctol.net*

Kerka, Sandra. "Distance Learning, the Internet, and the World Wide Web." *ERIC Digest* (1996): pp. 1–4. (ED395214.)

Kronholz, June. "Teacher Retirements Portend Acute Shortage." *Wall Street Journal*, July 24, 1997, p. B1.

Schamber, Linda. "Distance Education and the Changing Role of the Library Media Specialist." *ERIC Digest* (November 1990). (ED327221.)

Updegrove, Kimberly H. "Teaching on the Internet." Research paper, August 1995. *http://dolphin.upcnn.edu/~kimu/teaching.html*

Veltze, Linda A., and John H. Tasher. "Distance Learning: The Impact of Telecommunications on Cross-Cultural and Cross-Generational Educational Settings." *Reference Librarian* 44 (1994): pp. 115–121.

Watabe, Kazuo, Matti Hamalainen, and Andrew B. Whinston. "An Internet Based Collaborative Distance Learning System: Codiless." *Computers and Education* 24, 3 (April 1995): pp. 141–155.

Wilson, Jack M. "Distance Learning for Continuing Education." *Educom Review* 32, 2 (March–April 1997): pp. 12–16. (ERIC EJ539753.)

Internet Sites

AT&T/Lucent Technologies, Center for Excellence in Distance Learning (has the overall goal of advancing state-of-the-art distance education). *http://www.lucent.com/cedl/index.html*

Commonwealth of Learning (contains numerous links to worldwide resources and documents). *http://www.col.org/*

Dennison Online Internet School (a for-profit, private high school offering courses through CD-ROM and the Internet). *http://www.dennisononline.com*

Educom-Edupage Index, current issue. *http://www.educom.edu/web/pubs/ pubHomeFrame.html*

InfoSearch Broadcasting Links (an alphabetical directory of web sites for television networks, cable, and local broadcasting stations). *http://www.broadcastinglinks. com*

International Teleconferencing Association (professional association linking users, providers, strategists, educators, and managers that use teleconferencing, telecollaborative, and distance education technologies). *http://www.itca.org/*

Link Exchange Member Distance Learning. *http://www.collegiate.net/infoa9.html*

PBS Online (online support for over 100 PBS programs). *http://www.pbs.org*

PictureTel Applications. Select Education. *http://www.picturetel.com/apps/default.htm*

San Diego State University, Education First (describes educational applications for K–12 schools, community colleges, and public libraries). *http://www.kn.pacbell. com/wired/*

Schools and Libraries Corporation, Universal Service Fund Information. *http:// www.slcfund.org/*

Texas A&M University, Center for Distance Learning Research. *http://www.cdlr. tamu.edu/*

University of Wisconsin, Distance Education Clearinghouse (provides a wide range of information about distance education). *http://www.uwex.edu/disted/ satart.htm*

Of Practical Consideration: Scheduling, Study Halls, Substitutes, and Assessment

11

As library media specialists can attest, scheduling is a major factor in the success of the learning environment. We have become masters at facilitating and helping many groups of people with diverse needs simultaneously. In the traditional seven-period schedule, there was more control built in to plan more precisely for facility use by classes and study hall students. Now with the block schedule, the library media center and its staff have to be much more flexible to meet the immediate and changing needs of teachers and students. This chapter explores the need for flexibility and scheduling options and then focuses on study halls, substitutes, and assessment in the block.

SCHEDULING

When elementary libraries were established in the 1960s, the model was to schedule classes for a weekly period for library instruction. This rigidity was more for the convenience of the rest of the staff because the classroom teacher often used the library period as a time for planning. "Traditional, inflexible scheduling is based on administrative and institutional needs. . . . Flexible scheduling patterns are based on pedagogical practices, educational needs of students, and the professional needs of teachers" (Watts and Castle 1993, p. 307).

As integration of library skills, whole language, and other new learning adoptions became accepted, it was no longer appropriate to teach library skills in isolation. Media specialists coordinated utilization of the library facility, the elementary curriculum, and appropriate information and reading skills. The inflexible schedule was discarded for one whereby students could use the resources as needed and when appropriate. In June 1991 the American Association of School Librarians (AASL) adopted a position paper, "Position Statement on Flexible Scheduling," that speaks to the total integration of the library media program into the learning environment of the school. It is directed to all schools and all levels, and is particularly important to high school library media specialists about to embark on block scheduling. It reminds us that the library media program must adjust and fit the overall educational structure of the school to maximize learning goals and objectives.

Position Statement on Flexible Scheduling

Schools must adopt the educational philosophy that the library media program is fully integrated into the educational program. This integration strengthens the teaching/learning process so that students can develop the vital skills necessary to locate, analyze, evaluate, interpret, and communicate information and ideas. When the library media program is fully integrated into the instructional program of the school, students, teachers, and library media specialists become partners in learning. The library program is an extension of the classroom. Information skills are taught and learned within the context of the classroom curriculum. The wide range of resources, technologies, and services needed to meet students' learning and information needs are readily available in a cost-effective manner.

The integrated library media program philosophy requires that an open schedule must be maintained. Classes cannot be scheduled in the library media center to provide teacher release or preparation time. Students and teachers must be able to come to the center throughout the day to use information sources, to read for pleasure, and to meet and work with other students and teachers.

Planning between the library media specialist and the classroom teacher, which encourages both scheduled and informal visits, is the catalyst that makes this integrated library program work. The teacher brings to the planning process a knowledge of subject content and student needs. The library media specialist contributes a broad knowledge of resources and technology, an understanding of teaching methods, and a wide range of strategies that may be employed to help students learn information skills. Cooperative planning by the teacher and library media specialist integrates information skills and materials into the classroom curriculum and results in the development of assignments that encourage open inquiry.

The responsibility for flexibly scheduled library media programs must be shared by the entire school community.

The Board of Education endorses the philosophy that the library program is an integral part of the district's educational program and ensures that flexible scheduling for library media centers is maintained in all buildings and at all levels.

The District Administration supports this philosophy and monitors staff assignments to ensure appropriate staffing levels so that all teachers, including the library media specialists, can fulfill their professional responsibilities.

The Principal creates the appropriate climate within the school by advocating the benefits of flexible scheduling to the faculty, by monitoring scheduling, by ensuring appropriate staffing levels, and by providing joint planning time for classroom teachers and library media specialists.

The Teacher uses resource-based instruction and views the library media program as a integral part of that instruction.

The Library Media Specialist is knowledgeable about curriculum and classroom activities, and works cooperatively with the classroom teacher to integrate information skills into the curriculum.

There are many definitions of flexible scheduling. Jean Donham van Deusen (1995) states that flexible scheduling is a plan that encourages classes to meet for instruction in the library media center when they have a specific need, driven by activity in the classroom. She suggests there are five key elements required to make flexible scheduling successful:

1. Information skills curriculum that matches content-area curriculum
2. Flexible access
3. Team planning
4. Principal expectations
5. Commitment to resource-based learning (pp. 16–17)

These criteria are also essential for successful implementation of library media services in a block-scheduled high school. Some of the ways high schools can be more flexible is to work at the building level with the scheduling committee or group of people responsible for planning block scheduling and look at the way students move throughout the building. Flexible access encourages students to go to the library media center whenever they have a need, even when the class as a whole is not scheduled.

The transition team must recognize the need for students to be mobile and flexible during the block. It is not realistic for a student to sit in the same seat for 90 minutes doing the same activity, nor is it feasible for a high school student to sit at a table in the library media center silently engaged in learning for 90 minutes without the need to stretch, move around, or perhaps visit another location in the school for a teacher conference or to use a specific technology.

Coupled with the need to examine how study halls will take place is the need to rethink how students move from one location to another in the building. In a traditional high school, the student must have a pass from a teacher to be out of a classroom and in the hallways. Our block-scheduling transition team determined that teachers would be spending an inordinate amount of time writing passes. Prior to the block schedule it was a marathon experience in the library media center of checking and writing passes for students. It was decided to eliminate passes and make students accountable for their whereabouts by having sign-in and sign-out sheets in every room in the school, including the library media center. These sheets are turned in at the end of the day to the assistant principals in charge of discipline. By implementing this simple student sign-in and sign-out log, several things were accomplished:

- Teacher time was saved for more important tasks.
- Paperwork was reduced considerably.
- Students gained flexibility to move to many locations, including during their study hall.
- Students were made accountable for themselves.

Research Passes

For a few teachers who want to communicate individual students' research needs or have immediate feedback from the library media specialist, a research pass was developed. Paul Helvig, an English teacher at East Lyme High School, decided that he needed to give his ninth-grade students more flexibility in using the library media center. No longer was it appropriate to his instruction to have the entire class be scheduled in the library at one time. He experimented in a variety of ways and learned that he needed to have feedback from the library media specialist as to how his students used their time. Concurrently, the library media specialist asked for information about the needs his students were bringing with them. Upon concluding his or her research, the student now fills out the last section of a note that tells the teacher what was accomplished by coming to the library media center. That information can be filed in the student work portfolio. The information pass shown in Figure 11.1 has been used successfully as a communication device among the teacher, the library media specialist, and the student.

The teacher accepts the pass back from his students when they return to class. It serves as a communication device for the teacher and the student to determine how successful the student was in the library media center.

Scheduling Classes

Teachers need flexibility for whole- or half-class scheduling. In the first years of the block, I tried to use my traditional planning book and found that even though I knew what all my cryptic notes meant, the teachers who wanted to scan availability had difficulty viewing in a glance the planned activity of the library media center. This year, with the help of Lenore White, the science curriculum instructional leader at our school, the daily planning forms shown in Figure 11.2 were devised. Many positive comments have been made about their organization, options, and ease

Figure 11.1
Library Resource Request

Fill out top part; get teacher to initial; present to librarian upon entering library; pick up from librarian before leaving; present to teacher upon returning to class.

Name:_____

Date:_____

Purpose for using Library:_____

_____

_____

_____

Assistance needed from Library Staff: _____ yes   _____no

Librarian's signature and time when leaving_____

Use of time and resources: _____

_____

_____

_____

Source: Courtesy Paul Helvig.

Figure 11.2
Daily Planning Forms

DAILY SCHEDULE -- DAY 1

Name/Block	Check for *when* and *how many students*:	Date:_____ Activity/Library Staff and Materials Needed
Block 1 _____ _____	Block: Full ___1st half ___ 2nd half___ Class: Full ___ Half class____ Block: Full ___1st half ___ 2nd half___ Class: Full ___ Half class____ Block: Full ___1st half ___ 2nd half___ Class: Full ___ Half class____	_____ _____
Block 2 _____ _____	Block: Full ___1st half ___ 2nd half___ Class: Full ___ Half class____ Block: Full ___1st half ___ 2nd half___ Class: Full ___ Half class____ Block: Full ___1st half ___ 2nd half___ Class: Full ___ Half class____	_____
Block 3 _____ _____	Block: Full ___1st half ___ 2nd half___ Class: Full ___ Half class____ Block: Full ___1st half ___ 2nd half___ Class: Full ___ Half class____ Block: Full ___1st half ___ 2nd half___ Class: Full ___ Half class____	_____
Block 4 _____ _____	Block: Full ___1st half ___ 2nd half___ Class: Full ___ Half class____ Block: Full ___1st half ___ 2nd half___ Class: Full ___ Half class____ Block: Full ___1st half ___ 2nd half___ Class: Full ___ Half class____	_____ _____

Figure 11.2 Continued

DAILY SCHEDULE -- DAY 2

Name/Block	Check for *when* and *how many students*:	Date:_____ Activity/Library Staff and Materials Needed
Block 5 ——————— ———————	Block: Full ___1st half ___ 2nd half___ Class: Full ___ Half class____ Block: Full ___1st half ___ 2nd half___ Class: Full ___ Half class____ Block: Full ___1st half ___ 2nd half___ Class: Full ___ Half class____	
Block 6 ——————— ———————	Block: Full ___1st half ___ 2nd half___ Class: Full ___ Half class____ Block: Full ___1st half ___ 2nd half___ Class: Full ___ Half class____ Block: Full ___1st half ___ 2nd half___ Class: Full ___ Half class____	
Block 7 ——————— ———————	Block: Full ___1st half ___ 2nd half___ Class: Full ___ Half class____ Block: Full ___1st half ___ 2nd half___ Class: Full ___ Half class____ Block: Full ___1st half ___ 2nd half___ Class: Full ___ Half class____	
Block 8 ——————— ———————	Block: Full ___1st half ___ 2nd half___ Class: Full ___ Half class____ Block: Full ___1st half ___ 2nd half___ Class: Full ___ Half class____ Block: Full ___1st half ___ 2nd half___ Class: Full ___ Half class____	

Source: Courtesy Lenore L. White.

of reading. Because East Lyme High School is on an alternate-day schedule (A/B), the pages are collated in the planning book. The majority of
teachers keep to their time commitment, and the staff works well together
for maximum access. Often a teacher can be flexible as to whether he or
she brings the class in either the first or second half of the block. I do not
have a separate room for library skill instruction, so I like to coordinate my
time when I need the library media center fairly quiet with all the teachers who sign in for a block. The teachers understand and cooperate fully to
have everyone's needs accommodated.

There has been recent interest in how library media specialists schedule
classes via the listserv BLOCKLIST. The responses varied—some stating a
requirement of either 24 hours or teacher contact with the library media
specialist was required so that materials and support would be available
to the class. Others let total flexibility prevail. Each school is different; library media specialists, through trial and error, discover what is best for
their school.

THE STUDY HALL

One of the first questions library media specialists ask is, "How do you
manage study hall students with block scheduling?" There is great concern that what can be the bane of our existence will magnify and become
worse. How could it not when students will have now twice as much free
time on their hands? Can you imagine having that unruly student now for
90 minutes? What will you do? The concerns of study halls should be
looked at and planned for by the planning team.

Abolishing the Study Hall

Some schools that move to block scheduling decide that this is an excellent time to abolish study halls altogether. Many teachers would prefer to
teach an extra class rather than have study hall duty. If study halls are not
offered, students will need an alternative that would give them an opportunity to schedule conferences with teachers and help them manage their
time so they can fortify their learning through homework assignments.
Some schools have carved out a half-hour period in combination with
lunch, called an "administrative period," that allows students some time
to go to the library media center, talk to teachers, and keep appointments
with counselors. A downside of the entire school's having this common
period is that the library media center and the other resources get "maxed
out" very soon, and the benefit is questionable when the competition is so
keen for limited access for such a short amount of time.

The library media center is affected when the study hall is abolished.
Some schools report that circulation and student access decrease, even

with resource-based learning. Teachers will have to be made aware of the importance for them to plan access to the library media center from their classroom. "The elimination of study halls promotes guided practice and enrichment activities within the confines of the regular classroom" (Huff 1995, p. 22). If teachers do not make regular arrangements for compensation of study hall time, the students may use the library media center less than in a traditional schedule, an unacceptable proposal in the increasing requirement that all students be information literate.

If no classes are scheduled in the library media center, it may be a very empty place, except for small numbers of individuals arriving from classrooms to do research. Northampton High School in Massachusetts reported, "The overall impact with regard to the number of students using the library . . . is difficult to quantify. What is vastly different is the overall pattern of use. . . . The library is either nearly empty or nearly full, seldom anything in between" (Keenan 1997, p. 8). The downtime when the facility is empty provides an excellent opportunity for the library media staff to consult with teachers, catalog, work on acquisitions, and so forth. Certainly we all would welcome time during the school day to work on special projects and not always feel rushed to get everything done when time does not permit. Another upside is that with no study hall students to supervise, the library media specialist has less of a role and responsibility for monitoring student behavior.

Access for students was a concern at this school, and to open up opportunities, Northampton extended its hours before and after school. Other schools have added evening hours so students can use the library media center outside the school day.

Retaining the Study Hall

If your school plans to maintain the study hall, the library media specialist should approach the transition team and the administration with data about the usage and the kinds of activities that now take place during study hall periods for students in the library. What are the issues? Is space already a concern? If so, it will only become more of a concern because these students will compete with an increased number of classes in the library media center. Is student purpose and behavior a concern? With block scheduling and resource-based learning, teachers will assign many more research questions. This will change the kinds of activities and homework required from students, thus lending a greater need for students to have access to the library. I now see many teachers in my school requiring students to bring information, such as literary criticism, controversial scientific articles, or even statistical data, to the classroom for major tests and examinations. Students need flexible access to meet these information needs for assessment purposes.

Prior to going to the block schedule, document the current purpose and benefits of the study hall. This information will assist you in making a recommendation to the planning or transition team.

Assessing Study Hall Usage

1. Keep student study hall usage data for a year prior to block scheduling. If this is not possible, try to reconstruct a series of typical days throughout the year.
2. Look at several days in each quarter and determine the percentage of study hall students who use the library of the total student body. For example, a typical day in March showed 20 percent of the total student body in my school visited the library media center from study hall.
3. Determine if the usage is greater during certain times of the year. Third quarter used to be a crunch time for us because that is when most major research papers were assigned.
4. Recollect what kinds of activities study hall students perform in the library media center. Do an analysis such as this: "10 percent come to read the newspaper, 50 percent to do homework, 15 percent to research, 20 percent to use computers, 5 percent to socialize."

Once you determine why students come to the library media center from study hall, you can work creatively with the planning team to determine alternatives and opportunities. Remember that the library media center will be much more in demand by teachers with their classes using the facilities and program during instructional time.

If you determine that computer use is high, analyze what the computers are being used for. If it is word processing, perhaps a writing lab can be created that students can go to for this activity, thus reserving the library media center computers for research, Internet, and CD-ROM use. If you determine that the library media center has become a social hall, the transition team may be able to identify another location in the school where students can legitimately relax, eat, and visit. The block schedule does intensify learning, and it is important to remember that no adult would be able to function in an environment that never provided moments of downtime.

At East Lyme High School, study hall students do not have to stay in the library media center for the whole block. They are encouraged to use it only for their legitimate educational needs. When we implemented block scheduling, we also opened up a "social study hall" in the cafeteria for students who are in good academic standing. Those who are not are assigned to traditional quiet study halls. Those from the "social study hall" now use the library for information research or preparing multimedia. Those who want to visit and eat have a place to do that in the social study hall located in the cafeteria. Students in poor academic standing may use the library media center for a designated period of time with a stated research purpose. If they abridge this responsibility, they lose the privilege for a defined time. Working closely with the administration has kept our mission focused and students appropriately using the library media center from study hall.

SUBSTITUTE TEACHERS

On the LM_NET and BLOCKLIST listservs, there are occasional comments from library media specialists about unsatisfactory times when a substitute brings a class to the library media center for an entire block. Some library media specialists do not allow classes with substitutes unless the teacher has prearranged with them. Others will not allow classes with substitutes because they believe that without the teacher present for their content knowledge, the students do not use the time effectively.

The issue of substitute teachers and block scheduling is thorny. There is too much valuable time to waste when a teacher is out not to continue with the lesson, and block scheduling places even more importance on having knowledgeable and capable substitute teachers. Professional development for teachers is critical to their success in teaching in the block, and we expect no loss of instructional time when a substitute is required. When my school began the block, our intentions were to have our substitute teachers go through a training period so that they would have some strategies and understand our goals with the block. This training was short lived, I believe, because of the transiency of substitute teachers. The roster changes, and it would be an insurmountable task to train all newcomers.

Recently a situation arose in our library media center that involved a substitute, lesson plans, and motivation of students. It was a very busy block, with two other classes using the facility simultaneously. The class with the substitute had been in before, and the teacher's lesson plan noted that her students were to continue their research. I was comfortable with that plan because I knew the expected learning outcomes; however, the teacher did not leave precise instructions for the substitute about the research. After the fact, I learned how uncomfortable the substitute was with that lesson plan. At the next curriculum instructional leaders (CIL) meeting, the recommendation was made that the CIL for each department who works with the substitutes for teachers in the department contact the library media specialist directly if the plans call for library research. I make the time to talk to the substitute teacher before the class comes to the library. If the plans are unspecified, I institute a product requirement, such as the students will have to turn in to their substitute at the end of the block a specified minimum number of pages of notes, a bibliography, or whatever else seems appropriate. I have noticed that with a rapport already established earlier in the day with the substitute, I have a willing partner to help ensure that the students work to the best of their ability.

Students respond to a quantitative requirement, and teachers accept that we will modify the plan slightly to help ensure that their students remain on task.

ASSESSMENT

High school educators today are constantly looking "out of the box" of the traditional test and trying new methods of student assessment. A restructured school is an opportune time to expand student assessment that is appropriate to both the learning activities and the long-range goals for student retention and use of knowledge and information. Teachers should "assess academic progress in a variety of ways for a clear, valid picture of what students know and can do" ("Breaking Ranks" 1996, p. 6). Assessment is the skill of assessing the product and process for either improved instruction or to document what a student has learned.

The Association for Supervision and Curriculum Development (ASCD) web site offers an abundance of excellent materials on assessment. Not only are there summaries of past conferences on assessment, but there are also published articles by leaders in the field and announcements of future conferences. At a recent ASCD conference on assessment held in Boston, Jay McTighe, a featured speaker, suggested that the teacher must have a clear idea of what he or she wants the students to understand and do. Depending on the learning objective, the teacher selects an appropriate assessment technique. McTighe advocates traditional testing when the knowledge is worth the students' being familiar with or even if it is essential to know and do. In social studies, students can be tested on paper for their recollection of dates, events, and so forth. These are worth knowing or being familiar with. However, when the student should have an "enduring understanding" of a concept, then performance assessment is an excellent means to enable the student to understand this concept and be able to use it in later life. McTighe's example of an enduring understanding in social studies is a student's understanding of civil rights and one's ability to determine when a right has been violated.

For the most part, library media specialists do not assess students in the same manner that classroom teachers do. I believe, however, that we have a role to assess students' information skills as well as to help teachers in the development of assessment techniques, particularly performance assessment and the building of the student portfolio.

Performance Assessment

"Performance assessment is an activity that requires students to construct a response, create a product, or perform a demonstration. Since performance assessments generally do not yield a single correct answer or solution method, evaluations of student products or performances are based on judgments guided by criteria" (McTighe 1997, p. 5).

Teaching in the block schedule promotes learning activities, many of which are conducted, researched, or created in the library media center. With "performance assessment . . . students know at the outset that they will need to demonstrate mastery of their subjects at an agreed-upon level. . . . Teachers see new ways to plan learning activities" (Cawelti 1996, p. 245). Foremost, the library media specialist should be aware of the purpose of the activity or why the student is seeking information or creating a project. The longer my school has been on block scheduling, the more I find myself surprised by what appears to be a simple request actually turning out to be a very important component that will contribute to the larger assessment of the student's knowledge or skills.

An example is what I thought was a simple request was really a component of a student's understanding of communicable diseases. Passing in the hallway, a sophomore girl asked me to get her something on Typhoid Mary. The student is not a frequenter of the library media center, so I was a little flattered she would stop me and ask for help. I gave her a couple of articles, but she came back for more. This went on for two days—without really knowing what she needed, I would hand the student information that was accepted gratefully. She never fully disclosed why she was in such need of this information on Typhoid Mary. It was only after talking with her teacher that I discovered that she was preparing for her midterm examination in biology and that part of the exam was to be performance based with the information she brought with her to the test. Performance assessment has raised the stakes for students for the quality and quantity of information they obtain, particularly if they will be required to make a product, construct a response, or demonstrate their larger understanding of a concept. The library media specialist can be a valuable provider to students when assessment requires information literacy.

Technology and Organization Support for the Portfolio

The portfolio is not a new concept to professionals in the arts or to our elementary school colleagues. A portfolio is "an organized means of monitoring students' progress." It also serves to align curriculum, instruction, and assessment (Nidds and McGerald 1997, p. 47–48). The portfolio has also been called a "purposeful collection of student work that tells the story of student achievement or growth" (Arter et al. 1995).

If your high school is at the beginning stages of seriously using portfolio assessment for areas other than writing and the arts, the library media specialist can help in the process with his or her specialized skills. In the near future, when portfolios will be meant to be transferable with the student from grade to grade, or even from school to school, data or assessments that we have kept on paper will more practically be housed electronically in a digital format. The organizational and technology skills the library media specialist has with scanning, data entry, data organization, and retrieval could be very helpful in a school that is developing student portfolios. We are the people in the school who have expertise on storing information in multiple formats that can be shared. Portfolios are an ever-expanding means for students to show what they know and what they can do.

Information Literacy

One of our primary responsibilities as teachers is to ensure that students are information literate. Assessing students' knowledge and skills can be difficult when we do not have the same set of students regularly to monitor their continued progress. Nor do we routinely give students grades for their information skills. Resource-based learning incorporates information literacy, and it is important that library media specialists view this as an opportunity to assess students' progress with their development of information skills whenever practical:

Another factor which can improve the success of flexible scheduling is a design for student assessment of information-process skills. Having an assessment plan provides a means for the teacher-librarian and teachers to monitor the information skills curriculum. Such monitoring is particularly important for an infused curriculum; that is a curriculum taught as an integral component of a content area. The assessment plan should identify the characteristics of successful performance of the information processes and should include a system for assessing student progress toward success, as well as a system for record-keeping. (van Deusen 1995, p. 19)

I am encouraged when I plan a lesson with a teacher by the enthusiastic response the teacher gives me when I offer to assess the students on their information skills. Sometimes it is no more than a scale of 1 to 5. The more feedback we can give students about their performance, the more clearly they will understand their competencies as well as the areas they need to work on.

Rubrics

Rubrics are an ideal way to assess information literacy. Figure 11.3 is an example of a rubric used in a block-scheduled high school. It can be adapted to suit a variety of content areas or needs. It comes from Karen Libby, library media specialist at Kingswood Regional High School.

Figure 11.3
Analytic Scoring Rubric

Student:_____

Grade/Course_____

Performance Title: Information Literacy Competencies

Scoring Criteria	Excellent	Good Standard	Needs Some Improvement	Needs Much Improvement	NA
Research Statement--Define and refine the research statement. List questions that will be proven in the thesis statement.					
Search Strategy--Understand the need for a search strategy, developed search strategy (descriptors, key words, web, potential sources, evaluation of source and information)					
Location of Sources--Location of sources and information within sources: index, CD-ROM, PAC, ILL, periodicals, Internet, primary sources. Determine appropriateness and relevance.					
Use of Information Determination of usefulness of information: differentiate between primary and secondary sources, fact, opinion. Record information and bibliographic information. Determine authoriativeness, currency, and reliability of information.					
Synthesis -- Draw conclusions and generalizations. Organized information using web, outline, notes or questions. Identified and selected appropriate format for presentation, including graphs, multimedia, and charts.					
Evaluation -- Assessment and identification of the process of the search strategy and problem solving.					

Self-Assessment Through Growth Plans

It is up to us, the library media specialists, to learn about school restructuring, block scheduling, and the positive implications these movements can have on the quality of library media services and the support we can give students in a new learning environment. Our professional growth plans or goal statements can be used as a formal device to learn about the role we have in school reform and to evaluate our teaching and services. Each district has its own supervision model, and many of the criteria teachers are assessed on are appropriate for us. In addition, the following four areas are suggested:

1. Quality of the daily operation of the library media center
2. Relationship with students, staff, and school program
3. Internal operation of the library media center
4. Personal/professional development (Boardman 1997, p. 15)

I recommend a fifth area as a personal goal, and that is to develop action plans that address all the opportunities the library media center now has with the block schedule to provide better learning opportunities for students. The block is the most systemic change in the structure of high schools in over one hundred years, and we need to make the most of it.

BIBLIOGRAPHY

Print Sources

Arter, Judith A., et al. "Portfolios for Assessment and Instruction." *ERIC Digest* (1995): pp. 1–4. (ED388890.)

Boardman, Edna M. "Your Personal Goals Statement: A Powerful Tool in Your Evaluation." *Book Report* 15, 5 (March–April 1997): pp. 15–16.

"Breaking Ranks for High School Reform." Commission on the Restructuring of the American High School. *Education Digest* 62, 2 (October 1996): pp. 4–9.

Cawelti, Gordon. "A Model for High School Restructuring." *Educational Forum* 60 (Spring 1996): pp. 244–48.

Huff, A. Leroy. "Flexible Block Scheduling: It Works for Us!" *NASSP Bulletin* 79, 571 (May 1995): pp. 19–22.

Keenan, John. "Block Scheduling and the LMC." *Media Forum Newsletter* (Massachusetts School Library Media Association) 19, 1 (January 1997): pp. 7–8.

McTighe, Jay, speaker. Association for Supervision and Curriculum Development Conference, "Designing Performance Assessment Tasks: Tools and Templates for Developers." Boston, December 5, 1997.

McTighe, Jay. *Performance-Based Assessment: Principles and Practice.* Ijamsville, MD: Maryland Assessment Consortium, 1997.

Nidds, Johna, and James McGerald. "How Functional Is Portfolio Assessment Anyway?" *Education Digest* 62, 5 (January 1997): pp. 47–50.

Northeast Affiliates ASCD Conference. "Making Meaning of Assessment." Boston, December 5–6, 1997.
van Deusen, Jean Donham. "Prerequisites to Flexible Planning." *Emergency Librarian* 23, 1 (September–October 1995): pp. 16–19.
Watts, Gary D., and Shari Castle. "The Time Dilemma in School Restructuring." *Phi Delta Kappan* 75, 4 (December 1993): pp. 306–10.

Internet Sites

American Association of School Librarians, position paper. *www.ala.org/aasl/positions/PS_flexible.html*
Association for Supervision and Curriculum Development. *http://www.ascd.org*
Classroom assessment. *http://www.ehhs.cmich.edu/clsasst*
ERIC Clearinghouse on Assessment and Evaluation. *http://ericae.net*
ERIC/AE On-line Library (Papers) (essays, papers, books, online journal articles, and other collections on assessment). *http://ericae.net/lib/*
National Center for Research on Evaluation, Standards, and Student Testing (CRESST) (performance assessment). Select Assessment or keyword search Performance Assessment. *http://www.cresst96.cse.ucla.edu/teacher.htmrl*
University of Minnesota, College of Education and Human Development (CAREI), block scheduling. *http://carei.coled.umn.edu/BSmain.htm*

Case Studies

12

This chapter looks at the professional and personal experiences of high school restructuring with the block scheduling. Karen Libby from New Hampshire had been at Kingswood Regional High School only one year when it changed to block scheduling. Linda Brake at Evergreen High School in Vancouver, Washington, and Pat Gautier of Edward Little High School in Auburn, Maine, are veteran high school school media specialists who found that the needs of students and faculty dramatically changed with block scheduling. East Lyme High School in Connecticut was one of the first high schools in the state to adopt block scheduling.

I posed a set of questions to give consistency to the format of the case studies. The opinions and advice vary, depending on the readiness of the faculties to accept restructuring, the level and depth of professional development afforded the staff, and the planning and perceived role of the library media center in a block-scheduled school. The respondents were asked the following questions:

General school information
- Name of school, location, size, distinguishing facts about the school.
- Year school went to block scheduling.
- Type of block scheduling your school uses.
- What was the school trying to achieve (goals) by changing to the block?
- Did they meet these goals, or did something else occur, or is it too soon to tell?
- Describe the process used for studying and implementing the block.
- Was the library media specialist on the planning committee?
- If so, how did you contribute to the work of the committee?
- Other information.

Library media center
- Describe the LMC—philosophy statement, goals.
- Describe how the LMC was primarily used prior to block scheduling. Include types of uses, such as class instruction and study hall monitoring.
- What did you have to do to get the library media program ready for block scheduling?
- What were the expectations of the planning committee for the LMC with block scheduling? That is, was there a defined role for the LMC in the anticipated change?
- Did your budget change? If so, how? Why did it change? If it increased, what did you have to do to increase it? Who championed the increase?
- Describe the technology in the LMC. How important a role does it play with the changes that occurred because of the block?
- What have been the major changes to the LMC program after block scheduling was implemented?
- How did you prepare your support staff in the LMC for block scheduling? Speak about their role and the impact that block scheduling has had on them.
- What kind of training do you recommend for library support staff in a block-scheduled school?

Staff development
- Describe how your school correlated staff development with block scheduling. Be specific about workshops and presenters, opportunities afforded teachers to visit other schools, and so forth.
- What staff development of the last few years was most helpful to you as the library media specialist in a block-scheduled school? Be specific.
- What would you recommend for continuing staff development related to block scheduling for the faculty?
- What would you recommend for continuing staff development related to block scheduling for the library media specialist?

Curriculum
- Describe how curriculum changed (if it did) because of block scheduling and the role of the LMC program in curriculum change.

Instruction
- Describe how instruction changed (if it did) because of block scheduling, and the role of the library media specialist in differentiated instruction and support to the teachers.

What works the best in your school with block scheduling?

What are the drawbacks in your school with block scheduling?

What are the successes in the library media center because of block scheduling?

What are the problems in the library media center because of block scheduling?

Advice and recommendations
- In four to five paragraphs, give your best advice or recommendations to a library media specialist who works at a school that is changing to block scheduling.

- If you were at the planning stages for block scheduling, what would you do differently that would have had a more positive impact on library services for your students and faculty?

EDWARD LITTLE HIGH SCHOOL
Auburn, Maine

Patricia M. Gautier,
Library Media Specialist

GENERAL SCHOOL INFORMATION

Edward Little High School is a four-year high school located in the small city of Auburn in south-central Maine. With 1,200 students and a staff of over 130, the school is one of the largest in the state. Students come from all socioeconomic backgrounds, and various ethnic groups are represented. The school department spends $4,658 per pupil per year at the high school level, and the student-to-teacher ratio is 25:1. In 1996 54 percent of the Edward Little High School graduates went on to higher education, and 4 percent went into the military. Edward Little is part of the Androscoggin Valley Education Collaborative of five high schools that share computer technology, the regional vocational high school, and many interschool resources.

Located twenty-five miles north of Portland and 30 minutes from Freeport and L.L. Bean, Auburn, a city of 30,000, is better known as part of the twin cities of Lewiston-Auburn, where the combined population is close to 75,000. There are many recreational opportunities in the area, which is becoming known as the gateway to the western mountain and lakes region of the state. The community is basically residential and contains some farmlands on the outskirts of the area. Industrial development is ongoing, and businesses take an active role in the educational process. Most schools are affiliated with a local concern, and it is becoming commonplace to have business representatives on committees and focus groups that are making changes in the Auburn schools.

Edward Little High School implemented block scheduling in the fall of 1995. Initially the schedule was made up of four 80-minute blocks per day. Each student had three classes per day that met every other day. Students were required to take six classes. The fourth block of each day was a connection period; each class met once every six days. The first 40 minutes of the connection period were open for all students to have time to study, read, participate in extracurricular activities, or connect with another teacher for help or to make up work. The second 40 minutes were devoted to class teaching time.

Currently the block is made up of eight classes rotating over a two-day period (A/B schedule). The blocks are still 80 minutes in length, and each student must take a minimum of six classes. In scheduling students, an effort is made to give students only one learning lab or study hall a day. The switch to the eight-period schedule was made to allow students to take more than the six courses allowed in the original format. Also, it was an administrative, library, and guidance nightmare to have all students in a study hall at the same time. Students could not access the library media center or Guidance Department easily. Teachers were asked what initiatives they would like to implement in the future, and the administration converted to the eight-period schedule to accommodate those plans. We went to the eight-period schedule in September 1997, so currently only class size, teacher schedules, and students course selection have been affected. Some teachers regret losing the connection because it gave them 40 more minutes of class time that was lost when the block was initially implemented. Some had used it for enrichment, which they no longer have time for with the new format. Students who take an extra course or two are profiting from the change, as are the Guidance Department and library media center. Time will hopefully see various options and projects come to fruition.

Edward Little went to block scheduling after much investigation on the part of the high school administration. In 1991 a group had gone to Masconomet Regional High School in Boxford, Massachusetts, which is on the Copernican Plan developed by Joseph Carroll. In the spring of 1992 the team at Walton School (where our ninth-grade program was housed until this September) piloted block scheduling with seventy-five students. They liked it and began to investigate and research it more fully. The entire Walton staff agreed to implement it in the fall of 1994. They used four 80-minute blocks per day that allowed three classes and a uniform study hall each day. Students took six classes over two days.

While the entire ninth-grade program piloted the block, the full high school staff began to investigate the idea. Many staff members went to other schools in the area that were using the block. The Walton staff acted as a resource for others in each department. The administration had studied and was excited about the block from the moment they had seen the Copernican Plan in 1991. They researched the philosophy, set out clearly why they wanted to change to the block, and investigated many ways to do it.

Teaching to the block was eventually implemented in 1995 to accomplish a wide variety of improvements in education at Edward Little High School. The primary reason to change to the block was to allow for more student-centered learning, a major shift in instructional strategies. Also, students with different learning styles could be better accommodated because the block would allow three to four different activities to be used to teach a broad concept. This would allow all students to learn more productively. Teachers would be less lecture oriented and would be able to facilitate student learning better. Time would be available to implement long-term projects and cooperative learning. Information and research skills could be developed and taught in the longer time period. Many different paths could be taken to get to the knowledge and skills the curriculum called for.

The second reason to change to the block related to improvements in day-to-day class atmosphere and teacher-student relationships. It was hoped that teachers would have half of the students and preparation to deal with on a daily basis. This would allow teachers more time for personal involvement with each student and more opportunities to troubleshoot learning problems or personal issues. Students would have to deal with only three homework preparations a day rather than six. Class sizes would be lowered, everyone hoped. There would be a better use of the facilities and fewer transitions each day to deal with. This meant more productive time for both students and teachers.

The process of changing to the block is not finished at Edward Little High School. In fact, there is doubt that this process will ever be perfected or completed. Some of the goals have been met by most of the staff. Some came to the block kicking and screaming because they did not want to change after many years of doing things one way. Others jumped in, got the training they needed, and started to make the shift. Administrators have noticed that room layouts have begun to change as different configurations of desks enable students to work in groups. Teachers are developing interesting units in many different subject areas. Students have adjusted to the time frame that allows more activities to occur. The process has only begun, but we are beginning to see a shift to more student-centered learning that we hope will bring with it the skills and improved learning that the block was supposed to facilitate.

LIBRARY MEDIA CENTER

The library media center is committed to providing a relaxed and comfortable work space where students and staff can work, study, research, and learn productively. The collection of materials and resources is intended to support the curriculum and give users the tools they need for research, investigation, and analysis that will enhance their educational experiences. The library media center is open from 7:15 A.M. to 8:00 P.M. four days a week, and until 3:00 P.M. on Fridays. Serving the needs of staff and students is a priority for the library media center staff. There are four people on staff: one professional librarian with a master's degree in library science and three educational technicians, all of whom have a four-year degree. The library media center is centrally located directly across from the main office and the front entrance; it seats approximately sixty-five people. It has a collection of approximately 25,000 books, 4,000 paperbacks, 150 videos, and 20 CD-ROM discs. It subscribes to 61 magazines, 4 daily newspapers, Newsbank, and EBSCO's MAS Full Text Elite indexes on CD-ROM. There are twelve computers available, six of them with Internet and e-mail capabilities.

Prior to block scheduling, the library media center was used by teachers who wanted students to get materials they would need for specific assignments. Sometimes the class would come in when the students needed teacher-directed help in completing an assignment. Most assignments, however, were done outside class, on the students' free time. Study hall access was heavy, and some students used the library media center as a place to meet friends or "get out of study hall." Some did work, but the staff was constantly monitoring students whose need for library services was minimal. Class instruction was informal, and the staff worked mostly on a one-to-one basis with individual students. Students used library resources to write their papers or reports, and sometimes they did group projects. Usually the material found by one student was not shared with the rest of the class and was outside the specific information that the teacher was trying to cover in the class.

When the school switched to block scheduling, the library media center staff were unsure as to how things would change. We were not part of the initial investigations into block scheduling. Basic information about resource-based teaching, cooperative learning, and library research skill development was investigated. Pointers were passed on from other library media specialists in schools already on the block, but nothing formal was done before it was implemented in 1995.

The first year we waited to see what would evolve. Most faculty members were confused and not particularly enthusiastic about the changes they would have to make. Staff development was offered but not mandated, and teachers began to scramble to cover the material they had always covered but in a different time frame. It took several months before teachers began to grasp the concept that they were no longer to *cover* material but to *promote students' learning of it*. Some creative ones were able to let go of their former methods and began to develop lessons around the block. For those who ventured in, there was much trial and error, many successes and some failures. It did not happen overnight. Those who ventured out along with those at Walton who had piloted the program became mentors for the others who were more reluctant to change. Things are still developing, and we have a long way to go.

The first thing that we did in the library media center was restructure how students and teachers could access the library. Before the block, classes came down and students came from study halls, with the emphasis on study hall accessibility. When more teachers began using resource-based teaching and cooperative learning-teaching strategies, it became obvious that we had to have more room for classes and less room for study hall students. We needed to make sure that the computers that had indexes and CD-ROM programs on them were available for research and not being used for word processing. We had to accommodate more people who needed help with research. There was more commotion or activity than when students were studying individually. An increase in computer hardware came simultaneously with the block but not because of it. Fortunately, it allowed us to have more students doing productive research than before. We could still use more computers on our network, and we hope they will be forthcoming. It is obvious that we could use a larger room than we have. That is a long-range goal, but it is not immediately possible.

Our budget totals have not increased with block scheduling. The shift had already begun to spend more on reference materials and databases for research and less on books. The block has affirmed that shift, but to date has not resulted in any more money. The Newsbank and the MAS Full Text Elite periodical indexes are used constantly. Recent access to the Internet has provided students with many more sources of information. This in itself necessitates more time for research and library time. The block plays very well into this type of learning. Because of the block, students have more time to word-process and use the computers for assignments outside class. We have concluded that we need more desktop publishing computers in the library.

The number of library staff has remained constant, and we have found that since the block was implemented, we are serving students and teachers more frequently and in greater detail. We are finding that behind-the-scenes work, that is, cataloging, book orders, weeding, and so forth, is not getting done in a relaxed or orderly way. We are assessing this problem and trying to divide the tasks in a more realistic and productive manner.

The block has required the library staff to facilitate student research in many different ways. They have had to learn how to help students do keyword and Boolean searches needed for using electronic databases and the Internet. Now that students are more self-directed and their assignments are broader based, it is necessary to evaluate each student's needs and facilitate their research more than when the teacher gave them specific tasks or directions. The staff has had to initiate more one-on-one contact with individual students to ensure that they know how to find the most relevant material for their assignment. They have had to improve their skills of discerning where students are and what they need help in doing.

Students doing research and library work during the block have also necessitated a change in the way we handle reserve books and reference materials. Things need to be here in the library media center for students to use. Before the block, reserve books, vertical files, and some reference books could be taken out overnight. Now we are trying to restrict usage to the library or the classroom so they are available for classes at all times and for the hours after school when we are open until 8:00 P.M. Over weekends and long vacations, we do allow students to take some of these materials out. The changes in how students work in a block schedule has also affected the number of students we serve each period and the number of computers that are in use. We can have three classes in the library media center at one time, but with sixty students doing lengthy research, our six database/Internet computers are not sufficient. We are beginning to recognize that we need more working space for students and faculty, more computer access, and more library staff work space. The configuration of our room was not planned around usage needs but by simply opening one classroom up and adding it to the previous space. Future changes will be dictated by the block and should help us with our need for quiet study for those doing traditional reading or writing, group work areas for those working together, and more computer access space for both research and word processing.

The switch to skill-based learning is ongoing. In fact, there is a major shift in that area on a state and national level as we look at learning results and standards in different subject areas. Teaching to the block should improve our ability to meet these new frontiers in education. The library media center will continue to address changes in teaching strategies, students' needs for materials that come from many different sources, and individual student levels of proficiency. The block has certainly enhanced the use of the library media center and the many resources that we have for students.

STAFF DEVELOPMENT

The Auburn school system felt that teaching to the block was dependent on the development of good teaching strategies that could be used with students in any time frame. The switch that had to be made was changing the teachers' mind-set from teacher-centered learning to student-centered learning. Before the block was implemented, the staff development offerings were geared to presentations of varied teaching techniques that could be used when the block was put into place. One presenter, Bruce Wellman, gave workshops on multi-instructional techniques that included cooperative learning, problem solving, and interactive learning. There was an ongoing, reflective practice group that worked on cooperative learning techniques. Several teachers visited other schools that had already implemented the block. They observed, asked questions, and brought the information back to others in the building. These teachers became resources for other teachers who were slower to become comfortable with the block.

When the block was first implemented, staff development time was used by individual departments to work on their curriculum and examine how their content was going to have to be adapted to fit the block schedule. The biggest success came from teachers who embraced the multi-instructional technique concept and were able to shift to the student-centered learning approach. They embraced the concept that student-directed learning would result in the students' learning and retaining what they had learned more readily than when a teacher simply imparts the knowledge for the students to retain. Incorporated in the student-centered learning approach are several other skills, such as problem solving, information skills, and analysis of information skills, that encourage students to make inquiries and learn beyond the school environment. That is what we should be doing as educators, not just imparting a particular piece of knowledge. The teacher has to determine the broad content of what the students learn so that the curriculum is covered. But with the block, students are not confined to specifics; they are free to explore and investigate more. That in itself can be a major challenge to teachers, and that is where the successes of the block come: not being afraid to give students the skills they need to learn all they can learn.

Teachers who found it difficult to let go of individual control of what the students learn and who were not able to vary from the straight lecture teaching technique found the shift to the block the most difficult. It remains for some a philosophical difference, and they have not been successful with the block.

The library media staff were not included in any specific teaching technique workshops. Nevertheless, we had to learn about the block and the philosophical shift that was occurring in the presentation material and the skill development that was supposed to be generated. It fit right into what library media specialists have wanted to do for years. To get students to learn how to investigate a subject, how to find the best sources to substantiate their work, how to evaluate a source, and how to glean material for substance and information have been the objectives of the library skills curriculum for years. With the block came time for students to spend in the library media center to do this kind of work and for their teachers to be there to guide them. It has been gratifying to see students learn and then come back later to attack another subject with search skills they recently mastered.

One teacher in particular has been very successful with the block. She had been an education technology teacher in the Walton School's grade 9 program before she was hired to teach social studies the second year we had implemented the block. She jumped in and was not afraid to use the multi-instructional approaches that she had been taught. She was not tied to the lecture method that inhibited some of the more experienced teachers, nor had she spent several years working with a specific body of knowledge that she felt had to be imparted to her students. That seemed to free her to try new things. In her Maine studies class, she would develop a worksheet or list of questions about a particular era or activity and bring her class to the library media center, where they would spend the block searching through the books we have on the history of Maine. She often knew what they would be finding, but not always, and she was eager to learn right along with them. It was great to see them look in our various sources and struggle to find the best source. Sometimes they experienced failure and realized that we didn't have all their answers and they might have to go to a specialty library or make some phone inquiries.

When we could finally access the Internet, their research got exciting. One day the teacher asked me if we had any information about legislation and how a bill was made. She did not mention that it was her Maine studies class that was coming in, and we assumed she wanted her students to find out how a bill is developed and progresses through the U.S. Congress. When she arrived, we realized had the wrong resources ready for her students. Her students started looking through the Maine books and pamphlets. We started digging in encyclopedias and other reference books that might help. The kids were watching and participating in all this frustration. When we decided to check the Internet, we found on the State of Maine government home page a ten-page document that detailed the process through which a bill becomes law in the state of Maine. The class was impressed with the research, as the adults were.

This teacher has continued to use the library media center and student-centered, resource-based teaching techniques. She is not afraid to structure five broad questions about the major religions of the world and assign a group of students to come to the library to investigate each one. They learn a lot, and so does she. She knows that whatever they uncover for themselves will be retained much longer than her telling them the information. She then has them report out to each other so that others in the class can reflect on what was found. This teacher has truly learned to "teach to the block" by facilitating student learning and by using the library media center as a place for her students to learn how and where to find information.

Staff development is ongoing in our school. Teachers are all at different stages of adapting to the block schedule. The administration is aware of this uneven pattern and is striving to continue to meet the various needs. Workshops on teaching strategies continue. Teachers who are more successful or more comfortable with the block continue to act as mentors for those who are in need of assistance. The library media center staff is working individually with teachers who ask for assistance with individual projects or lessons. We also maintain and order resources that support the subjects and skill development that the curriculum calls for.

CONCLUSION

With block scheduling, the most success has been with teachers who are not afraid to let go of their old teaching strategies and blend them with the new ones that allow their students to work with material in many different ways. Seeing students succeed in a small way becomes an encouragement to the teacher to go one step further into the process. The biggest drawback appears to be the few teachers who are philosophically opposed to the change in teaching strategies that the block calls for. Perhaps those who have begun to integrate the differentiated teaching into their classes will act as encouragement and impetus for the others. Success usually builds on success. Time will tell.

The library media center is excited about the block and is trying to accommodate the increased usage and the constant research by both staff and students. Learning to know just what a student needs for assistance has been a challenge, as has juggling the numbers of classes that want library access. The biggest problems we have are space and budget, both of which need to increase considerably to meet the increased needs of classes and resources. If all the teachers in the building get hooked on resource-based teaching and differentiated instruction, we would not be able to accommodate them. As we approach the ideal called for in block scheduling, we hope to grow to meet it.

EVERGREEN HIGH SCHOOL
Vancouver, Washington

Linda Brake,
Library Media Specialist

GENERAL INFORMATION

Evergreen High School promotes the belief that "all youth can learn and succeed." The mission of the Evergreen School District is to "provide, in concert with the family, a balanced education that challenges and prepares the individual to think, learn, and achieve success in a changing environment." This high school, with approximately 2,000 students in grades 10, 11, and 12, traditionally was on a six-period-day semester system until the 1994–95 school year, when a major change was made. The school now follows a four-period day with one lunch and three trimesters. Each period is 80 minutes long, with 10 minutes of passing time.

The goals of changing to the block are to:

- Allow students to concentrate on fewer subjects each day for longer time frames.
- Personalize and improve staff and student relationships.
- Allow enough time for labs, projects, and in-depth learning.
- Give opportunities to teachers for common and longer planning times.
- Eliminate the number of passing times in the hall so the school would be calmer.
- Allow some tutorial time during a longer lunch.

- Improve instruction and necessitate innovative teaching.
- Reduce stress for students and staff.

Most of these goals have been met. As the student population grew, it has been difficult to give teachers common planning time. Many teachers have tried innovative teaching under the block, but some are still using lecture as the basis for their instruction.

Evergreen High School formed a restructuring committee to study the block, and it met for two years prior to making the change. They consulted and studied the literature and research, and visited other schools that were already using the block. They read material issued by the Coalition of Essential Schools, including *Horace's Compromise* by Ted Sizer. I was on the committee both years and was co-chair the first year. Surveys were given to parents, students, and staff to obtain opinions about the change. Parents were also invited to evening meetings that explained the change. Staff voted to adopt block scheduling at the end of the second year of study.

LIBRARY MEDIA CENTER

The Evergreen district goal for library media centers is to support and enrich teaching and learning. Students use the library media center resources to locate, evaluate, and utilize information to explore ideas in greater depth from varying points of view and in a variety of formats. They also use the media center resources to strengthen literacy skills and explore a wide variety of literature.

The collection consists of 14,000 books and 120 periodical subscriptions. The library media center is networked and has access to the Internet and over a dozen CD-ROM databases. In 1993–94, 9,240 items were checked out. Two years later, 7,868 were circulated. I believe that this reduction was not a result of the block schedule but of the ability of students to find the information they need from digital resources.

The media center seats eighty students. Prior to the block, orientation, book talks, and media instruction were emphasized with sophomores through their English classes. Social studies students in the Current World Problems class did a major research paper in sociology, psychology, or economics. Individuals and groups used the library for research, as did classes that were scheduled as needed.

Class use decreased with block scheduling. During the 1993–94 year, 609 classes were scheduled into the library media center. During the 1995–96 year, 452 classes were booked in under the four-period day. In 1996–97 there were 482 classes that reserved space. Class use numbers decreased under the new system, but library staff feel the center is just as busy. Where possible, the 80-minute block is split into two 40-minute blocks to accommodate more classes. Teachers can sign up for half a block (40 minutes) with the understanding that if no other class requests to use the library during the same block, the class may extend its stay through the entire block if needed. Study hall usage was not affected with the change to block scheduling because there had not been study halls at Evergreen High School for over fifteen years.

Teachers are allowed to send up to five students per class on a pass to work in the media center. The use of the center by individuals and groups increased dramatically under the four-period day, but without an exit counter, I had no way to track these statistics. This year, the staff is keeping a tally on the number of students who come into the media center on passes, and it is averaging well over 1,000 per month. With the longer blocks of time, teachers are designing 20- to 30-minute activities for students, so group use continues to increase. This means more library staff time is spent checking passes of students as they enter. The change also means that the library can be full of students, with each group working on something different, but with no teachers to help with supervision.

A common lunch time for almost 2,000 students created its own issues for the library media center. With the whole student body at lunch at the same time, some changes had to be made in lunch supervision. More students now come to the library media center during part of their lunch, thus requiring two staff to be on duty at all times. Staff are vigilant about banning food and drink from the library during lunch. The cafeteria can seat only about 800, and so the remaining students are eating everywhere in the building. The litter problem is significant.

In preparing for block scheduling, the expectation for the media center was that students would be doing more project-based work and more cooperative learning. This would affect the media center and audiovisual department with an increase in small-group use and a variety of projects beyond the traditional research paper. There were no budget changes for the library media center since the budget is based on a per pupil expenditure at the school.

The media center has had an automated circulation system with Follett for over five years, and the school was networked about the same time it went to the block. The district also approved a technology bond during this time. Teachers have telephones and computers in each classroom. The technology is very important to the implementation of block scheduling. Students are working on so many different projects, and they need access to computers for word processing, information databases, CD-ROMs, and the Internet. The Audio-Visual Department saw a great increase in Power-Point presentations, video editing, slide shows, and so forth. Teachers and media staff began using e-mail as the preferred method to communicate and to book classes into the library media center. The photocopying service of the library media center is very popular, although there has been a noticeable shift to an increased use of computer printing. Both the copying and printing use require significant staff time.

In 1993–94 the library media center had one certified school media specialist and one adult clerical aide. The audiovisual area had one certified specialist and one technician. Due to a change of policy, staffing is currently one certified library media specialist, two clerical aides, and two audiovisual technicians. The block was a large part of the motivation for this change. More teachers began expecting students to do multimedia presentations, which require more coordination between the library and the audiovisual staff. The increased research by groups also requires more staff help with keyword searching, printing, and downloading computer information.

For the first two years of the block, the staff consisted of one media specialist, one clerical worker, and one extra lunch adult supervisor. It was so busy that a strong case was made for an extra support staff position. Last year, an additional person was added full time, which freed the library media specialist to spend more time working with teachers and doing instruction rather than running the photocopier and fixing printers. Support staff did not change their job description in a major way under the block, but student supervision became more important with fewer teacher-directed classes scheduled and more small groups coming to the library media center.

Support staff needed to be in on the reasons for changing to block scheduling. I communicate information from the restructuring committee to the media staff to keep them up-to-date on all school programs during staff meetings.

The media center uses two student aides each period. Under the six-period system, we had twelve aides. We kept to the two students per period, but now have only eight aides, so the tasks have been structured to accommodate fewer helpers. Student aides have to be trained three times a year under the trimester system rather than two times a year with semesters. We sometimes feel that we just get one group trained, and it is time to start all over with a new group. The media center has had a harder time getting enough student aides to fill the positions. Some students seem worried that they will not have enough room in their schedule for aide jobs under the four-block day.

STAFF DEVELOPMENT

The teachers had a number of in-service sessions and training during staff meetings to get ready for block scheduling. Instruction in cooperative learning, critical thinking skills, and multiple intelligence training was given. Some outside instructors were brought in, and some teaching was done by district staff. After-school classes were also offered for college credit. I took one of the classes, Teaching in a Coalition Classroom, which stressed the teacher as mentor and the student as learner. One of the faculty members did her education master's thesis on strategies to be successful in the block, and she produced a booklet with the results of her research. All staff received a copy of this booklet and were divided into study groups to discuss the information. The booklet included information on research on restructuring, suggestions for pacing learning in an 80-minute block, varying activity samples, information on learning styles, critical thinking, cooperative learning, and the instructional process. Support staff were also given some training in these areas. Many staff meetings were held to give people a chance to ask questions and voice concerns before the final decision was made to change to the block. I felt the administration did a good job of preparing the community for this major change in the school day.

The best way to train media staff for the block is to make sure they are included in all general staff training. I also found it helpful to be a member of LM_NET, where I could read the postings of others who had similar situations. It was useful to go into classrooms and give book talks or give computer instruction. It gave me a chance to see how long 80 minutes can be!

Staff development needs to be ongoing. We all need information on the latest in learning research and reminders to use strategies that we know work but that we tend to ignore in favor of the old, comfortable methods of instruction. I still use lecture too much when I instruct a class in the use of the Internet and the evaluation of web pages. It seems to take more time to incorporate cooperative learning into instruction, but I am trying.

Evergreen High School has begun Critical Friends groups this year: groups of eight to ten teachers who meet several times a month and observe each other in the classroom. The goal is to discuss ways to improve teaching and learning. In the library, teachers have always observed my lessons, and I am picking up some good ideas for my own teaching by visiting art, science, music, and vocational classes. I am also getting more specific feedback from teachers who observe my teaching.

CURRICULUM AND INSTRUCTION

The library media staff have noticed increased use of the reference and reserve collections since changing to four periods each day. Students are doing more supplementary research on topics studied in class, and they want basic information, but not necessarily a whole book. The curriculum seems to be more project based under block scheduling. This will become even more pronounced in two years when Evergreen requires senior projects for graduation. There is more hands-on learning. Teachers are also aligning the curriculum more carefully so that the same thing is not taught in three different classes. The whole district is undertaking the large project of writing frameworks and outcomes for each subject area. I am on the committee to work on the media frameworks, and this has made me aware that there is not always a good flow from elementary to junior high to high school with the curriculum. Under the block, it is less likely there will be a huge range of courses that used to make up the "shopping mall" high school curriculum. Students must first master speaking, reading, and writing skills before they are offered classes such as film study or advanced Shakespeare.

There is a great deal more use of cooperative learning in the classrooms than before, although this is not entirely due to the block. Cooperative learning is being emphasized by our district for all schools. I still do many book talks and some classroom instruction. For example, during Banned Books Week, I talk to several classes about selection of library books and the process for challenging a book in the district. I also instruct as requested for specialized units, such as Vietnamese literature, library orientation, keyword search, and Internet lessons.

WHAT WORKS BEST?

The longer period gives more flexibility for library research. Groups and individuals are coming and going all day long, and they are all working on different topics.

Drawbacks of Block Scheduling

Library staff do more supervision and checking of library passes under the block. When the teacher comes with the whole class and all are working on the same basic topic, the supervision by the staff is minimal. When five or six are coming in from classes all over the school, the supervisory duties increase. We have noticed that it is harder to get student library aides each period under the block. With the trimester system, we just get student aides trained and then the trimester is over.

The library media staff sometimes feel overwhelmed with the number of different research projects going on at once. Finally, the photocopier and computer printers seem to be going nonstop all day and require a lot of maintenance and supervision by the staff.

Successes Because of Block Scheduling

The school has become calmer, and there seem to be fewer disruptions, fights, and other difficulties. Students like the longer lunch period, and many are using part of this time for tutorials with staff or to study in the library media center. The teaching staff are happier with a longer preparation and a longer lunch; library staff, however, do not get a longer lunch.

More students are doing projects and choosing areas of interest to study. The curriculum is being examined more carefully and is being aligned.

Staff are using a variety of information-gathering techniques beside lecture and this includes library use.

Under the block, students can stay longer in the library media center to finish a research project. Staff seem to be using my services as an information consultant more frequently.

ADVICE AND RECOMMENDATIONS

Media specialists who are working at schools considering block scheduling should be sure they are involved in all the prior planning. I would not have gotten extra lunch help if I had not been on the restructuring committee. Specialists should also gather statistics before the change is made so they have a basis for comparison with their statistics afterward. Circulation and class use statistics, printer use, and so forth may change dramatically under block scheduling. I advise library media specialists to record all their observations carefully during the first year of change and include these in monthly reports to administrators. It is important to document needs, problems, and successes. Library media specialists in schools considering change should also gather and read all pertinent information about block scheduling from research, periodicals, and other schools. Visits to block schools in the area are very helpful.

Generally the teachers at Evergreen High School like the block schedule. They now have a longer preparation period and fewer students to deal with each day. The whole school seems calmer with fewer hall passing times. The library media staff also see advantages to the four-period day, and they have attempted to adjust the staffing and collection to meet the changed needs.

I do not know that I would have done anything differently to prepare for the block. There are always surprises once a school actually changes, and no amount of study can get you ready for everything.

KINGSWOOD REGIONAL HIGH SCHOOL
Wolfeboro, New Hampshire

Karen Libby,
School Media Specialist

GENERAL SCHOOL INFORMATION

Kingswood Regional High School, located in Wolfeboro, New Hampshire, is a four-year school, grades 9 through 12, with a population of 819 students and 56 staff members. This school adopted block scheduling in 1995, and it uses a modified 4 × 4 schedule. In 1997–98, the first-year foreign language classes, some ninth-grade English classes, and American government for tenth grade went back to 45-minute periods. This helps the band schedule. It also became apparent that some learners, especially ninth graders, needed some classes for the full year. The school is trying to use more applied learning situations. I believe it is too soon to tell if the majority of the school population is succeeding in creating independent learners who will possess real skills. More teachers are attempting this type of methodology because of block scheduling, and some have been successful. The block scheduling committee is in the process of developing an assessment tool to evaluate the success of block scheduling.

Two years prior to going to block scheduling, a committee was formed to study this innovative practice. Visits were made to schools that already had block scheduling. I participated in one such visit. Teachers were encouraged to participate in staff development opportunities that focused on block scheduling. A few in-house in-service sessions were offered. At the same time the district was midway through the process of developing a strategic plan. This restructuring endeavor should have been embraced as a vehicle to develop curriculum that used the block-scheduling time allotments and integrative study practices. Unfortunately, the majority of faculty did not seize this opportunity and considered the work being done on developing benchmarks, performance tasks, and resource-based educational modules (units) as additional burdens. A great opportunity was missed that would have altered the perception that block scheduling is more than a time change but a real paradigm shift in delivery of content and instruction. The library media specialist at that time was not on the committee, but the following year, the new library media specialist (myself) joined the staff and the block scheduling committee. As a new member to the staff, I performed research and reported results, and I assisted teachers in identifying instructional strategies and resources for the transition. I collected and added resources to the library media center's circulating and professional collection that would be valuable for the transition. I have a background in elementary education, so my experience with holistic learning gave me an advantage in being able to see the big picture.

LIBRARY MEDIA CENTER

Our mission statement follows:

The library media center at Kingswood Regional High School supports the philosophy and the goals of the high school. The mission of the Library media center is to ensure that students and staff are effective users of ideas and information. The school library media program provides a wide range of resources and information that satisfy the educational needs and interests of students. The library media center is the laboratory where students may explore, more fully, classroom subjects that interest them, expand their imagination, delve into areas of personal interest, and develop the ability to think clearly, critically, and creatively.

The school library media center provides a setting where students develop skills they will need as adults to locate, analyze, evaluate, interpret and communicate information and ideas in an information rich world. Students are encouraged to realize their potential as informed citizens who think critically and solve problems, to observe rights and responsibilities relating to the generation and flow of information and ideas, and to appreciate the value of literature in an educated society.

I was the library media specialist at Kingswood Regional High School for only one year prior to block scheduling, and due to the efforts of the previous specialist, the library media center was beginning to become a learning laboratory. Classroom teachers were beginning to schedule time in the library media center for projects, but the library media specialist did not plan consistently with teachers or participate in instruction. Students were allowed access from study hall if there were no classes scheduled.

Prior to block scheduling with seven classes per day, it was usual to schedule one class each period in the library media center and to close the room to other classes and to study halls. With only four classes per day, it became apparent that frequently two classes would need to use the facilities simultaneously. The library media center consists of a large (2,944 square feet) room, three small (300 square feet) rooms, and an office area. The large room houses the main body of the print collection and has a seating capacity of sixty-six students, including six individual study carrels and a computer bank that accommodates nineteen students. I needed to divide the room so that we would be able to accommodate two classes of active learners, as well as students who were in the library media center for independent study. I created three areas divided by low bookshelves. Because there was no increase in budget, the collection did not change drastically, and there was no additional staff.

The block scheduling planning committee did not consider that there would be a great impact on the library media center since at the time, its role had not been an issue. There was no defined role for the library media center in anticipation of the block scheduling change. The budget has not increased beyond the normal increments of 5 percent.

Through grant funding, there has been a marked increase in the technology available in the library media center in the past three years, mostly due to my involvement on the technology task force, a visionary planning committee. The use of the library media center has increased so dramatically that it has become the center of the school for instructional technology. The use of technology with block scheduling has become a natural integrated learning strategy in most content areas. Students have the time to explore the Internet and practice and complete Boolean searching with CD-ROM databases. They can express the results of their research using different applications as well as presentation software. I do not believe that the change to block scheduling is the reason for the increased acquisition of technology, but because it is available to students, the increased use of technology is apparent.

The library media center is scheduled four blocks a day, with two and sometimes three classes per block. During the first year, many classes were scheduled because teachers were anxious about having enough transitions in their class to fill 90 minutes. I offered to assist in applied learning situations, so most teachers felt comfortable with a team teaching approach. I volunteered to work with many disciplines in curriculum R-BEM writing. This Results-Based Education Model is an outcomes-based program that unifies instruction, learning and assessment. It ensured an integrated information problem-solving component to be collaboratively planned and taught. Again, it is difficult to determine whether this type of planning would have occurred without the development of the strategic plan when there was a forced element of curriculum revision going on. There is more contact time and an emphasis on applied learning. Therefore, the library program has shifted emphasis to more in-depth development of process and synthesis than access and product.

The support staff in the library media center consists of a full-time library associate who has ten years' experience at the high school and a 10-hour-per-week assistant whose duties are primarily clerical. There was no preparation for my trusted and invaluable associate. I would share the information I gleaned, and I took her questions with me on a visit to a library media center with block scheduling. Her flexibility and highly organized approach have eased the operational procedures into this change. I believe that the support staff need to participate in visits to library media centers that are using block scheduling. Observing various methods and organizations will allow for easier troubleshooting when problems occur. It is valuable to have time to prepare as a group for and evaluate the change process.

STAFF DEVELOPMENT

Prior to the transition, teachers were advised to visit schools with block scheduling. Research was collected and disseminated, and a committee was formed to investigate concerns and problems. Speakers were invited to discuss the philosophy, but little was done concerning the strategies necessary to compact curriculum and deliver content. A partnership was developed in the first year of block scheduling with five other schools in New Hampshire that are similar in size and were in the first or second year of restructuring. Several times that year, facilitators were hired and workshops given for all the teachers of a particular discipline to attend.

I do not feel that any staff development I received prepared me specifically for block scheduling. Curriculum development and the work on the strategic plan were helpful for me to develop a perspective of the student expectations in each discipline. It enabled me to create a thread of information problem-solving skills in many units of various disciplines. The visits provided me ideas for creative scheduling and maintenance, but I was not involved in any workshops to prepare for the transition. The reason for this may be my confidence that this was necessary and appropriate. I had no anxiety over the transition; therefore, my principal did not suggest that I attend.

I believe that our faculty should have had more training prior to the transition. Many still do not understand applied learning and other instructional strategies that would enhance student learning. The focus is on time versus learning. An instructional practices task force has been developed that researches, reports on, and recommends instructional practices and their applications. I believe that this group should create mentors to assist teachers who are having difficulty adjusting to block scheduling. I am not sure how or why staff development would be different for library media specialists. The preparation of school librarians is more holistic and process oriented than for most high school teachers, so it is easier for us to adapt. Library media specialists are not stuck on content; we do not have ownership of pieces of knowledge but rather discover excitement in the quest of answers to all the unasked questions. Staff development for library media specialists may need to focus on the expansion of the role of the instructional consultant, our critical role in this period of transition.

CURRICULUM

Our school district has been undergoing a restructuring process that began about the same time as the block scheduling (perceived as a time change versus pedagogical change). Curriculum alignment and revision was not addressed because of block scheduling. Resource-based education was being implemented regardless of the amount of time teachers had in their day. In some instances, block scheduling reaped the benefits of developing process and applied learning activities due to the strategic plan development. Kingswood Regional High School made a commitment to keep block scheduling for three years and then as a staff reevaluate its effectiveness. The arguments against block scheduling all have to do with time; curriculum has only been affected due to the development of the strategic plan. I seized this opportunity to integrate information problem-solving skills and assessment tools in many units of instruction. Essentially the library media center instructional strategies have remained the same. Block scheduling has improved the potential for students to practice skills and gain real understanding of practice so that eventually these skills will become habit.

INSTRUCTION

Ideally delivery of curriculum in a 90-minute block should have three transitions. Students should have the opportunity to practice what they have been instructed. I have found that the library media center has become the laboratory to test new knowledge. Teachers send individual students to the library media center with a research question or information problem-solving endeavor. This is the perfect time to test prior knowledge and preparedness. Preplanning, feedback, and communication with the classroom teacher is important so the collaborative process evolves. There is more time for students to develop an understanding of the process of research, experience each step, synthesize results, and evaluate information. The depth of instruction should be increased while some content needs to be covered in self-directed searches. The library media specialist needs to know the teacher's expectations in order to extend the classroom to the library media center. In 90 minutes teachers are able to recognize students as individuals and address learning styles and multiple intelligences. Creating a flexible classroom and utilizing the library media center as a learning lab and the library media specialist as a team teacher demonstrate the intent of block scheduling.

THE BEST OF BLOCK SCHEDULING AT
KINGSWOOD REGIONAL HIGH SHOOL

The Social Studies Department has embraced block scheduling. It has created many resource-based units with various methods of assessment to evaluate student proficiency. One semester of study has compromised the scope of content, yet the depth of understanding of essential concepts has flourished. Students know more than dates; they understand why and how. The department has organized content thematically and forces students to construct meaning with a real depth of understanding. Students are responsible for their learning and individual projects with demonstrable outcomes measured. In the third year of block scheduling, the Social Studies Department has integrated with the English Department for a one-year, 90-minute block of study for American studies. This is the essence of the best of using block scheduling to restructure education.

DRAWBACKS

Other departments are reluctant to give up content. In some cases, block scheduling impedes the ability of teachers to cover every unit of study. Some teachers resent curriculum compacting or revision and have doubled the work that students complete so that they can finish the book in one semester. I believe this is the proof that we should have taken more time to restructure and revise curriculum before changing the schedule. I understand that there is a concern that students will not be prepared for the SAT or ACT depending on the test dates and students' schedules. For some students, 90 minutes in one class such as algebra is very difficult. The time lapse between foreign languages is found to be undesirable; it is felt too much time must be spent on review. Systemic change has not occurred. The philosophy and pedagogical benefits of block scheduling are not understood or embraced by everyone at Kingswood Regional High School. As with evolution of ideas to species, the trickle-down (or -up) effect disrupts life and systems and causes far-reaching paradigm shifts and shock waves. Slow-moving educational reform may encumber innovative schools with block scheduling to compete in the standardized testing realm.

LIBRARY MEDIA CENTER SUCCESSES

The use and integration of technology into curriculum and learning has been facilitated by block scheduling. The *process* of information problem solving versus collecting information sources has become recognized and implemented. Students are synthesizing and evaluating information with guidance. They are able to explore and experiment in the library media center without the pressure of time. Their skills are developed and refined, and process often leads to impressive product. The library media specialist is often sought after to become a collaborator and team member because our expertise is relied on and respected. My work with the Social Studies Department to create units of study that incorporate and validate independent problem-solving skills to create lifelong learning habits has been the apex of success for the library media program.

CONCERNS

Initially some of the use of the library media center was unwarranted. Teachers, anxious about filling time, would schedule time in the library media center that was unneeded without learner expectations. The library media center would be filled with sixty students who had nothing to do. It was chaotic! Conflicts still arise over scheduling the library media center as a classroom. With only four blocks per day, teachers need to be flexible about sending students who need to access information rather than bringing a whole class. It has become difficult to juggle student and teacher needs. Burnout of the library media specialist and staff is very real. I do not have a planning period and do not close for lunch. It is energizing to see the learning that occurs in the library media center yet exhausting to be the facilitator for so many learners. My hope is that with time, independent learning behaviors will become habit, and my role will be more in the background. The increased teaching time has an effect on the time spent organizing, selecting, and disseminating the library media center collection. The addition of technology has greatly affected the access to information and has added many troubleshooting headaches to my day. I have asked for but not been given increased staffing in the last three years. Educating teachers will relieve some of the pressures of the library media staff.

ADVICE

I have an excellent library media center program, and the staff and administration realize that it is the hub of the school and learning process. This success is due to serendipitous timing.

It is important to be involved in the planning of block scheduling from the beginning. The library media specialist must gain respect from faculty and administrators. The education of school librarians focuses on applied learning practices and integration, so we have a jump-start on many teachers. We need to convey our confidence and support to our faculty.

If curriculum reform is part of the process, volunteer to collaborate with content teachers to ensure integration of information problem-solving skills. Offer assistance with resource and applied learning situations. Be involved in the staff workshops and visits. At times the library media specialist's participation is overlooked, but it is necessary to experience what our peers are experiencing. Look for creative ways to schedule the library media center and to use space. Work toward increasing your budget and staffing. The total number of students you serve is not increasing, but the volume using the library media center at one time may be. The most important piece of advice I can offer is to volunteer to help write curriculum, to collaborate, and to team teach.

Teacher training and curriculum revision should be the focus of planning for this reform movement. Unfortunately, most faculty members are concerned with the time versus the learning. To begin this process again, I would be more organized and firm concerning the library media center use from the start. I was caught trying to facilitate too many students at one time and trying to accommodate every teacher request. This led to a tired librarian and frustrated students and teachers. I am thankful for the realization that the library media program is essential to the success of block scheduling and that I did not allow this resource to be overlooked.

East Lyme High School
East Lyme, Connecticut

Marie Keen Shaw,
Library Media Specialist

East Lyme High School is located in a shoreline town on Long Island Sound. East Lyme has long supported both commercial fishing and recreation, and Niantic Bay scallops are famous for their delectable quality. The summer population of East Lyme doubles in size due to the beautiful

beaches, boating, and recreational opportunities. The town serves as a
bedroom community to employees of major industrial sites in other towns
in the county. East Lyme is proud of its schools, and a large percentage of
our graduates further their education after high school.

Approximately 75 percent of our student population of 989 students live
in East Lyme; the remaining 25 percent live in the adjacent community of
Salem. A cooperative agreement exists between the two towns that desig-
nates East Lyme High School as Salem's school of choice.

East Lyme High School adopted block scheduling in September 1995 after two years of study. A common theme among the faculty was that we
never seemed to have enough time to conduct learning in the way that we
knew was right for our students. Our day was segmented into eight periods of 39 minutes each. There was barely enough time to introduce a concept before the bell rang and students were off to their next class. We had
an eight-period day in order to be a comprehensive high school with
strong academic offerings as well as a wide variety of electives. The day
was broken down into eight small bits so students could take advantage of
an enriched curriculum. But there were too many transitions and disruptions in this traditional schedule.

A study team formed in November 1995 attended a Coalition of Essential Schools conference in Chicago. This group included the principal, a
science teacher, a math teacher, a family and consumer life teacher, a social
studies teacher, the library media specialist, and a parent. Although no one
in the group suggested that our school become a CES school, we did like
what we learned about how block scheduling, process-oriented learning,
and performance assessment could restructure a high school. The conclusion of every member of the team after the conference was that East Lyme
High School was ripe to change to block scheduling. The team became the
basis for the planning committee to research and guide the staff to a decision about the block.

It was determined that the alternating-day, or A/B, format would be appropriate for our school. Because we already offered eight periods, it was
simple to cut the day in two and offer half the courses on alternating days.
It also was a comfort to us that if block scheduling failed, we could easily
go back to our old schedule without negatively affecting students. The
A/B format also relieved any anxiety about state standardized testing, AP
exams, SATs, and other tests because the curriculum is continuous during
the entire school year for one-credit courses. Half-credit courses are still
carried over a semester, as they had always been.

Our faculty and students are satisfied with block scheduling. We are
now undergoing a major construction and renovation project, and many
of the architectural designs were made primarily to accommodate
students in a block schedule, such as expanding the cafeteria so all students can eat at once and providing a large learning hall where students
can collaborate and meet over their studies. There is no indication that

teachers would prefer the old schedule or change to any other type of block schedule.

It was important for the library media specialist to be a member of the block scheduling planning team. Not only could I provide research and information to the faculty, but I could advocate for the kinds of technologies, staffing, and acquisitions that would be necessary for students to be successful with resource-based learning. By being a member of the team, my administration was very receptive to preparing the library media center for its important role in a block-scheduled high school.

LIBRARY MEDIA CENTER

The facility was recently officially named the Frances Hart Ewers Library Media Center, dedicated to a former English teacher who drew her everyday wisdom from her love of reading and literature. She also was one of the first promoters and users of technology in our school, thus making it fitting that she is permanently remembered in this way.

The philosophy of the Frances Hart Ewers Library reads:

The library media program supports student learning by providing up-to-date technology, multimedia, and print materials. By the end of twelfth grade, students will know how to find and utilize information and technology for acquiring content knowledge, communicating information and ideas, and solving problems. Life long reading skills for all students will be reinforced through quality literature.

Program goals are numerous and drive the day-to-day purpose of serving students and staff:

- The library media center will provide a wide range of educational technologies for students to conduct research, communicate information and ideas, secure materials through resource sharing, create original works, organize data, and solve problems.
- Students will apply the skills necessary to locate, evaluate, interpret, and synthesize information from print, nonprint, and electronic sources.
- Students will use technology to enhance essential skills and facilitate learning in content areas.
- The library media center and its materials will support instructional and curriculum changes due to block scheduling.
- The library media center will support interdisciplinary teaching.
- The library media center will support the East Lyme Technology Plan, "Target on Technology."
- The library media center will offer professional development opportunities to the staff to refine their information and educational technology skills in areas of changing curricula and personal growth.

- The library media center will provide and continually update a diverse collection of materials that represents various points of view on current and historical issues and provide quality literature for personal and required reading.

- The library media center will provide materials and opportunities to support the school-to-career initiative.

- The library media center will support the school requirement of a major research paper or writing assignment for each course offered.

On a recent Blue Ribbon application, the question was asked, "As students and teachers engage in active learning, how are resources made available for gathering information and sharing the results of their work?" Here is how we answered this question about our library media program and services:

This high school is recognized as a leader in our state for its exemplary library media center. Staff are encouraged to join professional activities both in and out of state. Ten years ago the high school library and the town public library received joint funding to become part of Libraries Online, a nonprofit organization of twenty college, public, and school libraries that share a computer system for the purposes of individual library management and resource sharing among the member institutions. By participating in this endeavor, students have access to an enormous variety of materials, and all citizens share in the local resources of the town.

In addition to belonging to a resource sharing consortium, the library subscribes to other on-line information sources including eight Internet connections, EBSCO Mas Elite, and the Electric Library. As of July 1, 1997 there were 1,451 registered patrons. The collection has 38,617 items, of which approximately 8,000 are back issues of periodicals. In the 1996–97 school year, 21,777 items were used or searched within the library. Actual items that were checked out in circulation numbered 11,349 or over 10 items per patron. Having the ability to borrow books from other libraries is critical to having appropriate materials for all students, and, during 1996–97, over 1,000 books were secured for students through interlibrary loans. Over 200 books from the high school collection were lent, in return, to citizens throughout the state.

There are eight networked computers in the library, six Pentium processors and two 486's, all with CD-ROM capability. There are two dedicated on-line public access computers (PACs) for searching the catalog databases of our school and those of the other members of Libraries Online. Also, on-line access to the majority of automated databases in the state can be obtained instantaneously through the PACs.

Ninety magazine subscriptions, along with five daily newspapers, are available to users. There is a professional library and an extensive retrospective periodical collection that can be accessed through microfiche holdings. The audiovisual collection includes kits, slides, and videotapes; however, our membership in LEARN, a regional educational resource center, gives teachers and students access to a full lending library of multimedia, computer software, and film with weekly delivery.

Students have access to the library before and after school. During the school day no passes are required: students simply sign in and sign out. The library staff successfully supports the initiatives of the block schedule by offering a flexible environment to as many students and teachers as possible within a given block. On any given day, as many as 450–500 students use the library facilities during class time.

Prior to block scheduling, the Frances Hart Ewers Library was well used by the students. On a daily basis, classes reserved room to use the facility, and simultaneously up to thirty students were permitted to come in lieu of study hall. The level of support was broad but for the majority of students did not have depth. For example, in the 39-minute periods that we were working under, a teacher could take attendance, go over homework, and explain the day's assignment in 10 minutes. It could easily absorb another 5 minutes to move twenty-five students from the classroom to the library media center. That left 24 minutes for any instruction by me, finding materials, and so forth. Meaningful note taking could occur only on the second or third visit. It was very frustrating to prepare the students to do research, only to be interrupted by the bell that sent the students to their next 39-minute class.

Study hall students were mine for 39 minutes, whether they had work to do or not. Because all study halls were structured and did not permit socialization, students competed to be in the library where they could meet their friends. It was a constant struggle to have these students buy into an academic reason to be in the room, and often a disciplinary referral resulted, much to both the students' and my frustration. Much time was taken up by the staff's tracking students and their passes. And we did this eight times a day.

I was on the building planning team for block scheduling, so I had the opportunity to evaluate the existing level of service and support and contrast it to what we wanted to happen under block scheduling. There were many changes we were looking to have occur with restructuring. Aside from the school climate and transitional changes, we knew from our research that the block could give us more instructional time per subject. It would provide the opportunity for teachers to use differentiated instruction, which would include cooperative and collaborative learning. At the same time, individual instruction could be enhanced because the teacher would have fewer students per day. It would also provide more choice for students in their educational program and how they could approach their own learning. This control that they would have would affect the library media center greatly because they were given, in degrees, freedom to determine sometimes the process, and often the product, of their learning.

The administration was extremely interested in seeing that the library media program advance the instructional and curricular goals we were formulating. Not only was the materials budget increased, but an additional part-time library media specialist position (.6) was created because we knew that the resources would be stretched if we could accomplish even a fraction of our goals. At the same time block scheduling was implemented, I accepted the position of curriculum instructional leader for five school departments, including the library media center. This position would take approximately a block a day of my time; therefore although there was a gain in staffing, the overall new professional staffing was in net to the program a little more than .2 of a position.

A humorous aside on my persistence in bringing the library media center to the forefront occurred in June 1995 prior to our beginning the block in September. A group of teachers and the principal went to speak to a faculty in a neighboring high school about our research and preparation for the block. We had recently been told that all budgets for the coming year would have 25 percent withheld due to financial constraints. I was frustrated that at a time when I knew we would need to purchase as many books as we could, the budget would be less.

During his presentation my principal mentioned that the library media center would need to purchase an even larger number of books under block scheduling. At the break, I reminded him of what he had said and was told that when we got back to school, he would restore the book budget by 25 percent. Needless to say, I followed my principal back to school that afternoon, and he made good on his promise. The book budget has been exempt from any reductions since we instituted block scheduling.

The Frances Hart Ewers Library Media Center had a well deserved reputation of being in the forefront of technology. In the mid-1980s, through the support of the superintendent, a library improvement plan for K–12 was developed by the three district media specialists. As part of our proposal, we received funding for online databases at the secondary schools, and the high school, through a cooperative grant, joined a consortium together for circulation and resource sharing.

We have improved our use of technology over the past ten years. Our limitation, like so many other schools, is not our enthusiasm or creative educational uses, but the budgetary constraints we are under. Nevertheless, we are in an excellent position with a major construction and renovation project at our fingertips that will result in our library media center's doubling in size, and it will be outfitted with state-of-the-art technologies.

The changes that have resulted in our changing to the block have been dramatic and subtle. The most dramatic change is the caliber of research that students are now doing and the higher level of thinking they must perform as they use a wide variety of information sources. No longer do we see the same research project again and again. Teachers are extremely creative and have been given the freedom to experiment and try new ideas. They are also much more collaborative as professionals, and good ideas are freely shared within and between departments. This new approach is invigorating and energizing because the library media program supports so many of these new initiatives. Another change is the pace.

What once was a very busy, productive room now *never* stops. Is it because of the block, or the technology, or the combination of both? I don't know if one drives the other, but the result is that the resources and staff have to be "on" every moment of the day. Most of the time this is fine, but occasionally it is frustrating that work doesn't get done in a timely manner or a staff member cannot be as thorough as she would like.

There was no formal training of the library support staff for block scheduling, and if I could do things over, this is one area that I would have done differently. I would have spent the time sharing my research and observations about how the block would change us, and I would have made contact for them with paraprofessionals in blocked schools. Over the years, I have tried to communicate daily to the staff the type of assignments students would be embarking on and the expectations of their teachers. The staff has access to a daily scheduling sheet, which they often consult to know what to expect in the upcoming block. The demand for services of the library has dramatically increased, and the staff have felt the impact, from interlibrary loan to supporting the LAN. Unfortunately support staff were not included in the excellent professional development workshops on differentiated instruction, curriculum development, and strategies for teaching in the block. They have not visited other schools that use a block schedule, nor do they have a network of peers outside the building in other libraries to question or commiserate with for exchanging ideas or garnishing support. Our high school was one of the first in the state to use block scheduling, so even in our geographic area, people come to us for the answers. It would be very beneficial if there were a formal networking group for support staff of block-scheduled libraries to exchange methodologies and ideas.

Because I cover staff development, curriculum, and instruction in other chapters, I will skip to the last questions of the case study format.

What works best in our school with block scheduling? The relationships students and teachers now have are the most important improvement with block scheduling. The classroom environment has changed to one that is far more collaborative, and teachers and students are partners in learning. This carries over to the library media center. I am often engaged in helping a student pursue an area of knowledge new to both the student and myself. The depth of the inquiry gives us all the impetus to stretch our minds and resources to understand issues and draw conclusions.

What are the drawbacks? There are two issues that need resolution. First, our school is too small for the student population and the type of learning environment we need to have to maximize the potential of the block. Many teachers move from room to room to teach, and most teachers do not have their own classrooms for use during their planning period. This will be corrected with a new facility, to be completed by the year 2000. On this road to completion, there will be even more stress as school carries on amid this major project. It will get worse before it gets better, but the result will be an educational facility that will be equipped to meet the educational challenges of the new millennium.

The second issue is a common one to many schools, and that has to do with funding. Although our school enjoys an excellent reputation, in the most recent figures from the Connecticut State Department of Education, it ranked far below most high schools in Connecticut in per pupil spending. The low allocation requires teachers and administrators to be very frugal at a time when we are encouraging our staff to create new instructional methodologies and activities more conducive to learning in the block. To the credit of our staff, our students do very well when compared to other schools, but like any other institution that is underfunded, there are resulting stresses in a time when we should be concentrating solely on curriculum and instructional changes.

What are the successes in the library media center because of block scheduling? We have experienced many successes in the library media center because of block scheduling, and most have already been written about in this book. In summary, areas that saw marked improvement are:

- An increase in teacher and student expectations and reliance on library media services. Our patrons expect more support from the staff, materials, and technologies because the teachers have redefined what is important in the curriculum with block scheduling. Our teachers have designed new, exciting, and engaging learning activities for students that require the resources of the library media center.

- Our circulation and student contact have more than doubled each year since we became a restructured high school. The increased use of materials and technology perhaps would have occurred over time, but I believe the stimulus of having the longer periods created this incredible immediate demand for library media services.

- Because our veteran teachers had to examine their instructional methodologies, and our staff dramatically changed with the inclusion of many new teachers in the past five years, there has been ongoing, positive collaboration between library media specialists and teachers in planning learning activities that are supported by the resources of the media center.

- The school changed many of its former practices with the inception of block scheduling, such as eliminating bells and passes and reconfiguring the study hall. Students have more responsibility for their actions and more choice in their movement in the school. All of this has resulted in a calmer atmosphere, and this has positively affected the purpose students have when they visit the library media center. On a whole, they are much more on task and have valid information needs. Incidents that required disciplinary interaction have been reduced drastically.

What are the problems in the library media center with the block schedule? We do not live in a perfect world, and with the block, there are some problems.

Again, many of these have previously been addressed in this book. A recap of the most noticeable are these:

- The incredibly exhausting pace that the block schedule has brought us in the library media center has not been mitigated. Although most teachers enjoy their extended planning time, for support services such as the library and computer services, the pace never stops. Common lunch time sees well over 300 to 400 students in and out the library, and most blocks have multiple classes reserving space. In addition, small groups of students from classes are encouraged to use the facility as well as study hall students. The seats barely have time to cool down before they are filled again.

- Relevant to the pace is the increased work associated with our increased circulation and use. All the staff time required to keep the resources in order or functional is stressed with the increased use.

- Technology, so important to the delivery of information services, requires a price in staff time to keep current with new software innovations, troubleshoot, instruct new users, unjam printers, and so forth.

Selected Lesson Plans for
Classes Using Block Scheduling

13

As a catalyst for change, block scheduling has provided the sustained time needed for comprehensive lessons or instructional opportunities at the high school level. In the library media center, we support differentiated instruction by all our teachers and the information needs of all students through resource-based learning. Chapters Three and Five focus on the impact of instruction and curriculum changes that may occur in a block-scheduled high school and how the library media program can support these changes. In conjunction with these chapters, there follow five lesson plans.

These lessons vary in content and structure. Each teacher has successfully designed a lesson that uses the extended time of the block schedule to challenge students to apply their skills to find and interpret information from the library media center. Each lesson is adaptable to suit other disciplines or themes within the curriculum.

PARAGONS AND PALADINS: A SEARCH FOR PERFECTION WITHOUT AND WITHIN
Discovering the Ideals of Society Through Literature

Edythe S. Rose and Marie K. Shaw

SYNOPSIS

This project is the culminating activity for a semester unit on heroes in the Bible and in Anglo-Saxon and medieval literature. Students have read selections from the Old and New Testaments, *Beowulf, Tristan and Isolt, Sir Gawain and the Green Knight*, and *Murder in the Cathedral*. Through literature, students recognize that ideals of a society are embodied in the deeds of a specific individual. The purpose of this project is for students to learn that for any society to progress, with concern for its members, there has to be a code of conduct and ethical standards. In groups, students research a chosen time period and narrow their investigation to a specific country/culture to identify all that is good and right in that society. Once students understand the positive qualities the society values, groups create a person who demonstrates these qualities throughout his or her own life. Because of these exemplars, students are able to make their own judgments about what is valuable within a society against which they are able to measure their own personal worth. Each group writes a mini-epic with exploits through which the paragon/ paladin proves the ideas of his or her society. Groups must visually and aurally perform their mini-epic, using a variety of methods, such as theatrical presentations, film, music, and art, thus utilizing multiple intelligences.

STUDENTS

Sixty-five college preparatory seniors participate in this project. Students select their own groups (no fewer than three members, no more than five). Each group chooses a chairperson, who serves as the leader. This person draws the time period of study, makes sure the group meets and communicates regularly, and completes the assigned tasks. A recorder organizes the group's ideals and notes. A typist is responsible for all drafts, final copies, and the saving of all information on computer disk. The entire group is responsible for proofreading, editing, and performing.

STAFF

One English teacher and one library media specialist guide the project. Staff in all other departments agree to serve as resources. The teachers use the instructional methodologies of guided practice, coaching, modeling, consultation and conferencing, and assisting with research.

MATERIALS, FACILITIES, AND RESOURCES

Students are required to use the library facilities, technology, and literature studied throughout the semester to accomplish the project. Students generate visuals and select historically accurate sound recordings for their presentations.

OVERALL VALUE

The innovative feature of the unit concentrates on the ideals of society as depicted through the Bible, Anglo-Saxon, and early medieval literature. Students learn about society by the way literary figures conduct their own lives. The unique quality of this project is that students are limited to the time period but unlimited as to gender, culture, geography, ethnic background, and deeds. Students are encouraged to research little-known areas of culture. By studying the literature of other cultures, students are aided in the development of their own moral code and ethical outlook.

This project has successfully been given as a nontraditional midterm enthusiastically embraced by students. The assessment is twofold: the written component is teacher evaluated for mastery of writing skills, and the performance component is peer and teacher assessed according to specific criteria. The project may be so versatile that it addresses almost every aspect of the Connecticut Common Core of Learning; but in this case, specifically students "understand that literature reflects and illuminates human experiences, motives, conflicts and values," "recognize the necessity for moral and ethical conduct in a society," and "gather, analyze, synthesize and evaluate information" to enable them to create their unique and personal paragon/paladin.

This is a two-week project. The time line and sequence of activities in the block schedule (five classes at 85 minutes each) are shown in Figure 13.1.

The lesson plans and student handouts follow.

LESSON PLAN ONE: DETERMINING IDEALS AND CHARACTERIZATIONS

TIME FRAME: This lesson is conducted in the classroom and library at the beginning of the project ($1\frac{1}{2}$ hours).

OBJECTIVES: The students:

- *Identify* the moral standards and ideals to which a country/culture aspires.
- *Demonstrate* these ideals by creating a paragon/paladin who embodies these characteristics.

MATERIALS: Old and New Testaments, Anglo-Saxon literature, early medieval literature, library resources.

LESSON DEVELOPMENT: The English teacher guides this lesson initially, turns it over to the library media specialist, and then serves primarily as consultant.

Background: Students have concentrated during the first semester on literary figures whose deeds have been of epic proportions and who have demonstrated the ideals of his/her country/culture.

1. Students are given a written overview of the project, objectives, suggested resources, ideas for presentations, and possible problems. [*application of knowledge*]
2. Students are given approximately 5 minutes to choose their groups (no fewer than three members, no greater than five). Each group must select a chairperson who will coordinate group activities such as meetings and tasks, a recorder to

Figure 13.1
Sequence of Activities

Class	Lesson Development	Activities
1	Project Overview Students are given written overview of the expectations of the project, objectives, suggested resources, ideas for presentations, and possible problems. Questions are addressed. The chairperson draws from a box a folded piece of paper on which the time period is written.	Students select their groups; each group selects a chairperson who acts as the project manager and who reports to the teacher, a recorder, and an editor. Groups are no larger than 5 but no fewer than 3. Each group draws a time period of study. Teacher is given a timeline from each group and the person responsible for each task within the group. Group sets up meeting dates outside of class.
2	Library Research Students are challenged to be inquisitive about their time period. Primary sources, historical chronologies, and biographical material are presented by library media specialist.	Students answer guided questions to establish a profile for hero/heroine. Students investigate the cultures of the assigned time period through historical and literary works.
3	Library Research Both the English teacher and Library Media Specialist consult and guide students in their research.	All group members must do research; however, the chairperson can designate individual assignments, such as Internet, EBSCO or print material. Students gather, analyze, evaluate and synthesize information. Chairperson of each group ensures that the members are on task and gathering meaningful information.
4	Teacher Consultation	Student outlines are reviewed, progress is assessed, problem solving within groups is done for logistics, such as scheduling video production and locating props.
5	Presentations (Students may make presentations either in two class blocks or as a mid-term examination)	Students perform a visual/aural presentation of the mini-epic created by the group.

take notes and organize information, and a typist to generate the written component, provide copies for all members, as well as final copy to be turned in, saved on computer disk. All group members are responsible for proofreading the final product and creating and performing their mini-epic. [*developing relationships, participation*]

3. The teacher prepares time periods from the year 1100 through 2000 on pieces of paper, which are folded and placed in a box to be drawn by the chairperson of each group. Division of time depends on technological and literary advancements. [*application, anticipation*]

4. Students and teacher discuss the written component, which must meet all the criteria for good writing and respond to questions generated by groups regarding presentation format and techniques. Students are reminded that they are limited to the time period chosen by the chairperson but unlimited in every other aspect of the project. Students are encouraged to look beyond traditional Eurocentric concepts. [*writing, risk taking*]

5. Students meet in the library to review research strategies with the media specialist. [*research*]

6. The teacher circulates through the groups to monitor focus, task orientation, suggest terminology for research, review ideals. [*modeling, monitoring, brainstorming*]

7. The lesson concludes with groups handing in the name of the country/culture they will research and a list of ideals to be explored through literature of that country/culture. [*closure*]

ASSESSMENT: The teacher observes students in the classroom and during library time to evaluate each group's comprehension, focus, and progress of character development. Students are able to provide organization for their written project and class presentation.

CORRELATION: The lesson gives students the overview for a two-week project, which in this case became a nontraditional midterm examination. Having studied heroes, heroines, epic and otherwise, and given the opportunity to create their own champions of virtue and present their creation to their peers, students were highly motivated to be as creative and yet as accurate—historically, currently, and futuristically—as possible.

Student Handout, Lesson One

OBJECTIVE: Research a particular time period to discover the ideals and qualities that people admired and tried to emulate. Create a hero or heroine and write a mini-epic or short story with at least three major exploits that prove your character upholds these ideals. Your hero or heroine may be from any country (unless specified otherwise on your time period) and from any area of society: sports, politics, monarchy, science, industry, literature, art, music, religion, or any combination of these areas. Your choices are virtually unlimited. The length of your written component should be approximately fifteen to twenty-five pages.

SOURCES: Note: You will not be permitted to use encyclopedias of any kind.

Internet

Individual biography/autobiography

Histories

Online newspapers and magazines, such as the Electric Library or Dow Jones

Periodicals

Historical fiction

Additionally, you may want to browse:

Collected biographies

Historical chronologies (time lines)

Travel, geography, and history stacks

Finally, you will make a visual/oral presentation to the class to show off your creation. Your visual component may be a video, puppet show, posters, live reenactment, or . . . You are limited only by your collective imaginations. Remember to utilize your human resources as well.

LESSON PLAN TWO: RESEARCH STRATEGIES

TIME FRAME: This lesson occurs at the beginning of the project because students must be able to identify the ideals and standards prevalent in a country/culture during a particular time period. (40-minute lesson presentation, 25-minute initial research time)

OBJECTIVES: The students:

- *Locate* and *use* primary source documentation, historical chronologies, and biographical resources.
- *Gather, analyze, synthesize,* and *evaluate* information from traditional and electronic formats.
- *Develop* criteria for the creation of the individual who will demonstrate ideals and ethical standards of a society.

MATERIALS: Criteria worksheet, reference books, online periodical databases, Internet, multimedia, electronic bibliography format, and other library resources.

LESSON DEVELOPMENT: The library media specialist demonstrates research strategies.

Background: The English teacher has previously prepared students with overall lesson objectives and time periods. Students have self-selected their groups.

1. Chronologies are placed on reserve for student exploration of time periods and cultures. *[learning skills]*
2. Library media specialist demonstrates appropriate research strategies and resources using transparencies and criteria worksheets. *[demonstration, application of knowledge]*
3. Library media specialist gives individual groups guided practice on how to formulate research questions and models examples. *[demonstration, modeling, application of knowledge]*
4. Teacher, library media specialist, and students review questions designed to guide thinking to create the individual who will represent the ideals of a particular society. *[discussion, reflection]*
5. Library media specialist instructs students in the appropriate selection and use of electronic databases and the Internet. *[demonstration, monitoring]*
6. Library media specialist instructs students on the proper formulation of a bibliography for electronic databases and the Internet. *[demonstration]*
7. Lesson concludes with groups' selecting the country/culture and appropriate resources. *[closure]*

ASSESSMENT: The teacher and library media specialist monitor student understanding and progress toward completing the criteria form and selecting a country/culture for study. Groups make appointments for research consultations.

CORRELATION: Library research was the jump-start to the project. Based on their group collaboration and findings, students were able to select their country/culture, research ideals and standards of the society, and begin to develop the mini-epic and visual presentation.

Student Handout, Lesson Two

There is no single source that will give you the information you will need to write a mini-epic or short story. You must have at least three major exploits that prove your hero or heroine upholds the ideals or qualities admired by society during your selected time period. Be prepared to utilize many different avenues of research!

Be inquisitive about the time period in history. This handout is designed to have you respond to questions that will guide you through your selections. As seniors, you are very familiar with the research process, and we will expand on your solid knowledge base.

Use the questions on this handout as criteria to determine whether you have completely researched your time period and the possibilities it offers for creating a paragon or paladin.

Time period: _____

What were the more interesting events taking place? _____

_____

Was there war or peace? If war, which one(s), and who were the heroes/heroines? Why?

_____

Was it a time of prosperity or poverty? Who influenced the economy? _____

_____

What countries dominated the globe, and who were the power players? _____

_____

Who were the sports and entertainment figures of the time? Were they admired? _____

_____

Who were the political figures of the time? _____

_____

Were there technological, mathematical, or scientific advances made that affected society? If
so, what were they, and who were the inventors? _____

_____

Writers and poets often become the spokespeople for a generation. Can you name major authors, what they wrote, and why they affected their audience? _____

_____

Who were the humanitarians of the time period, and what did they do? _____

_____

Don't forget to research (if appropriate) major prizes and awards, such as the Nobel prizes,
Pulitzer prizes, Purple Heart, etc. _____

_____

Are there memorable songs or works of art of this time period? What are they, and who were
the artists? _____

_____

Will the contributions be viewed as positively influencing society? How? _____

_____

Were there natural or man-made disasters that elicited heroism? _____

_____

Have people affected our environment in a positive way because of a stand they took, an
organization they founded, or a piece of legislation they were able to have enacted?

_____

_____

What was the form of communication? Can we obtain primary source material (i.e., speeches,
videos, documentaries, etc.) _____

_____

ASSESSMENT

Performance assessment for this project is based on students' experiences with aural and visual presentations and group writing assignments. (See Figure 13.2.)

Scoring Guide for Mini-Epic (Written Component)

Each paper must have:

Criteria	Assessment
1.	Introduction with character's background.
2.	How/when the society's value system is learned.
3.	Exploits that follow logically from the society's value system.
4.	Character clearly dynamic or static.
5.	Use of dialogue, language appropriate to time period, clarity of expression.
6.	Unified plot with resolution of all conflicts or not.
7.	Bibliography.

Each chairperson draws a number for the group for the order of presentations. Three volunteers from the last group, along with the teacher, serve as assessors for the first group. Three volunteers from each preceding group then serve as assessors for the next group. The teacher's assessment carries the same weight as the student assessors. Each group's performance assessment is based upon an average of the four assessors' evaluations. Teacher and assessors invariably have the same assessment!

RIVER VALLEY CIVILIZATIONS

Alice Pembrook and Marie Shaw

SYNOPSIS

This first-quarter major research assignment for ninth-grade students is to provide the foundation of the research process using the topics of the River Valley civilizations. We have been studying prehistory and the River Valleys, Mesopotamia, Egypt, China, and India. The students are to select three topics from these areas and write a paragraph describing why they made these choices. This assignment has oral, written, and project components. The main purpose is to provide students with the beginning skills of the research process. Their schooling thus far has been mainly reports. The students' goal is to gather their sources and begin to evaluate them. They

Figure 13.2
Evaluation of Presentation

Rate each item below 1 through 5, with 1 = unsatisfactory, 5 = excellent

Articulation/Volume	Energy/Focus	Structural Unity of Plot	Thoroughness of Research
1 = poor diction, indistinct, hesitations 5 = clear, loud, believable	1 = dull, unenthusiastic 5 = energized, dramatic	1 = unconnected events 5 = unified plot sequence	1 = no connections between individual and society 5 = clear connections between individual and society

Group Members:_____

Group Time Period:_____

CONTENT:

1. List three ideals you recognize from the plot as belonging to the above time period:

    a._____

    b._____

    c._____

2. Describe at least one exploit during which the hero/heroine displays these ideals:

_____

_____

3. State one particularly effective technique which enabled you to understand these ideals:_____

_____

4. Describe one concept which could have been developed more fully:_____

_____

Rate each item below 1 through 5 with 1 = unsatisfactory, 5 = excellent

Articulation/Volume	Energy/Focus	Structural Unity of Plot	Thoroughness of Research

Overall Presentation Rating:_____

Comments:

_____

_____

_____

will determine the strengths and weaknesses of a variety of resources. Through an annotated bibliography, they will assess the caliber of the author and the validity of information on Internet web sites; the relevancy of date, qualification of authorship, and publisher of books and periodicals, as well as the importance of primary and secondary sources. There are many opportunities for teacher-student conferences during this project. The block schedule provides the time for these meaningful conferences to take place, which result in the development of rapport and trust between the teacher and student that continue throughout the year. The lesson plan is shown in Table 13.1.

Table 13.1
Lesson Plan for River Valley Civilizations

Lesson Development	Activities
Week 1: Teacher and student discuss project overview. Students are provided with Expectation Sheet.	Brainstorm ideas about possible topics. Homework assignment: Select 3 topics and in a paragraph tell why you made these choices.
Week 2: Conference with teacher about topic selection. Discuss research and the help students will need to be successful. Discuss the importance of gathering and evaluating sources. Library media specialist will visit class and give instruction on how to evaluate sources for students.	Students review Expectation Sheet. Students expand ideas about how to evaluate sources with teacher and library media specialist. Students provide their own input and criteria for evaluation of print and nonprint information. Students receive Library Research Handout.
Week 3: Library research.	Students begin research process with help of library staff. Research continues as a homework assignment.
Week 4: Conferencing with teacher for comments and suggestions of the research process. Assessment of work done to date.	Notetaking, homework.
Week 5: Conferencing with teacher.	Notetaking, homework.
Week 6: Conferencing with teacher.	Rough draft of paper due. Share project ideas with teacher in writing.
Week 7: Class discussion and assessment of work done to date.	Written description of project. Review progress on paper.
Week 8: Oral presentation about research, demonstrate project.	Class presentations.

LESSON PLAN DEVELOPMENT

TIME FRAME: This lesson takes place over an eight-week period during first quarter.

OBJECTIVE: Students will develop the skills for research by gathering and evaluating sources.

RESEARCH PROCESS: Students are required to ask the basic who, what, when, where, why, and how as they seek information on their topics. Further questions to be asked:

- What was unique or special about your topic?
- What was common about your topic?
- Make a comparison between today's civilization and the culture you are researching.
- How does your topic reflect the times in which it took place?
- How does your topic reflect the culture of the times?

STAFF: The social studies teacher and library media specialist are the instructors. Instructional methodology to be used is guided practice, conferencing, coaching, modeling, and directing or assisting.

MATERIALS: Library media center resources and technology for the social science areas. Community resources, such as interviews.

ASSIGNMENT COMPONENTS: There are three components:

1. Research paper (40 points)
   - 4–5 pages   (20 points)
   - typed or word processed
     double spaced
     Times or Helvetica 12 font   (5 points)
     Writer's Inc format
   - Annotated bibliography page,   (15 points)
     4 pages in length

2. Project (35 points)
   This is determined individually (no posters)

3. Oral Presentation (25 points)
   - 5–7 minutes
   - summary of research
   - project explanation
   - note cards may be used
   - hand in outline
   - speak clearly, concisely, emphatically

OVERALL VALUE

1. Set in place the elements of research.
2. Gather information about topics of a River Valley civilization and connect that topic to the present.
3. Establish the framework for themes and patterns throughout history.

Student Expectation Sheet

OBJECTIVE: You will learn how to select and evaluate information from books, magazines, and the computer. You will develop your research skills for our year-long study of world history and cultures.

PROCESS: Select three areas of interest in the River Valley civilizations. Write a paragraph for each explaining specifically why you are interested in these areas. In conference we will determine your topic.

In conjunction with the library media specialist, a source gathering and evaluation sheet (Library Research Handout, Figure 13.3) will be explained and used with our first visit to the library. This is step 1 for an annotated bibliography.

Research, take notes and focus on the basic *who, what, when, where, why, and how* as you seek information on your topics. Further questions to be asked:

- What was unique or special about your topic?
- What was common about your topic?
- Make a comparison between today's civilization and the culture you are researching.
- How does your topic reflect the times in which it took place?
- How does your topic reflect the culture of the times?

ASSIGNMENT COMPONENTS: There are three components:

1. Research paper (40 points)
   - 4–5 pages   (20 points)
   - typed or word processed
     double spaced
     Times or Helvetica 12 font   (5 points)
     Writer's Inc format
   - Annotated bibliography page,   (15 points)
     4 pages in length

2. Project (35 points)

   This is determined individually—no posters. You may create a video, music, or a dramatization. It could be a puppet show, sculpture, or diorama. Use your creativity!

Figure 13.3
Library Research Handout

NAME:_____

RIVER VALLEY CIVILIZATIONS
Library Research Handout

STUDENTS ARE TO USE THIS BLOCK TO INVESTIGATE THE RESOURCES IN THE
LIBRARY THAT YOU WILL LATER USE TO RESEARCH. **DO NOT TAKE NOTES TODAY—**
USE THE TIME TO EVALUATE BOOKS AND ONLINE INFORMATION FOR LATER USE.

Reference:

Cambridge Illustrated History of Archaeology	R930.1
Chronicle of the World	R909
McGraw-Hill Encyclopedia of World Biography	R920
The History of the Ancient and Medieval World	R930
History of the World	R909
Smithsonian Timelines of the Ancient World	R930.02
Hammond Past Worlds:The Times Atlas of Archaeology	R911
Key Monuments of the History of Art	R709
Larousse Encyclopedia of Archaeology	R913
Encyclopedia of World Art	R703

Select two reference books you will look at and use proper bibliography formatting:

Source: _____

Source: _____

**Here you are to comment about the above sources. Evaluate the book as to the author,
when it was published, who published it and its usefulness to you in this project.**

_____

_____

_____

Books:

Use the LION computers to find books on your *subject.* Books are located in the
nonfiction collection. **Subject keyword(s) is the best option for you to use!**

Search Strategies: Topic or Subject (Theater, Ancient Greece, Greek Drama)
   Place or Time (Stonehenge, England, History)

LION PAC:
1. Author
2. Title
3. Subject
4. Series
5. Title or Series keyword(s)
6. Subject keyword(s)
7. Content keyword(s)

Figure 13.3. Continued

Areas of the Library where you can look or browse:

200	-	Religion
400	-	Language and symbolism
709	-	Art
720	-	Architecture
909	-	World History
913	-	Ancient civilizations, Man's Origins, Mesopotamia
913.32	-	Ancient Egypt (description & travel)
920 or 921-		Biography
932	-	History of Egypt
951	-	History of China
954	-	History of India

Select three areas that you should look at for books: _____,

_____, _____.

Here you are to comment about the above sources. Evaluate the book as to the author, when it was published, who published it and its usefulness to you in this project.

_____

_____

_____

Periodicals:

1. Use the <u>National Geographic Index</u> to find magazine articles on your topic. Many ancient ruins have been written up in this magazine source.

2. The LION computers offer a magazine file called **EBSCO**. Here you can find magazine articles for many of your topics. **EBSCO** is found in the main menu:

11. Magazine Index

Search strategies: Name of object, place, or building
Descriptive words

Words to search: _____, _____, _____

_____, _____, _____

Figure 13.3 Continued

ere you are to comment about the above sources. Evaluate the book as to the author,
hen it was published, who published it and its usefulness to you in this project.

_____

_____

_____

ternet:

The Library has multiple Internet accounts. The most common usage is the world wide
eb or WWW. You need to use a search engine to conduct a www search. Here are some
iggestions to try:

Excite	**http://www.excite.com**
Hotbot	**http://www.hotbot.com**
Altavista	**http://www.altavista.digital.com**
Yahoo	**http://www.yahoo.com**

ɔr Excite, Altavista, and Yahoo, put " " around words that you want to be searched as a phrase.

e.g.   "Sphinx of Gaza"

ut a + before any word that you want to see often in the search results:

e.g.   +temple+Egyptian   (the order of words does not matter)

otbot lets you easily select the kind of search you do. Try it!!

'ords to search: _____, _____, _____

_____, _____, _____

ource: URL or Address you use:_____

Here you are to comment about the above sources. Evaluate the book as to the
uthor, when it was published, who published it and its usefulness to you in this project.

_____

_____

_____

Figure 13.4
Assessment Handout

RIVER VALLEY CIVILIZATIONS
Assessment of Project and Oral Presentation

Name:_____

Topic:_____

Did the presenter address:

who_____

what_____

when_____

where_____

why_____

how_____

How is the project similar to the presentation?_____

_____

Did the project and presentation reflect the culture?_____

_____

Evaluate for:

Creativity or Uniqueness_____
Clarity_____
Summary_____
Eye Contact_____
Pacing_____
Voice_____
Avoidance of words such as "um", "like",
        "you know" "ah"_____

3. Oral Presentation (25 points)
   - 5–7 minutes
   - summary of research
   - project explanation
   - note cards may be used
   - hand in outline
   - speak clearly, concisely, emphatically

JOURNEYS: THE CULTURAL MOSAIC
Kingswood Regional High School

Karen Libby, Deborah Bergeron, Ruth Bley, and Claire Hanlon

This integrated unit involves literature, social studies, information problem solving, and the arts. There are six supporting activities to be accomplished throughout the unit with a culminating or final exhibition. Activity 3 has been selected as one example of how the library media specialist participates on the instructional team.

THEME: Patterns of migration and assimilation contribute to a nation's cultural identity and an individual's self-concept.

RELATED CONCEPTS: Compromise, conflict, unity, division, human condition, leadership, civil rights.

EXAMPLES OF POSSIBLE PERFORMANCES: Tasks:

- Write and evaluate a variety of essay.
- Use information systems to research and report.
- Portray a historical figure.

Projects:

- Study and evaluate literature.
- Create a product, such as a reflective essay or visual or oral presentation, to share what was learned.

Exhibition:

- Write and publicly present an original piece of work.

PLANNING: Motivating Activity: Audio of Neil Diamond's "America" is playing in class. Discuss the lyrics. Supporting Activities:

1. Identify the motivation behind migration and journey.

Table 13.2
Researching the Attributes of a Leader

JOURNEYS: THE CULTURAL MOSAIC
SUPPORTING ACTIVITY 3

This is just one of several supporting activities for the unit.

OBJECTIVE: Select an important leader or group whose path has made positive change. Using the information problem-solving process, students will individually select and research one person or group who has made a positive change.

VOCABULARY: interior monologue
                        information problem-solving process

Prompts	Notes
What is a leader?	Teachers will provide background packet of information on patterns of immigration. Students will select a topic for research.
What are the qualities and characteristics of a leader?	Library media specialist will provide information problem-solving strategies to assist research.
Who are some leaders who have made positive change? Were any of them immigrants?	
What is an interior monologue?	Students will construct interior monologue based on completed research.
	Teacher will provide a model of an interior monologue.
What would some of these leaders or groups be thinking?	

ASSESSMENT: Student demonstrates an understanding of the information problem-solving process. (teacher observation)

Student exhibits an understanding of the background of the character, obstacles, experiences, and thoughts along the path toward change. (analytic scoring rubric)

ENRICHMENT DIMENSION: Offer an in-depth study of immigrant challenges in the legal system.

---

2. Using film and literature, demonstrate the difficulties and accomplishments of immigration.
3. Select an immigrant leader or group whose path has made positive change.
4. Investigate a natural occurrence that has caused movement of people, and study the path of relocation. (Define themes of geography.)

5. Study the effects of immigration and the human condition through the eyes of an artist (photo, music, poetry).
6. Examine the issue of assimilation vs. maintenance of cultural identity.

Culminating Activity: Create an exhibition that shows an appreciation of the essential understandings as they relate to migration and journey.

Table 13.2 shows an overview of the activity where students gain an understanding of the attributes of leadership.

FRESHMAN ACADEMY
East Lyme High School
Frances Hart Ewers Library Media Center

Marie Shaw

Freshman Academy is a ninth grade transition program developed and administered by Mrs. Freda Gianakos, a Family and Consumer Science teacher and Curriculum Instructional Leader at East Lyme High School.

GOAL: All ninth-grade students will have a positive introduction to the library media center and become familiar with the services it provides and the people who work there. This will also be an opportunity for students to broadly explore the resources of the library media center.

OBJECTIVES:

• Students will learn the more important procedures and policies of the library.
• Students will gain practice in outlining an oral presentation. They will create an outline that uses a research or a journalistic format.
• Students will use library materials and technology for information and presentation (project).

FORMAT: Students rotate among twenty elective teachers, counselors, assistant principals and support services, including the library media center, for one block for an explanation of existing curricular opportunities. The rotations occur during the first quarter of the school year during block 4. Students are assigned to a small group of approximately twelve students.

MATERIALS/TECHNOLOGY: Students have access to *anything* in the library media center for this lesson; however, they should be encouraged to use a variety of sources. Suggestions for obtaining information are: periodicals, CD-ROMs, books, reference books, Internet, online magazines and newspapers.

To create the small poster or transparency, students have available to them: PowerPoint software, computers for lettering, stencils, crayons, colored pencils, markers, glue, the picture file, scissors, photocopier, transparencies.

A lesson plan and a student checklist (Figure 13.5) for preparing presentations follow.

FRESHMAN ACADEMY LESSON FORMAT

1. Attendance, welcome, and introductions (5 minutes)

2. Top 12 policies/rules (25 minutes)

    Students are handed a short description (1 per student). They have 2 to 3 minutes to read it and decide how to present it to the group. Each policy is numbered, and a volunteer will draw a number slip from a box to determine the order of presentation.

3. "And for My Next Presentation . . ." (55 minutes)

    Students need practice in creating an outline for oral presentations. Throughout the year they will have many opportunities to talk in front of their class. The remainder of this class will be used to create an outline for a topic of interest. Teacher instruction includes the format of a presentation such as introduction, middle, closing ideas and the journalistic approach of the 5 W's (who, what, where, when, why, and how?).

    Presentations should follow either format. Each should have five distinct ideas for the presentation. Students do not have to present; they are getting practice for putting together an outline for a presentation. Students may select their own topic.

- Each transparency or paper must have at least one picture.
- Each should have at least three colors.
- Lettering should be neat and readable. (Neat does not mean uniform. Be creative!)
- Students must use at least three sources from the library.
- Students must have one library assistant initial that she helped them.
- Students can use anything electronic and are encouraged to do so—the Internet, scanner, photocopier, LION, etc.
- Topics must be approved by the library media specialist.

4. Closing (5 minutes)

    Students explain their five statements for their speech. Project must be accompanied with checklist.

Figure 13.5
Student Checklist

Name:_____

FRESHMAN ACADEMY
Checklist for Preparing Presentations

_____ Five phrases of information that guide the presentation.

_____ Use of 3 sources from the LMC for the information:

_____ Received help from a Librarian Assistant
(signature:_____)

_____ Use of at least one picture.

_____ Use of at least 3 colors.

_____ Lettering is readable.

_____ Creativity.

Sources used: (these must be from this Library)

1. Title:_____Call Number:_____

2. Title:_____Call Number:_____

3. Title:_____Call Number:_____

Grading Scale 1 - 3

3 =   Excellent work. Meets all criteria, good use of layout and design, outline for
      presentation follows either the research paper format or the journalism format.

2 =   Satisfactory work. There are one or two criteria missing.

1 =   Unsatisfactory work. Did not have 5 statements that could be used to develop a
      presentation. Did not meet requirements.

WORLD LITERATURE
East Lyme High School
Michael Landow

GOAL: This full-year independent project will give students the opportunity to enhance their understanding of the world in which we live.
OBJECTIVES:

• Employ creativity
• Develop an in-depth understanding of another country and its culture
• Improve time-management and organizational skills
• Improve research skills
• Improve reading and writing skills

GETTING STARTED: Beyond classroom periods devoted to introducing students to library resources and available technologies, this is an independent project to be worked on outside class time.

1. Students are to select a country of interest to them.
2. It is necessary to do extensive research. Students should take advantage of the following resources:

    • Libraries
    • Embassies/consulates
    • Internet/World Wide Web
    • Universities and professors of higher education
    • The United Nations
    • International organizations, such as Asia Society, Japan Society
    • Television news
    • Newspapers
    • Regional educational support services
    • Family/teachers/students
    • PBS, Discovery Channel, etc.

3. Students are to use outlines or graphic organizers, such as Venn diagrams, webs, and so forth, to help focus and organize their findings. Significant organizational categories may include religion, family life, education, holidays and festivals, gender roles, racial or ethnic relations, politics, economics, geography, historical events, sports, or others.
4. Each quarter, students submit an essay, a review, and a bibliography. Ultimately, students will rely on these sources when creating their culminating project.

Tables 13.3 and 13.4 show research requirements and student work that is due each quarter throughout the year.

Table 13.3
Quarterly Independent Research Requirements

1st Quarter	2nd Quarter	3rd Quarter	4th Quarter
200 points	*200 points*	*200 points*	*200 points*
Encyclopedia or CD-ROM	1 novel	1 play or 1 novel or 1 nonfiction text	music/instruments
5 related news or magazine articles (Internet or print)	4 short stories or 10–15 poems (or combination)	5 related news or magazine articles (Internet or print)	1 novel
1 documentary film (history, travel, biography)	art or architecture or photography (or combination)	1 film (fictional)	1 film (fictional)
1 nonfiction book (history, travel, biography)	1 interview (live, mail or e-mail)	1 interview (live, mail or e-mail)	1 interview (live, mail or e-mail)

Table 13.4
Quarterly Product Requirements

1st Quarter	2nd Quarter	3rd Quarter	4th Quarter
"What I learned" essay and bibliography	"What I learned" essay and bibliography	"What I learned" essay and bibliography	"What I learned" essay and bibliography
3 typed pages	3 typed pages	3 typed pages	3 typed pages
	1 text review (minimum 5 typed paragraphs)	1 text review (minimum 5 typed paragraphs)	Culminating project
Initial organizer	Initial organizer	Initial organizer	

CULMINATING PROJECT (200 POINTS): This culminating project must reflect the year-long independent reading and research. The project must include a typed bibliography using MLA or *Writer's Inc.* format. An asterisked project must be accompanied by a three-page typed rationale for and explanation of the project. A research paper or comparative literary analysis must incorporate a minimum of six supporting quotations.

Students may choose one of the following:

- Short story (seven to ten typed pages minimum)
- Research paper (seven to ten typed pages minimum)
- Comparative literary analysis (seven to ten typed pages minimum)
- One-act play
- Video
- Painting
- Sculpture
- Short screenplay
- Ten poems or songs

Index

About the Author

MARIE KEEN SHAW is curriculum instructional leader and a library media specialist at East Lyme High School in East Lyme, Connecticut. She took a leadership role in her school's adoption of block scheduling and has presented a number of workshops on the topic to school library media specialists. She was a member of the Connecticut Legislative Task Force on Telecommunications for Schools in 1997, and co-authored a district technology plan, "Target for Technology."